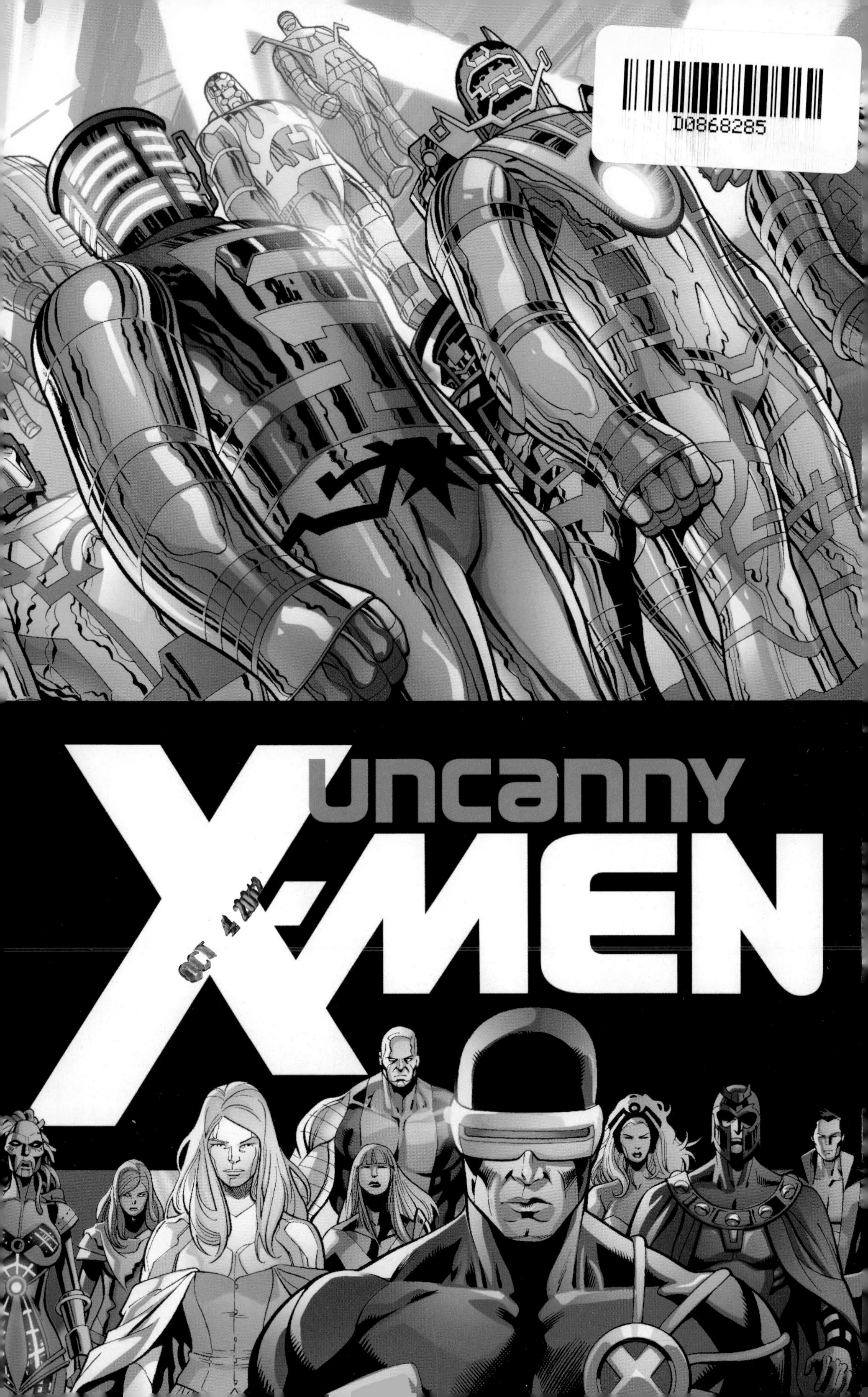
D0868285
UNCANNY
X-MEN
OCT 4 2012

WRITER: **KIERON GILLEN**

#1 PENCILS: **CARLOS PACHECO** • INKS: **CAM SMITH** • COLORS: **FRANK D'ARMATA**

#2 PENCILS: **CARLOS PACHECO, JORGE MOLINA** & **RODNEY BUCHEMI**
INKS: **CAM SMITH, ROGER BONET, WALDEN WONG** & **JORGE MOLINA**
COLORS: **FRANK D'ARMATA, RACHELLE ROSENBERG, JIM CHARALAMPIDIS**
& **JORGE MOLINA**

#3 PENCILS: **RODNEY BUSCEMI, PACO DIAZ** & **CARLOS PACHECO**
INKS: **CAM SMITH, WALDEN WONG** & **PACO DIAZ**
COLORS: **DOMMO, REX LOKUS** & **JIM CHARALAMPIDIS**

#4 ARTIST: **BRANDON PETERSON** • COLORS: **JUSTIN PONSOR**

LETTERS: **VC'S JOE CARAMAGNA** • COVER ART: **CARLOS PACHECO, CAM SMITH**
& **FRANK D'ARMATA** (#1-3); AND **BRANDON PETERSON** (#4)
ASSISTANT EDITORS: **SEBASTIAN GIRNER** & **JORDAN D. WHITE**
ASSOCIATE EDITOR: **DANIEL KETCHUM** • EDITOR: **NICK LOWE**

COLLECTION EDITOR: **JENNIFER GRÜNWALD** • ASSISTANT EDITORS: **ALEX STARBUCK** & **NELSON RIBEIRO**
EDITOR, SPECIAL PROJECTS: **MARK D. BEAZLEY** • SENIOR EDITOR, SPECIAL PROJECTS: **JEFF YOUNGQUIST**
SENIOR VICE PRESIDENT OF SALES: **DAVID GABRIEL**
SVP OF BRAND PLANNING & COMMUNICATIONS: **MICHAEL PASCIULLO**
BOOK DESIGNER: **RODOLFO MURAGUCHI**

EDITOR IN CHIEF: **AXEL ALONSO** • CHIEF CREATIVE OFFICER: **JOE QUESADA**
PUBLISHER: **DAN BUCKLEY** • EXECUTIVE PRODUCER: **ALAN FINE**

UNCANNY X-MEN BY KIERON GILLEN VOL. 1. Contains material originally published in magazine form as UNCANNY X-MEN #1-4. First printing 2012. Hardcover ISBN# 978-0-7851-5993-3. Softcover ISBN# 978-0-7851-5994-0. Published by MARVEL WORLDWIDE, INC., a subsidiary of MARVEL ENTERTAINMENT, LLC. OFFICE OF PUBLICATION: 135 West 50th Street, New York, NY 10020. Copyright © 2011 and 2012 Marvel Characters, Inc. All rights reserved. Hardcover: $19.99 per copy in the U.S. and $21.99 in Canada (GST #R127032852). Softcover: $16.99 per copy in the U.S. and $18.99 in Canada (GST #R127032852). Canadian Agreement #40668537. All characters featured in this issue and the distinctive names and likenesses thereof, and all related indicia are trademarks of Marvel Characters, Inc. No similarity between any of the names, characters, persons, and/or institutions in this magazine with those of any living or dead person or institution is intended, and any such similarity which may exist is purely coincidental. **Printed in the U.S.A.** ALAN FINE, EVP - Office of the President, Marvel Worldwide, Inc. and EVP & CMO Marvel Characters B.V.; DAN BUCKLEY, Publisher & President - Print, Animation & Digital Divisions; JOE QUESADA, Chief Creative Officer; DAVID BOGART, SVP of Business Affairs & Talent Management; TOM BREVOORT, SVP of Publishing; C.B. CEBULSKI, SVP of Creator & Content Development; DAVID GABRIEL, SVP of Publishing Sales & Circulation; MICHAEL PASCIULLO, SVP of Brand Planning & Communications; JIM O'KEEFE, VP of Operations & Logistics; DAN CARR, Executive Director of Publishing Technology; SUSAN CRESPI, Editorial Operations Manager; ALEX MORALES, Publishing Operations Manager; STAN LEE, Chairman Emeritus. For information regarding advertising in Marvel Comics or on Marvel.com, please contact John Dokes, SVP Integrated Sales and Marketing, at jdokes@marvel.com. For Marvel subscription inquiries, please call 800-217-9158. **Manufactured between 1/30/2012 and 2/27/2012 (hardcover), and 1/30/2012 and 8/27/2012 (softcover), by R.R. DONNELLEY, INC., SALEM, VA, USA.**

10 9 8 7 6 5 4 3 2 1

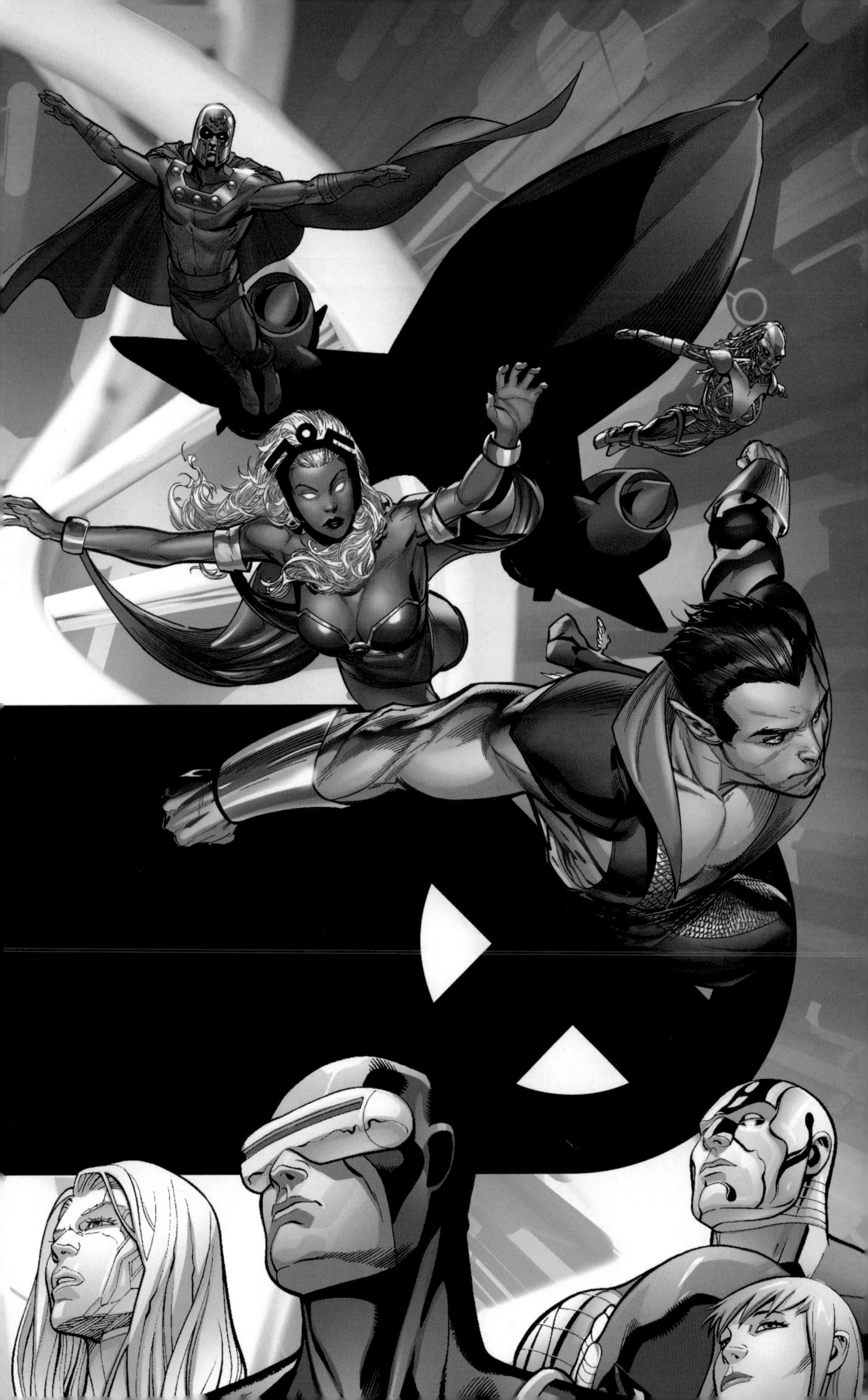

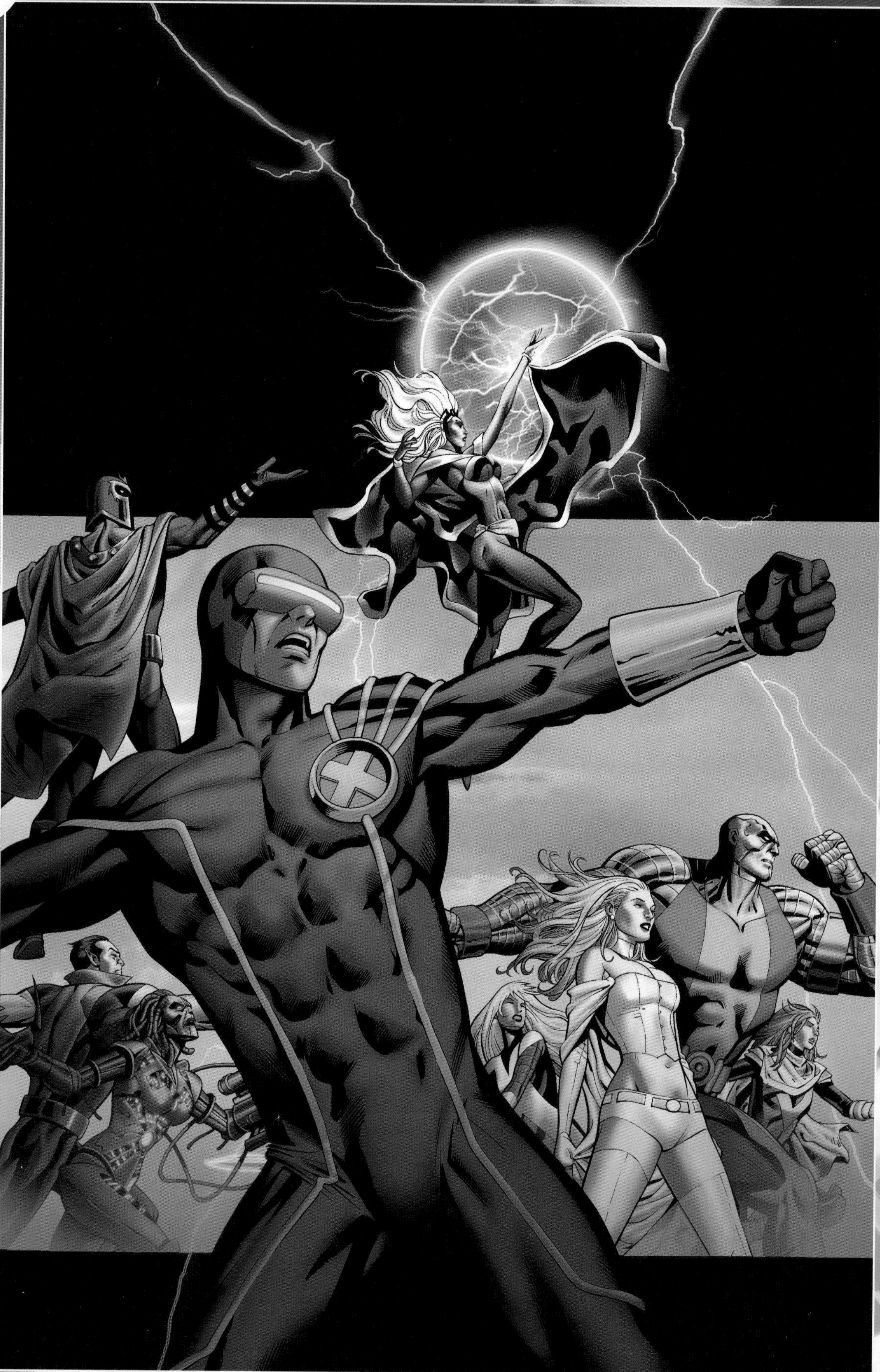

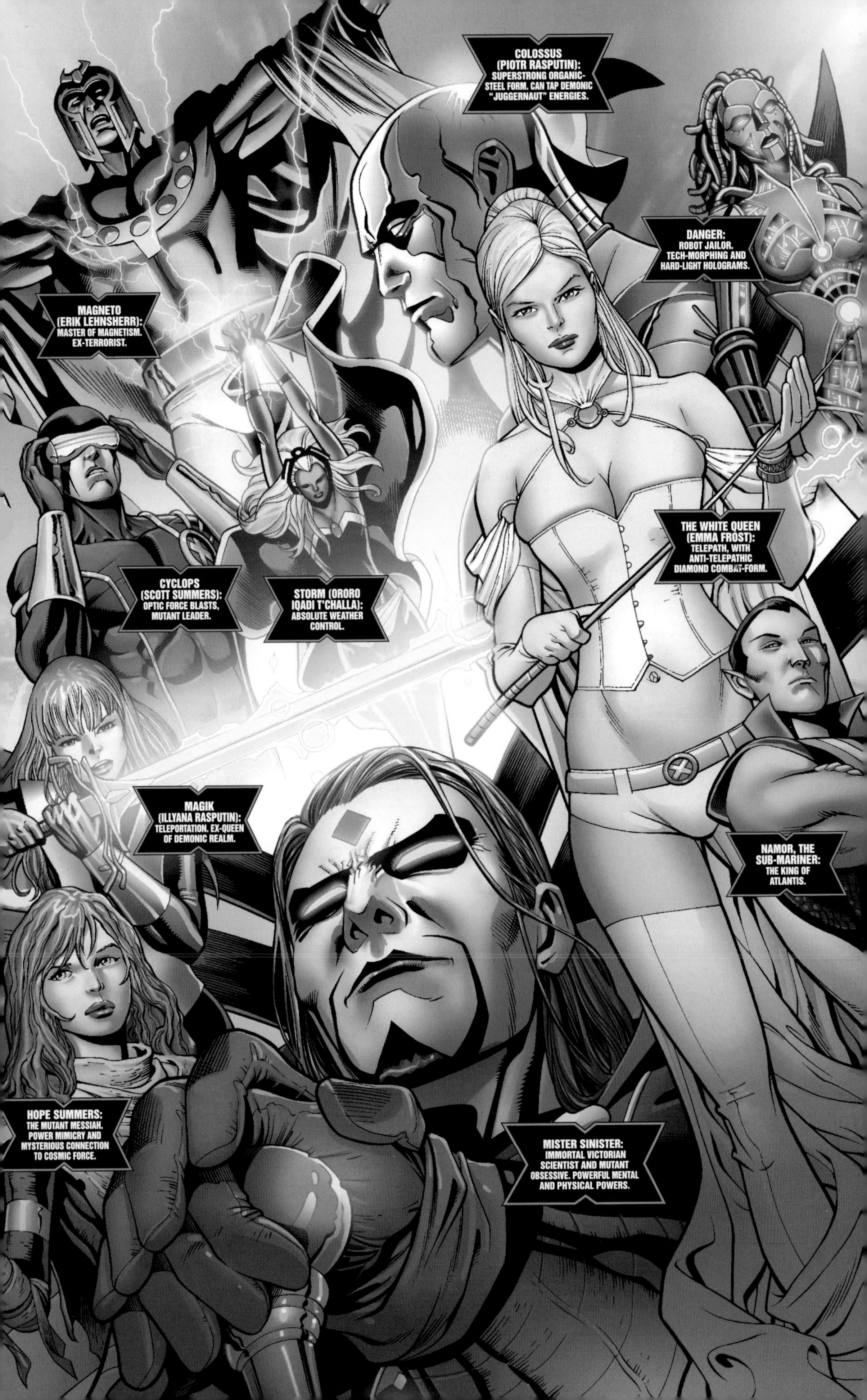
COLOSSUS (PIOTR RASPUTIN): SUPERSTRONG ORGANIC-STEEL FORM. CAN TAP DEMONIC "JUGGERNAUT" ENERGIES.
DANGER: ROBOT JAILOR. TECH-MORPHING AND HARD-LIGHT HOLOGRAMS.
MAGNETO (ERIK LEHNSHERR): MASTER OF MAGNETISM. EX-TERRORIST.
THE WHITE QUEEN (EMMA FROST): TELEPATH, WITH ANTI-TELEPATHIC DIAMOND COMBAT-FORM.
CYCLOPS (SCOTT SUMMERS): OPTIC FORCE BLASTS, MUTANT LEADER.
STORM (ORORO IQADI T'CHALLA): ABSOLUTE WEATHER CONTROL.
MAGIK (ILLYANA RASPUTIN): TELEPORTATION. EX-QUEEN OF DEMONIC REALM.
NAMOR, THE SUB-MARINER: THE KING OF ATLANTIS.
HOPE SUMMERS: THE MUTANT MESSIAH. POWER MIMICRY AND MYSTERIOUS CONNECTION TO COSMIC FORCE.
MISTER SINISTER: IMMORTAL VICTORIAN SCIENTIST AND MUTANT OBSESSIVE. POWERFUL MENTAL AND PHYSICAL POWERS.

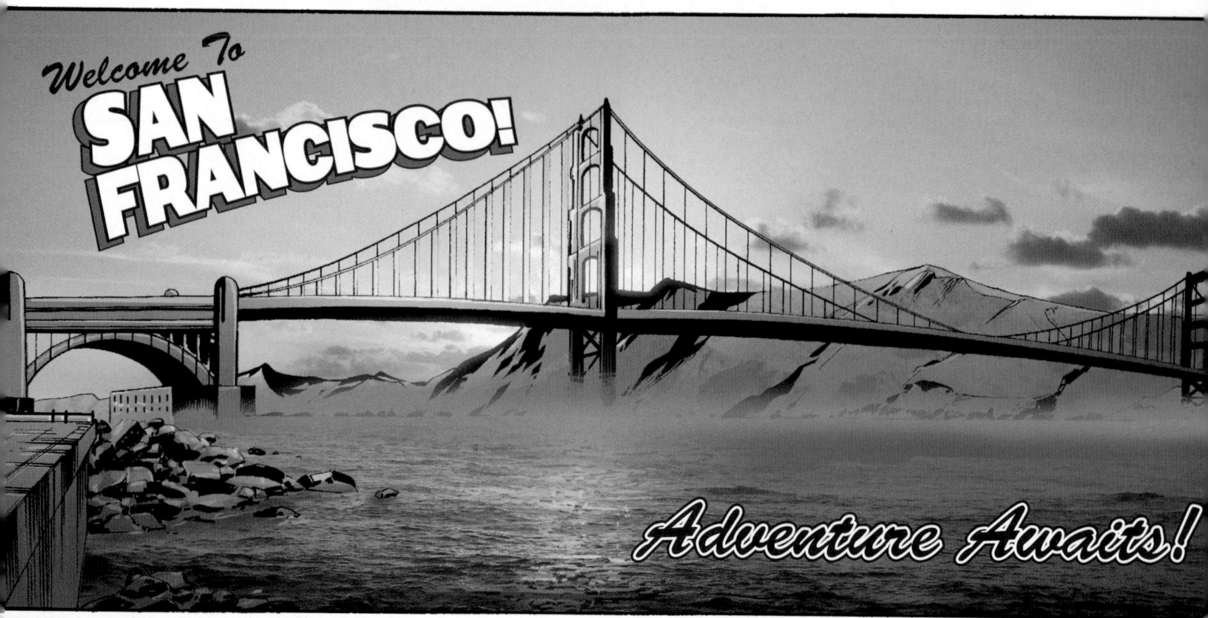
Welcome To
SAN FRANCISCO!
Adventure Awaits!

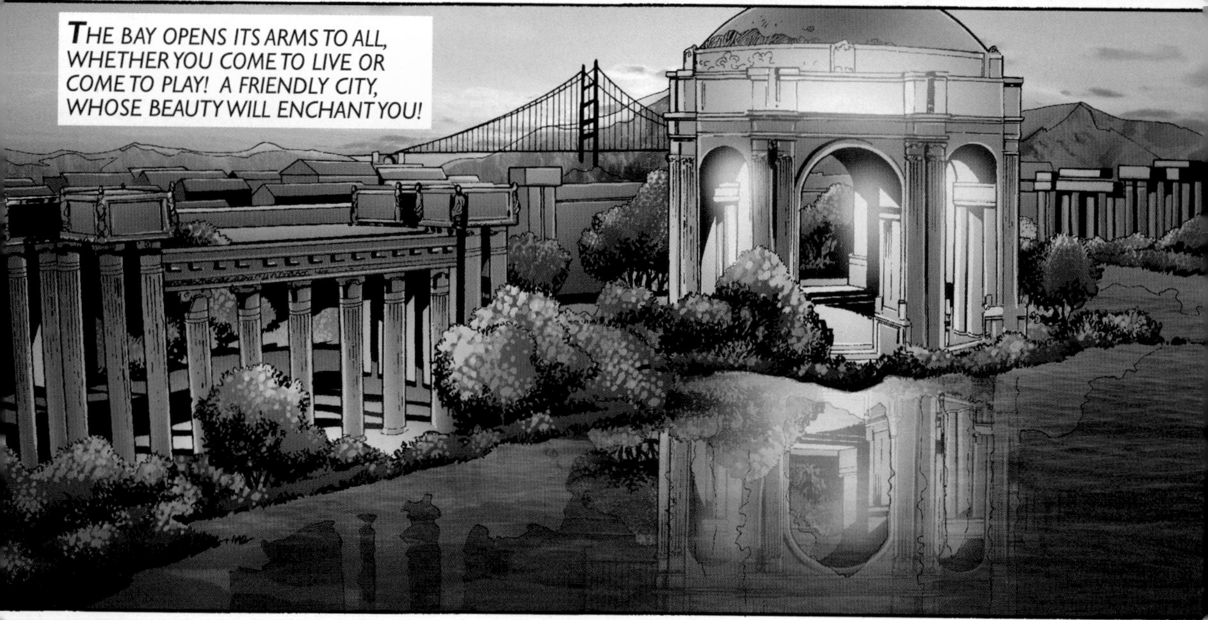
THE BAY OPENS ITS ARMS TO ALL, WHETHER YOU COME TO LIVE OR COME TO PLAY! A FRIENDLY CITY, WHOSE BEAUTY WILL ENCHANT YOU!

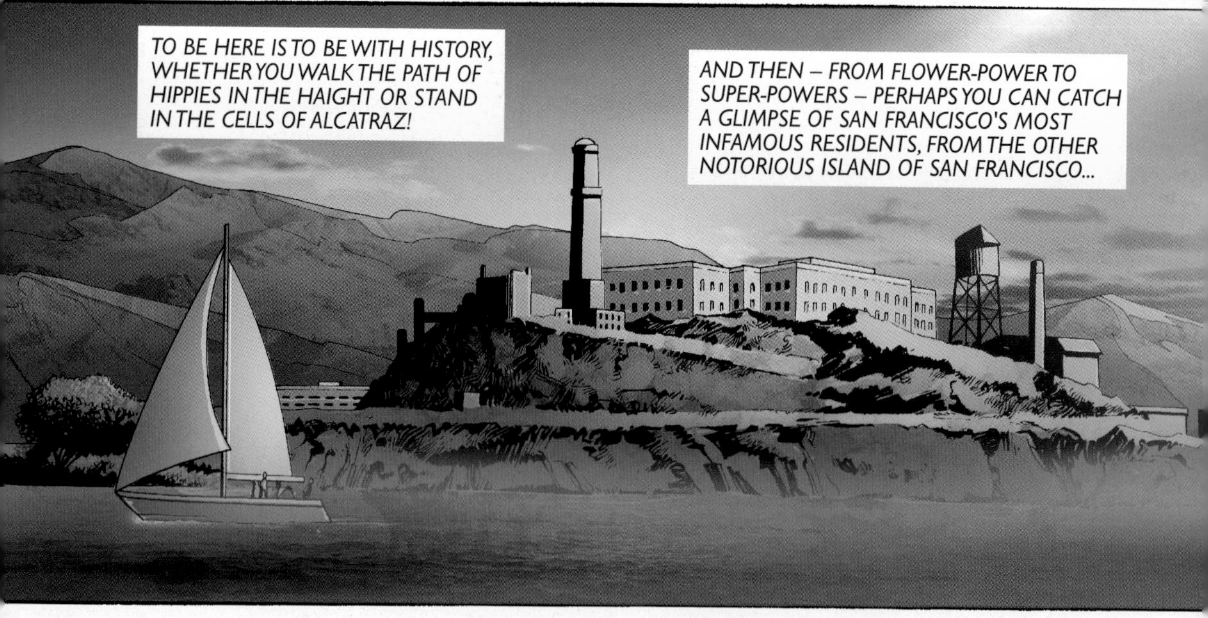
TO BE HERE IS TO BE WITH HISTORY, WHETHER YOU WALK THE PATH OF HIPPIES IN THE HAIGHT OR STAND IN THE CELLS OF ALCATRAZ!
AND THEN – FROM FLOWER-POWER TO SUPER-POWERS – PERHAPS YOU CAN CATCH A GLIMPSE OF SAN FRANCISCO'S MOST INFAMOUS RESIDENTS, FROM THE OTHER NOTORIOUS ISLAND OF SAN FRANCISCO...

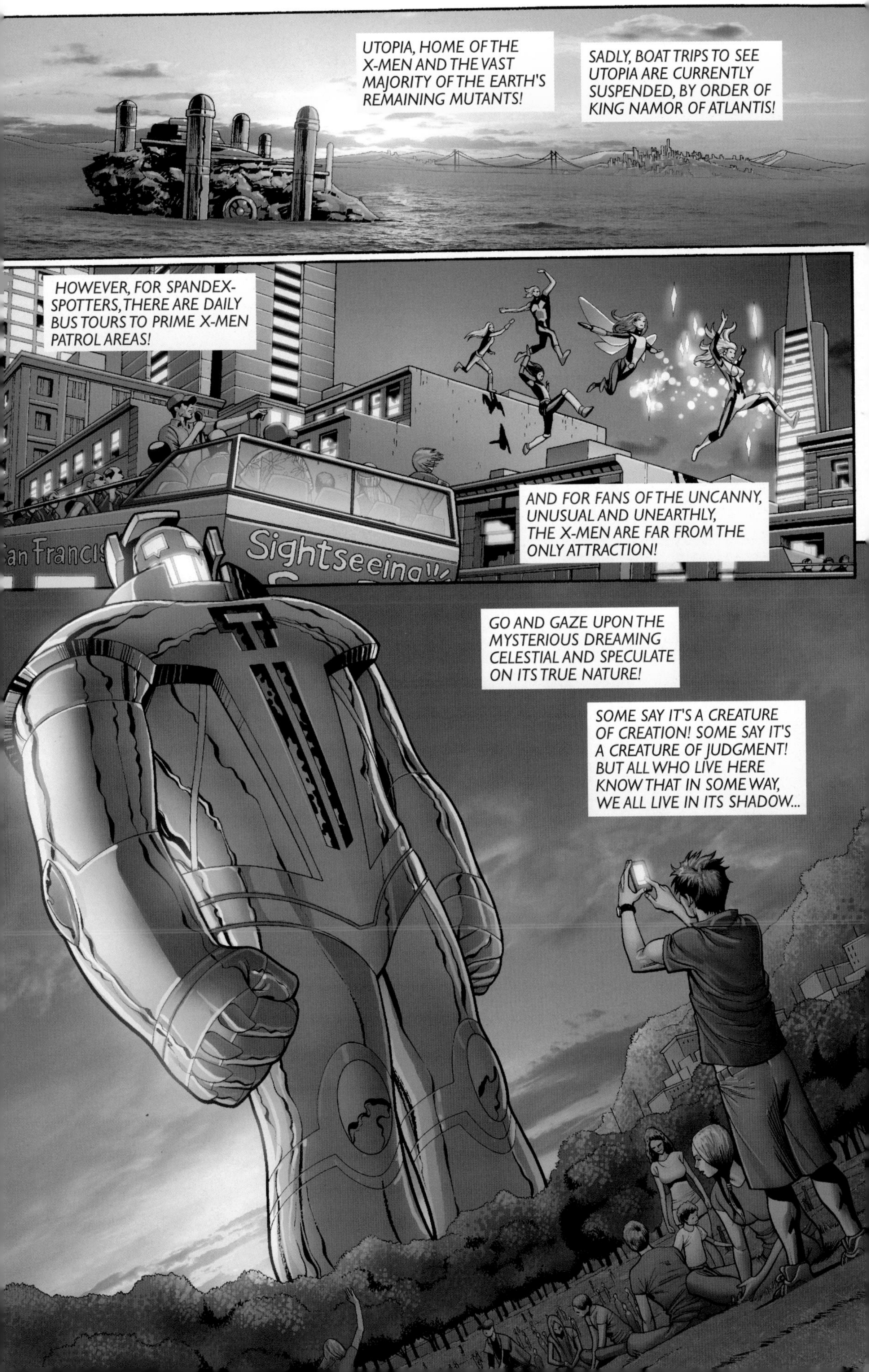
UTOPIA, HOME OF THE X-MEN AND THE VAST MAJORITY OF THE EARTH'S REMAINING MUTANTS!
SADLY, BOAT TRIPS TO SEE UTOPIA ARE CURRENTLY SUSPENDED, BY ORDER OF KING NAMOR OF ATLANTIS!
HOWEVER, FOR SPANDEX-SPOTTERS, THERE ARE DAILY BUS TOURS TO PRIME X-MEN PATROL AREAS!
San Francis
Sightseeing
AND FOR FANS OF THE UNCANNY, UNUSUAL AND UNEARTHLY, THE X-MEN ARE FAR FROM THE ONLY ATTRACTION!
GO AND GAZE UPON THE MYSTERIOUS DREAMING CELESTIAL AND SPECULATE ON ITS TRUE NATURE!
SOME SAY IT'S A CREATURE OF CREATION! SOME SAY IT'S A CREATURE OF JUDGMENT! BUT ALL WHO LIVE HERE KNOW THAT IN SOME WAY, WE ALL LIVE IN ITS SHADOW...

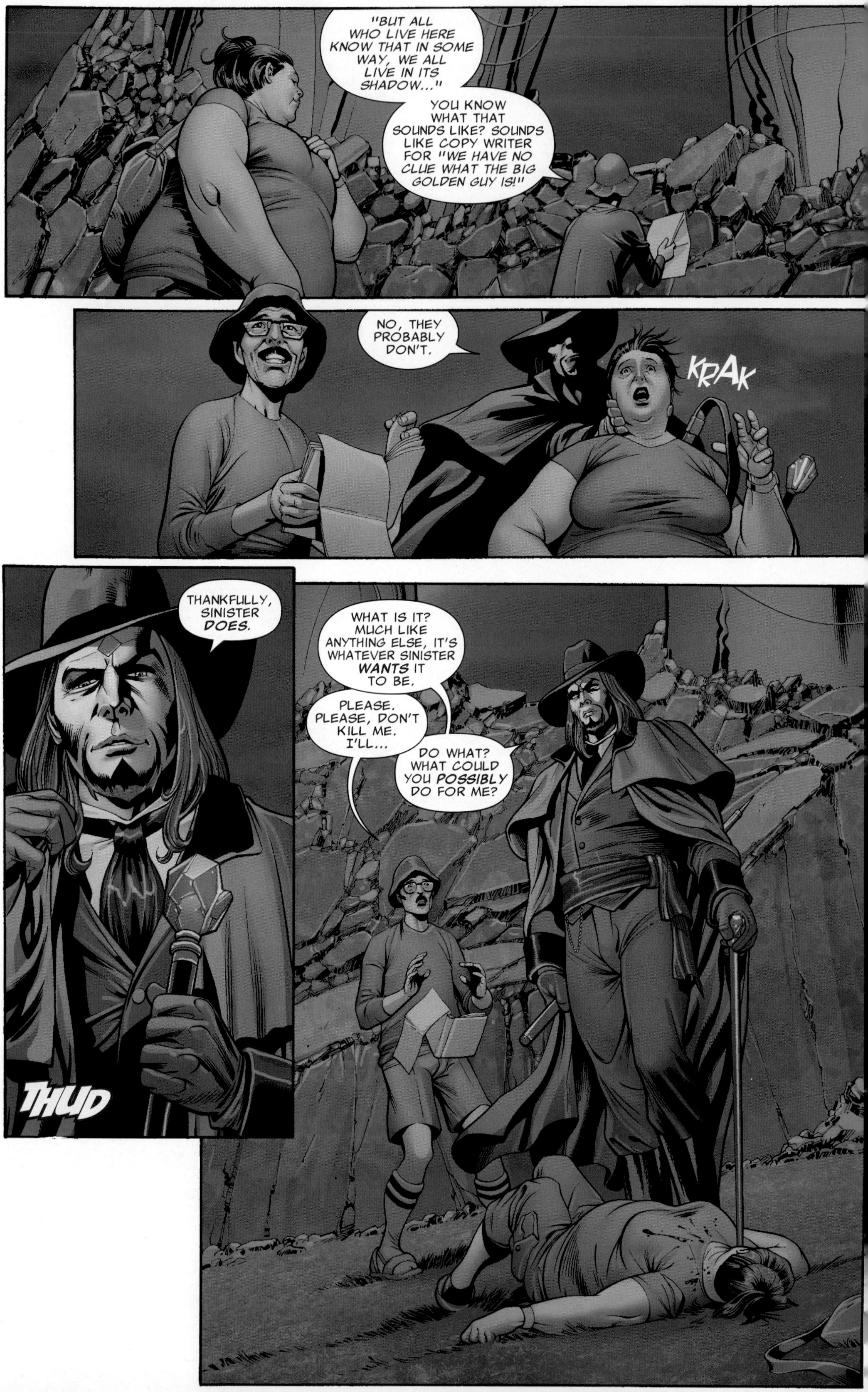
"BUT ALL WHO LIVE HERE KNOW THAT IN SOME WAY, WE ALL LIVE IN ITS SHADOW..."
YOU KNOW WHAT THAT SOUNDS LIKE? SOUNDS LIKE COPY WRITER FOR "WE HAVE NO CLUE WHAT THE BIG GOLDEN GUY IS!"
NO, THEY PROBABLY DON'T.
KRAK
THANKFULLY, SINISTER DOES.
THUD
WHAT IS IT? MUCH LIKE ANYTHING ELSE, IT'S WHATEVER SINISTER WANTS IT TO BE.
PLEASE. PLEASE, DON'T KILL ME. I'LL...
DO WHAT? WHAT COULD YOU POSSIBLY DO FOR ME?

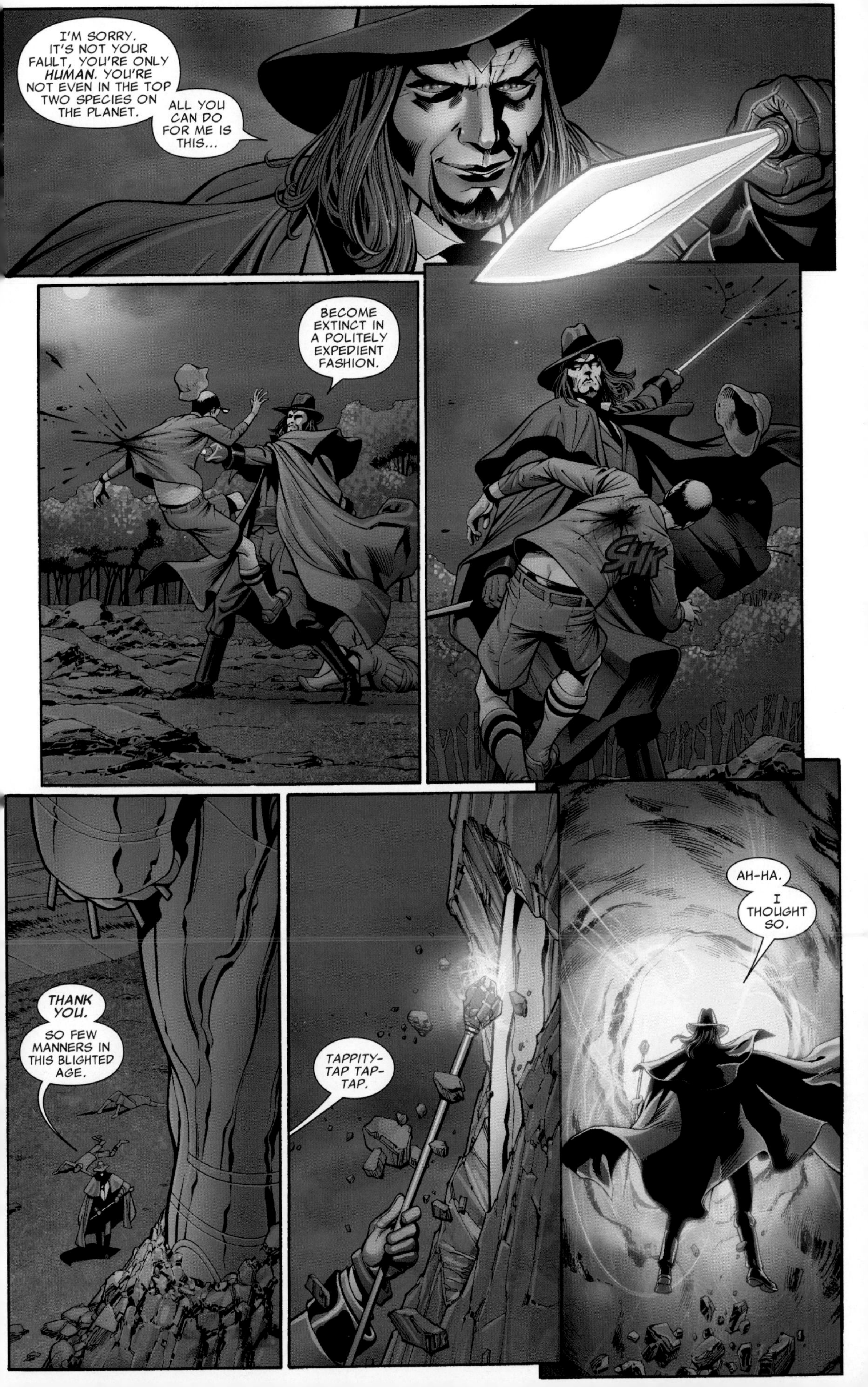
I'M SORRY. IT'S NOT YOUR FAULT, YOU'RE ONLY *HUMAN*. YOU'RE NOT EVEN IN THE TOP TWO SPECIES ON THE PLANET.
ALL YOU CAN DO FOR ME IS THIS...
BECOME EXTINCT IN A POLITELY EXPEDIENT FASHION.
SHK
THANK YOU.
SO FEW MANNERS IN THIS BLIGHTED AGE.
TAPPITY-TAP TAP-TAP.
AH-HA.
I THOUGHT SO.

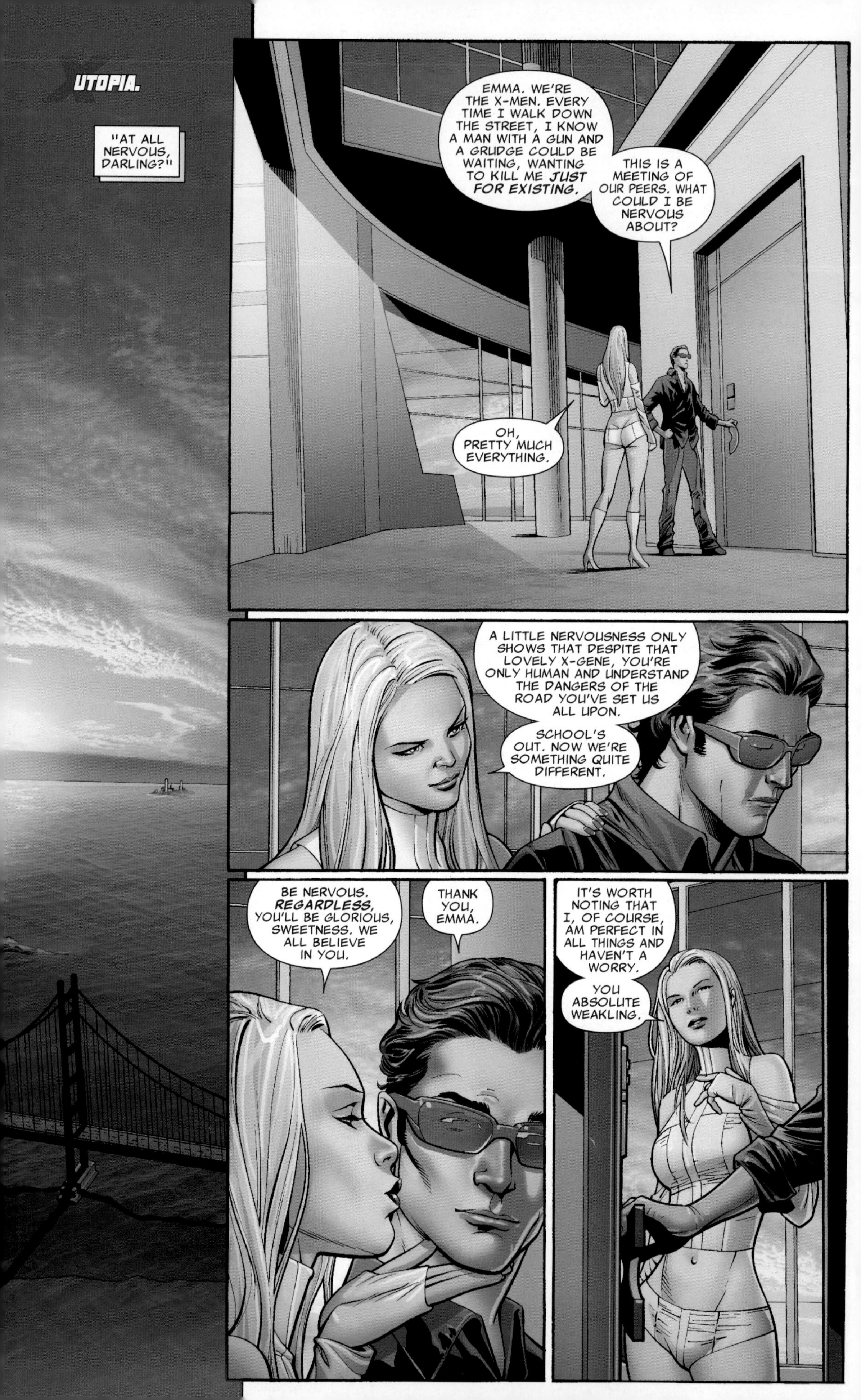
UTOPIA.
"AT ALL NERVOUS, DARLING?"
EMMA. WE'RE THE X-MEN. EVERY TIME I WALK DOWN THE STREET, I KNOW A MAN WITH A GUN AND A GRUDGE COULD BE WAITING, WANTING TO KILL ME JUST FOR EXISTING.
THIS IS A MEETING OF OUR PEERS. WHAT COULD I BE NERVOUS ABOUT?
OH, PRETTY MUCH EVERYTHING.
A LITTLE NERVOUSNESS ONLY SHOWS THAT DESPITE THAT LOVELY X-GENE, YOU'RE ONLY HUMAN AND UNDERSTAND THE DANGERS OF THE ROAD YOU'VE SET US ALL UPON.
SCHOOL'S OUT. NOW WE'RE SOMETHING QUITE DIFFERENT.
BE NERVOUS. REGARDLESS, YOU'LL BE GLORIOUS, SWEETNESS. WE ALL BELIEVE IN YOU.
THANK YOU, EMMA.
IT'S WORTH NOTING THAT I, OF COURSE, AM PERFECT IN ALL THINGS AND HAVEN'T A WORRY.
YOU ABSOLUTE WEAKLING.

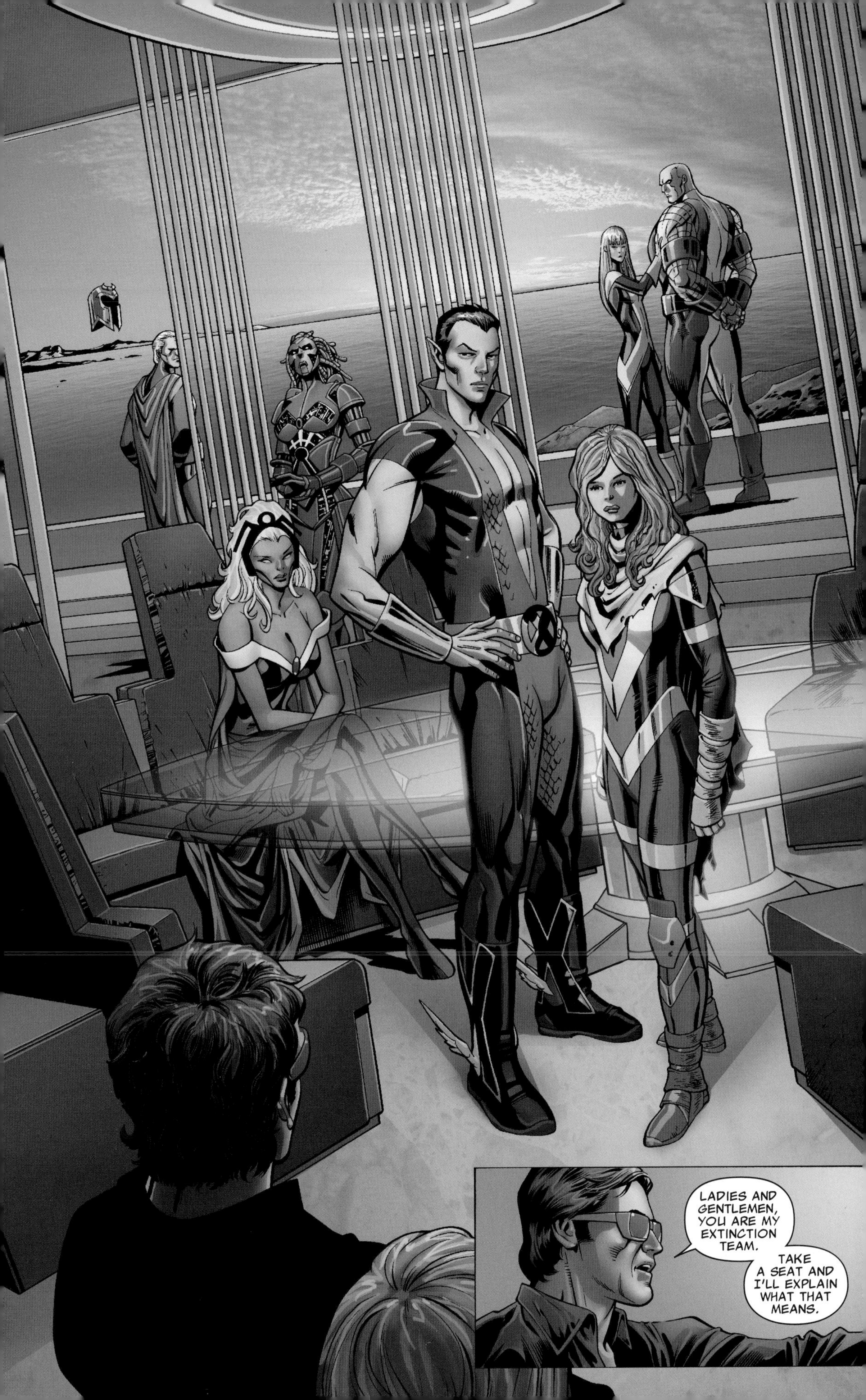
LADIES AND GENTLEMEN, YOU ARE MY EXTINCTION TEAM.
TAKE A SEAT AND I'LL EXPLAIN WHAT THAT MEANS.

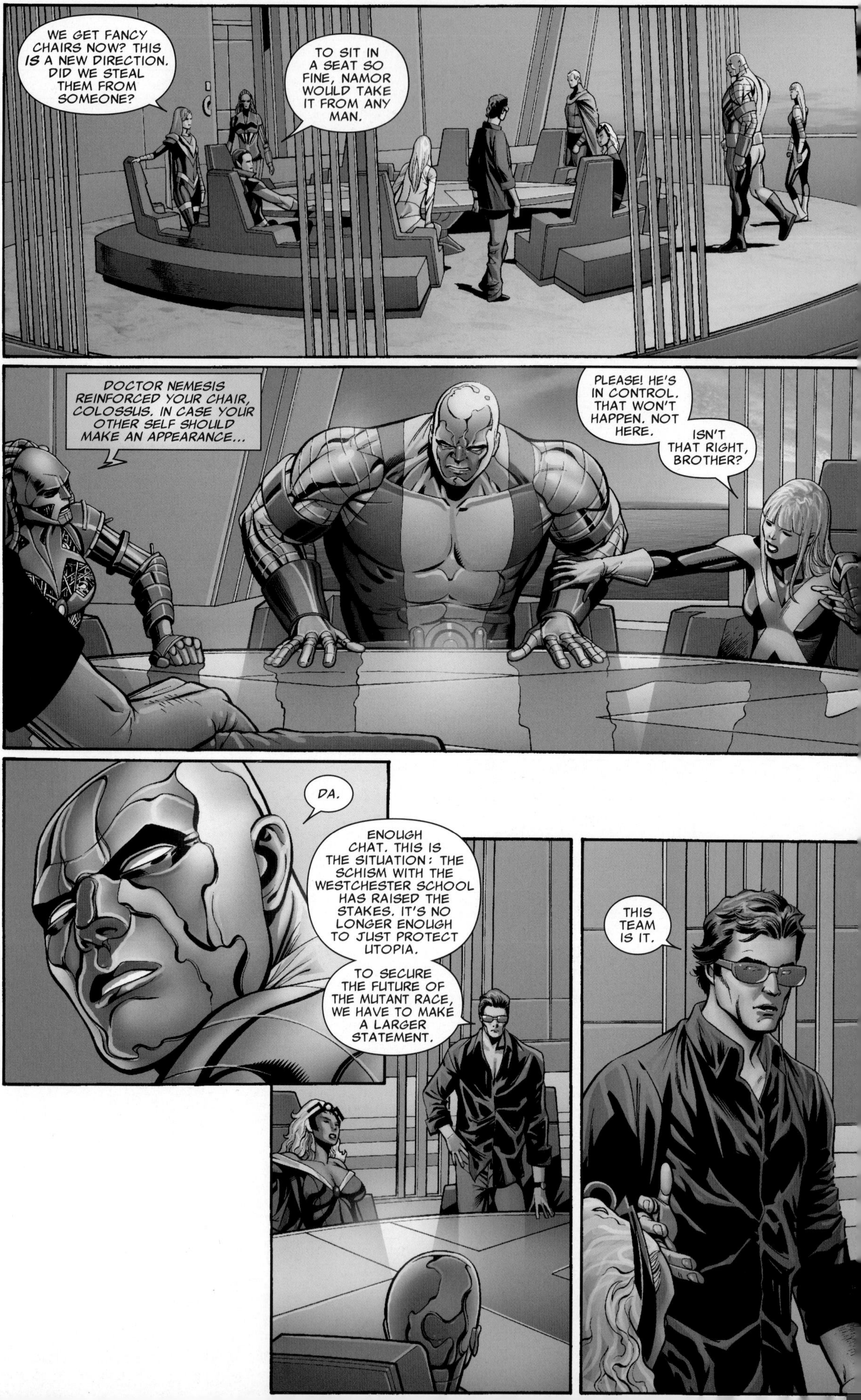
WE GET FANCY CHAIRS NOW? THIS IS A NEW DIRECTION. DID WE STEAL THEM FROM SOMEONE?
TO SIT IN A SEAT SO FINE, NAMOR WOULD TAKE IT FROM ANY MAN.
DOCTOR NEMESIS REINFORCED YOUR CHAIR, COLOSSUS. IN CASE YOUR OTHER SELF SHOULD MAKE AN APPEARANCE...
PLEASE! HE'S IN CONTROL. THAT WON'T HAPPEN. NOT HERE.
ISN'T THAT RIGHT, BROTHER?
DA.
ENOUGH CHAT. THIS IS THE SITUATION: THE SCHISM WITH THE WESTCHESTER SCHOOL HAS RAISED THE STAKES. IT'S NO LONGER ENOUGH TO JUST PROTECT UTOPIA.
TO SECURE THE FUTURE OF THE MUTANT RACE, WE HAVE TO MAKE A LARGER STATEMENT.
THIS TEAM IS IT.

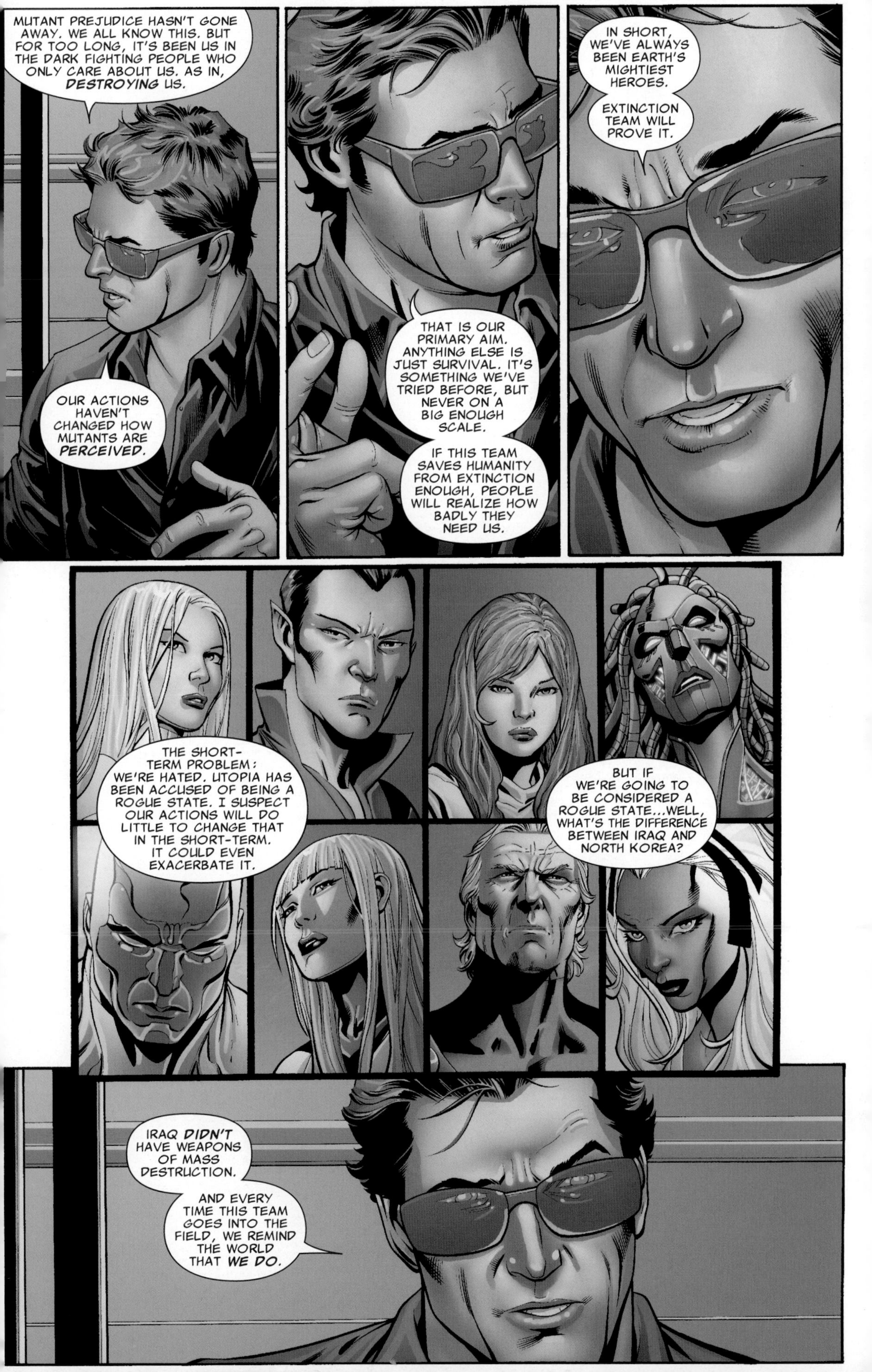
MUTANT PREJUDICE HASN'T GONE AWAY. WE ALL KNOW THIS. BUT FOR TOO LONG, IT'S BEEN US IN THE DARK FIGHTING PEOPLE WHO ONLY CARE ABOUT US. AS IN, DESTROYING US.
OUR ACTIONS HAVEN'T CHANGED HOW MUTANTS ARE PERCEIVED.
THAT IS OUR PRIMARY AIM. ANYTHING ELSE IS JUST SURVIVAL. IT'S SOMETHING WE'VE TRIED BEFORE, BUT NEVER ON A BIG ENOUGH SCALE.
IF THIS TEAM SAVES HUMANITY FROM EXTINCTION ENOUGH, PEOPLE WILL REALIZE HOW BADLY THEY NEED US.
IN SHORT, WE'VE ALWAYS BEEN EARTH'S MIGHTIEST HEROES.
EXTINCTION TEAM WILL PROVE IT.
THE SHORT-TERM PROBLEM: WE'RE HATED. UTOPIA HAS BEEN ACCUSED OF BEING A ROGUE STATE. I SUSPECT OUR ACTIONS WILL DO LITTLE TO CHANGE THAT IN THE SHORT-TERM. IT COULD EVEN EXACERBATE IT.
BUT IF WE'RE GOING TO BE CONSIDERED A ROGUE STATE...WELL, WHAT'S THE DIFFERENCE BETWEEN IRAQ AND NORTH KOREA?
IRAQ DIDN'T HAVE WEAPONS OF MASS DESTRUCTION.
AND EVERY TIME THIS TEAM GOES INTO THE FIELD, WE REMIND THE WORLD THAT WE DO.

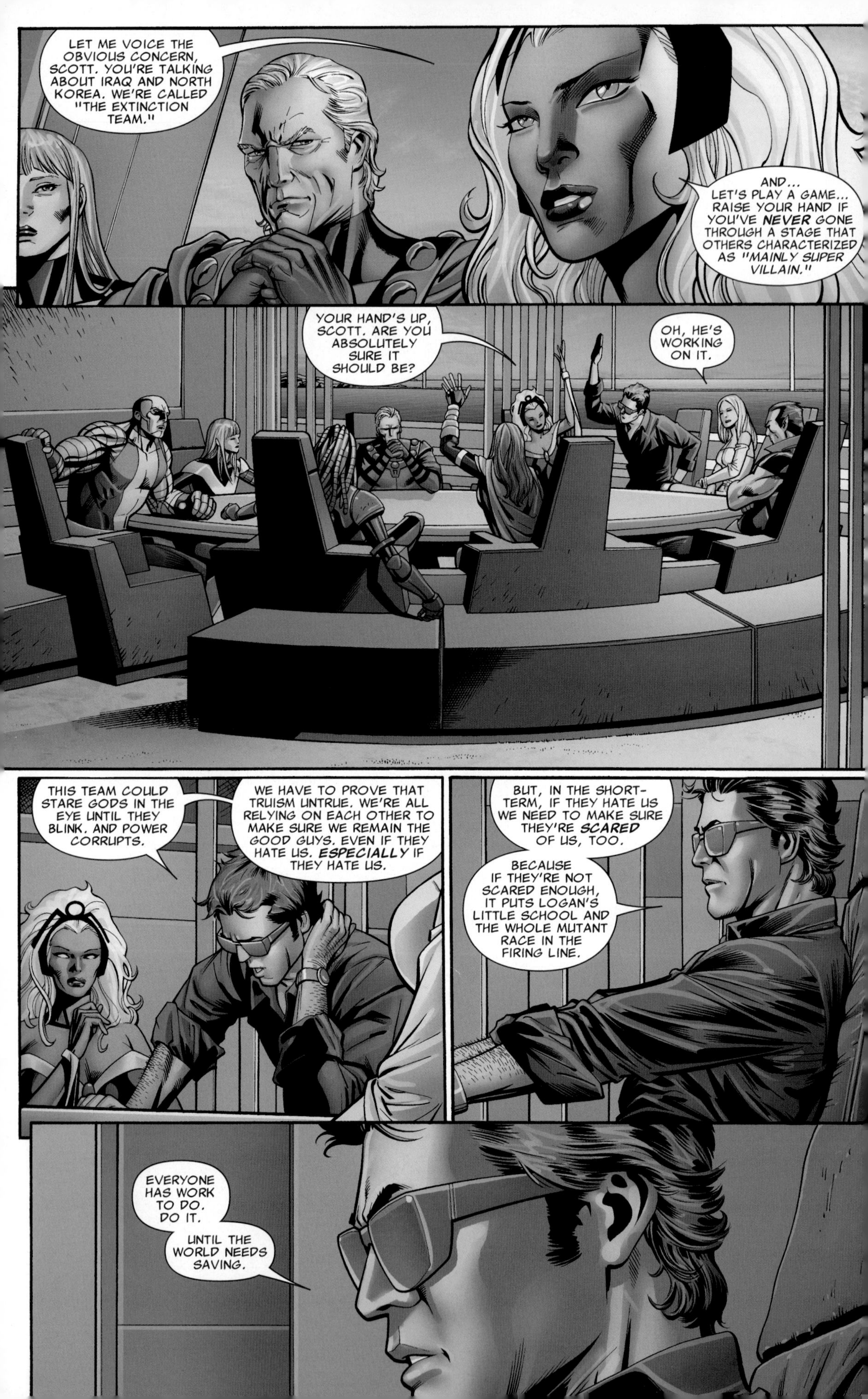
LET ME VOICE THE OBVIOUS CONCERN, SCOTT. YOU'RE TALKING ABOUT IRAQ AND NORTH KOREA. WE'RE CALLED "THE EXTINCTION TEAM."
AND... LET'S PLAY A GAME... RAISE YOUR HAND IF YOU'VE NEVER GONE THROUGH A STAGE THAT OTHERS CHARACTERIZED AS "MAINLY SUPER VILLAIN."
YOUR HAND'S UP, SCOTT. ARE YOU ABSOLUTELY SURE IT SHOULD BE?
OH, HE'S WORKING ON IT.
THIS TEAM COULD STARE GODS IN THE EYE UNTIL THEY BLINK. AND POWER CORRUPTS.
WE HAVE TO PROVE THAT TRUISM UNTRUE. WE'RE ALL RELYING ON EACH OTHER TO MAKE SURE WE REMAIN THE GOOD GUYS. EVEN IF THEY HATE US. ESPECIALLY IF THEY HATE US.
BUT, IN THE SHORT-TERM, IF THEY HATE US WE NEED TO MAKE SURE THEY'RE SCARED OF US, TOO.
BECAUSE IF THEY'RE NOT SCARED ENOUGH, IT PUTS LOGAN'S LITTLE SCHOOL AND THE WHOLE MUTANT RACE IN THE FIRING LINE.
EVERYONE HAS WORK TO DO. DO IT.
UNTIL THE WORLD NEEDS SAVING.

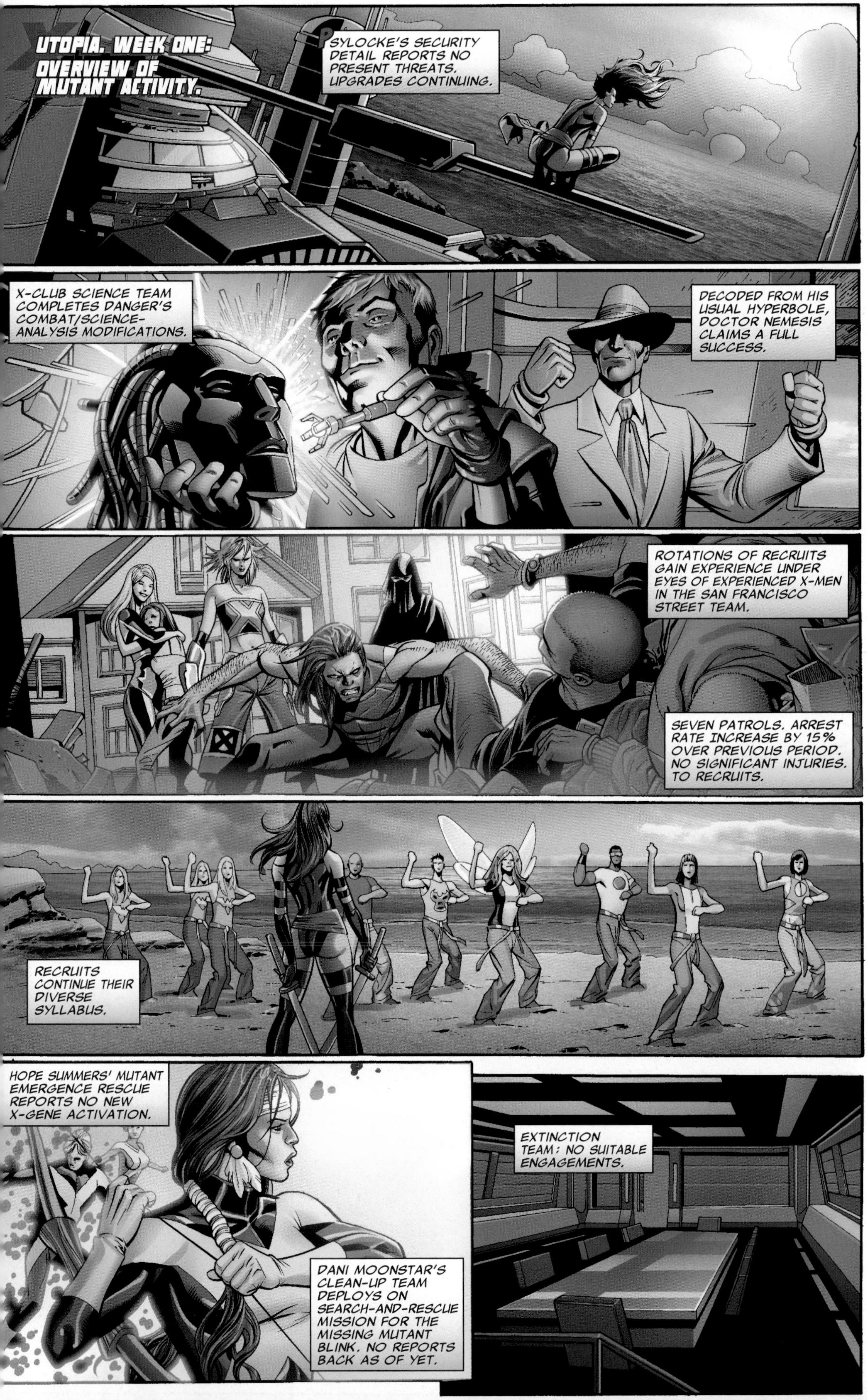
UTOPIA. WEEK ONE: OVERVIEW OF MUTANT ACTIVITY.
SYLOCKE'S SECURITY DETAIL REPORTS NO PRESENT THREATS. UPGRADES CONTINUING.
X-CLUB SCIENCE TEAM COMPLETES DANGER'S COMBAT/SCIENCE-ANALYSIS MODIFICATIONS.
DECODED FROM HIS USUAL HYPERBOLE, DOCTOR NEMESIS CLAIMS A FULL SUCCESS.
ROTATIONS OF RECRUITS GAIN EXPERIENCE UNDER EYES OF EXPERIENCED X-MEN IN THE SAN FRANCISCO STREET TEAM.
SEVEN PATROLS. ARREST RATE INCREASE BY 15% OVER PREVIOUS PERIOD. NO SIGNIFICANT INJURIES. TO RECRUITS.
RECRUITS CONTINUE THEIR DIVERSE SYLLABUS.
HOPE SUMMERS' MUTANT EMERGENCE RESCUE REPORTS NO NEW X-GENE ACTIVATION.
EXTINCTION TEAM: NO SUITABLE ENGAGEMENTS.
DANI MOONSTAR'S CLEAN-UP TEAM DEPLOYS ON SEARCH-AND-RESCUE MISSION FOR THE MISSING MUTANT BLINK. NO REPORTS BACK AS OF YET.

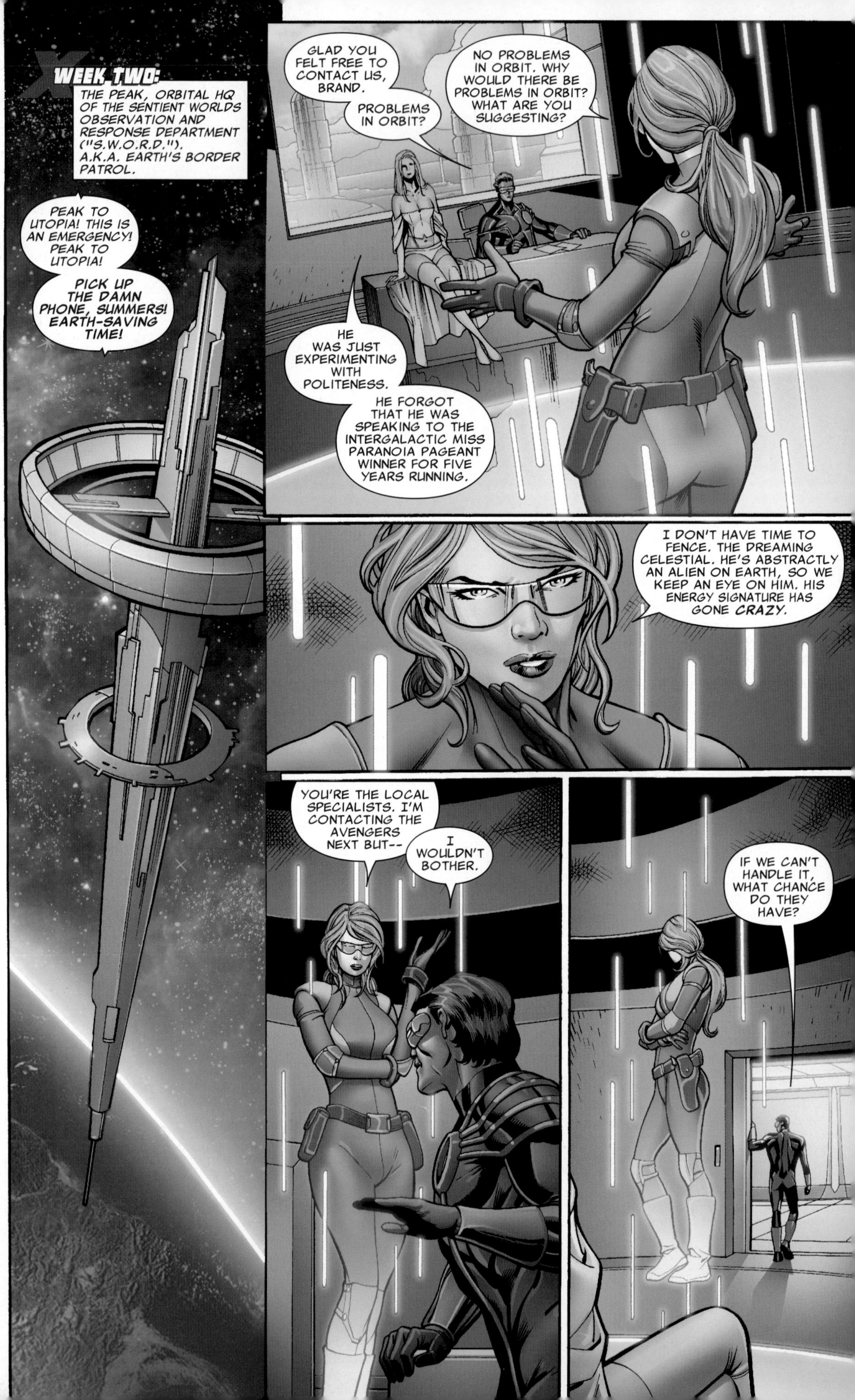
WEEK TWO:
THE PEAK, ORBITAL HQ OF THE SENTIENT WORLDS OBSERVATION AND RESPONSE DEPARTMENT ("S.W.O.R.D."). A.K.A. EARTH'S BORDER PATROL.
PEAK TO UTOPIA! THIS IS AN EMERGENCY! PEAK TO UTOPIA!
PICK UP THE DAMN PHONE, SUMMERS! EARTH-SAVING TIME!
GLAD YOU FELT FREE TO CONTACT US, BRAND.
PROBLEMS IN ORBIT?
NO PROBLEMS IN ORBIT. WHY WOULD THERE BE PROBLEMS IN ORBIT? WHAT ARE YOU SUGGESTING?
HE WAS JUST EXPERIMENTING WITH POLITENESS.
HE FORGOT THAT HE WAS SPEAKING TO THE INTERGALACTIC MISS PARANOIA PAGEANT WINNER FOR FIVE YEARS RUNNING.
I DON'T HAVE TIME TO FENCE. THE DREAMING CELESTIAL. HE'S ABSTRACTLY AN ALIEN ON EARTH, SO WE KEEP AN EYE ON HIM. HIS ENERGY SIGNATURE HAS GONE CRAZY.
YOU'RE THE LOCAL SPECIALISTS. I'M CONTACTING THE AVENGERS NEXT BUT--
I WOULDN'T BOTHER.
IF WE CAN'T HANDLE IT, WHAT CHANCE DO THEY HAVE?

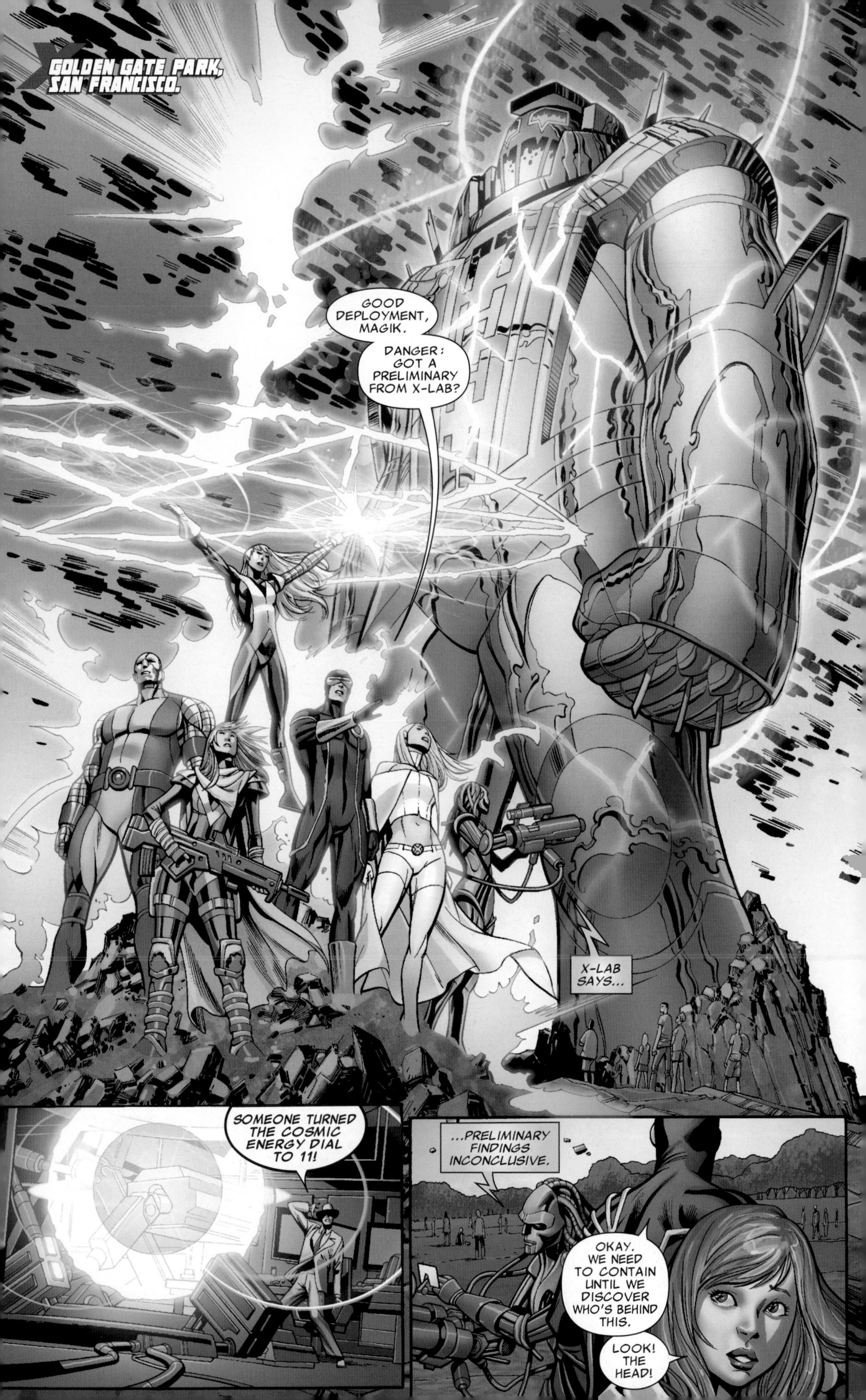
GOLDEN GATE PARK, SAN FRANCISCO.
GOOD DEPLOYMENT, MAGIK.
DANGER: GOT A PRELIMINARY FROM X-LAB?
X-LAB SAYS...
SOMEONE TURNED THE COSMIC ENERGY DIAL TO 11!
...PRELIMINARY FINDINGS INCONCLUSIVE.
OKAY. WE NEED TO CONTAIN UNTIL WE DISCOVER WHO'S BEHIND THIS.
LOOK! THE HEAD!

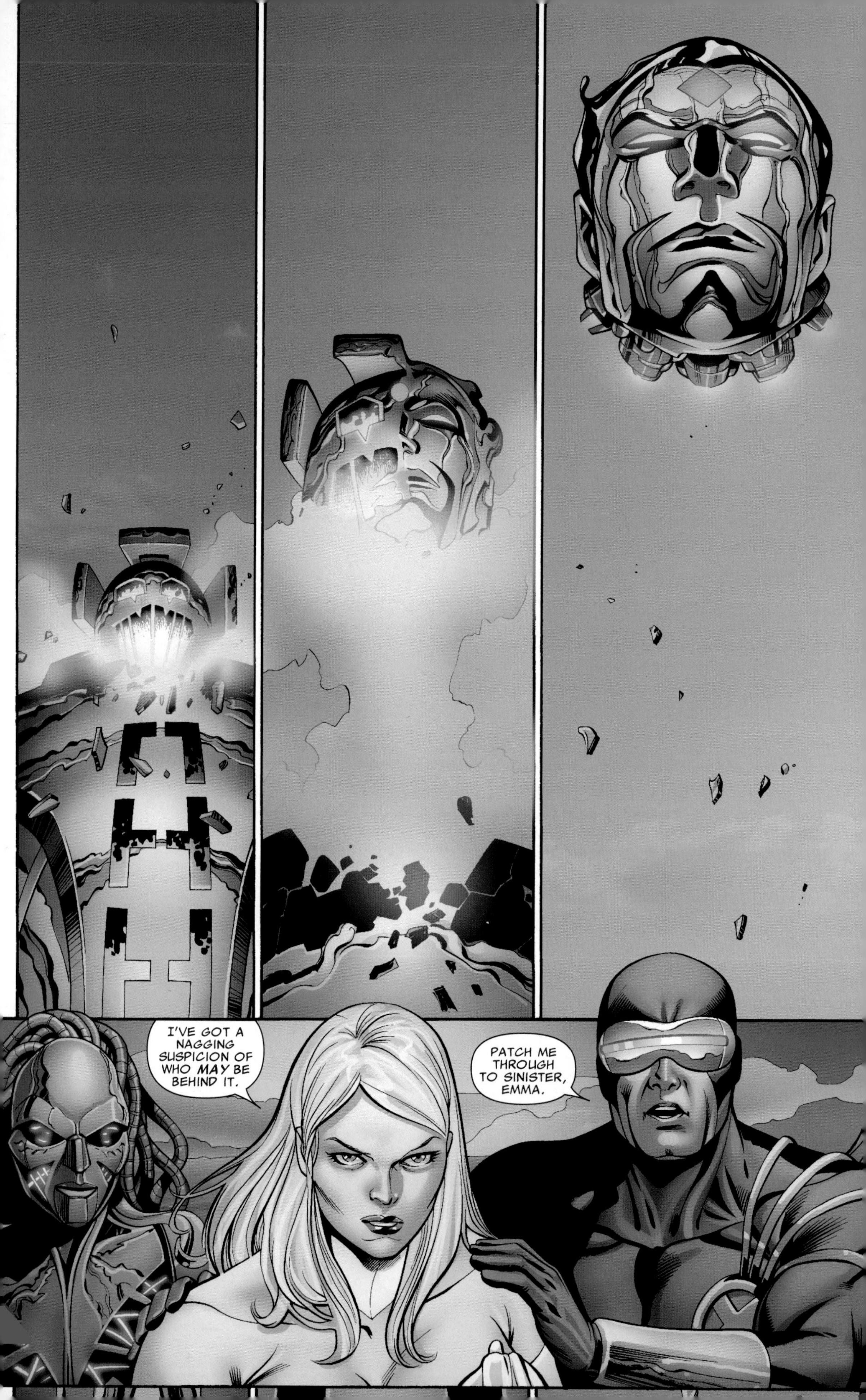
I'VE GOT A NAGGING SUSPICION OF WHO MAY BE BEHIND IT.
PATCH ME THROUGH TO SINISTER, EMMA.

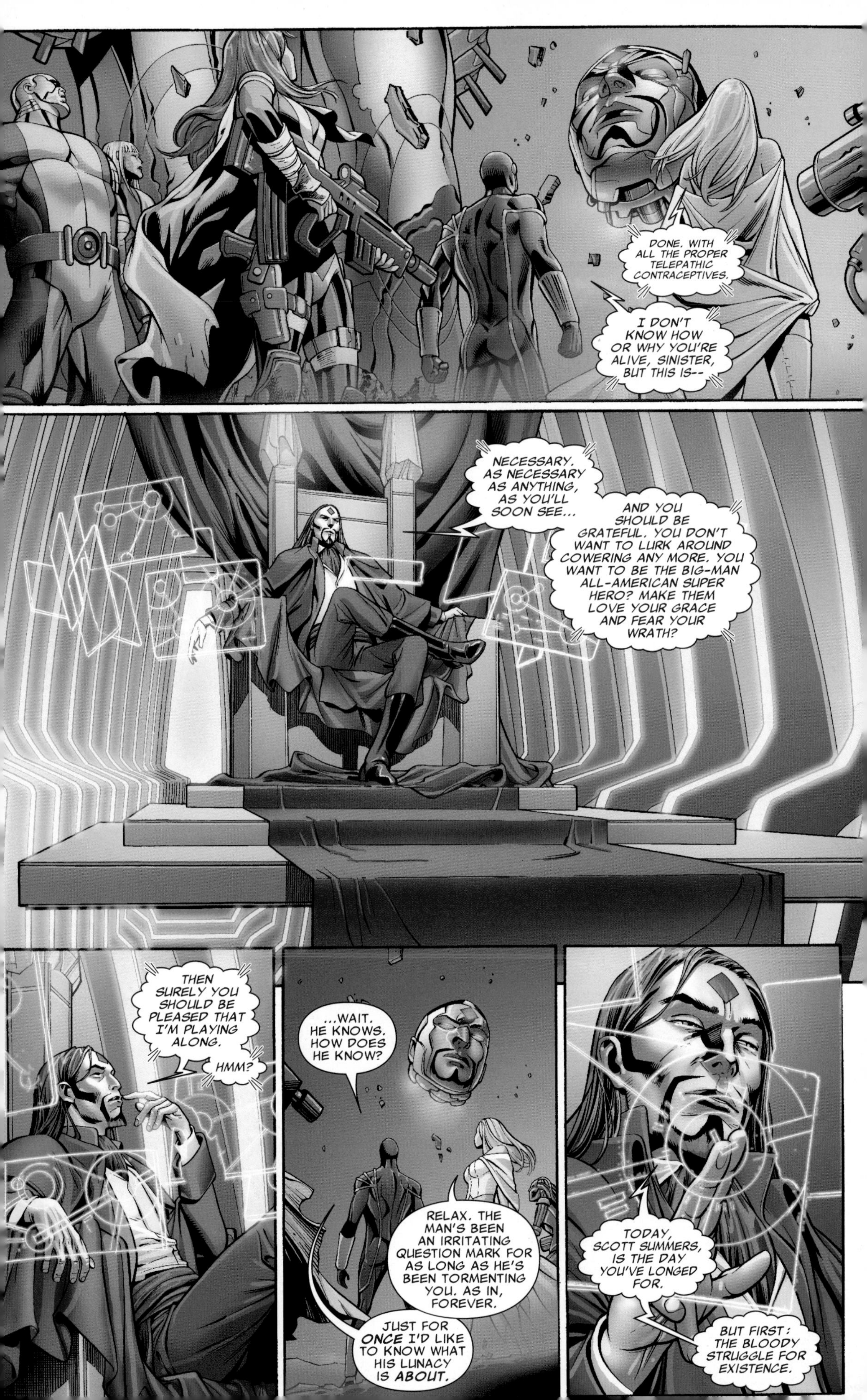
DONE. WITH ALL THE PROPER TELEPATHIC CONTRACEPTIVES.
I DON'T KNOW HOW OR WHY YOU'RE ALIVE, SINISTER, BUT THIS IS--
NECESSARY. AS NECESSARY AS ANYTHING, AS YOU'LL SOON SEE...
AND YOU SHOULD BE GRATEFUL. YOU DON'T WANT TO LURK AROUND COWERING ANY MORE. YOU WANT TO BE THE BIG-MAN ALL-AMERICAN SUPER HERO? MAKE THEM LOVE YOUR GRACE AND FEAR YOUR WRATH?
THEN SURELY YOU SHOULD BE PLEASED THAT I'M PLAYING ALONG.
HMM?
...WAIT. HE KNOWS. HOW DOES HE KNOW?
RELAX. THE MAN'S BEEN AN IRRITATING QUESTION MARK FOR AS LONG AS HE'S BEEN TORMENTING YOU. AS IN, FOREVER.
JUST FOR *ONCE* I'D LIKE TO KNOW WHAT HIS LUNACY IS *ABOUT*.
TODAY, SCOTT SUMMERS, IS THE DAY YOU'VE LONGED FOR.
BUT FIRST: THE BLOODY STRUGGLE FOR EXISTENCE.

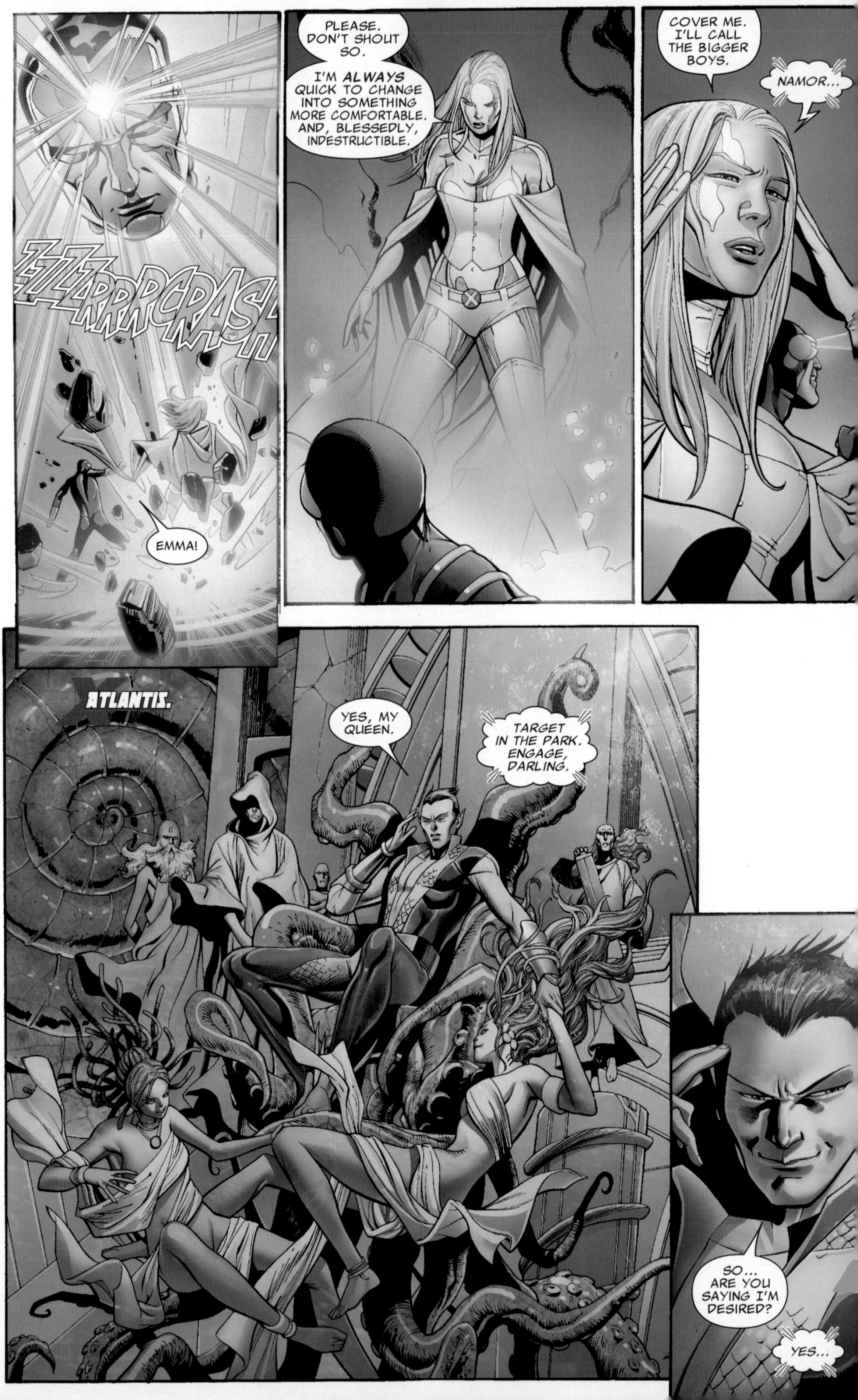
ZZZZZARRRRCRASH
EMMA!
PLEASE. DON'T SHOUT SO.
I'M ALWAYS QUICK TO CHANGE INTO SOMETHING MORE COMFORTABLE. AND, BLESSEDLY, INDESTRUCTIBLE.
COVER ME. I'LL CALL THE BIGGER BOYS.
NAMOR...
ATLANTIS.
YES, MY QUEEN.
TARGET IN THE PARK. ENGAGE, DARLING.
SO... ARE YOU SAYING I'M DESIRED?
YES...

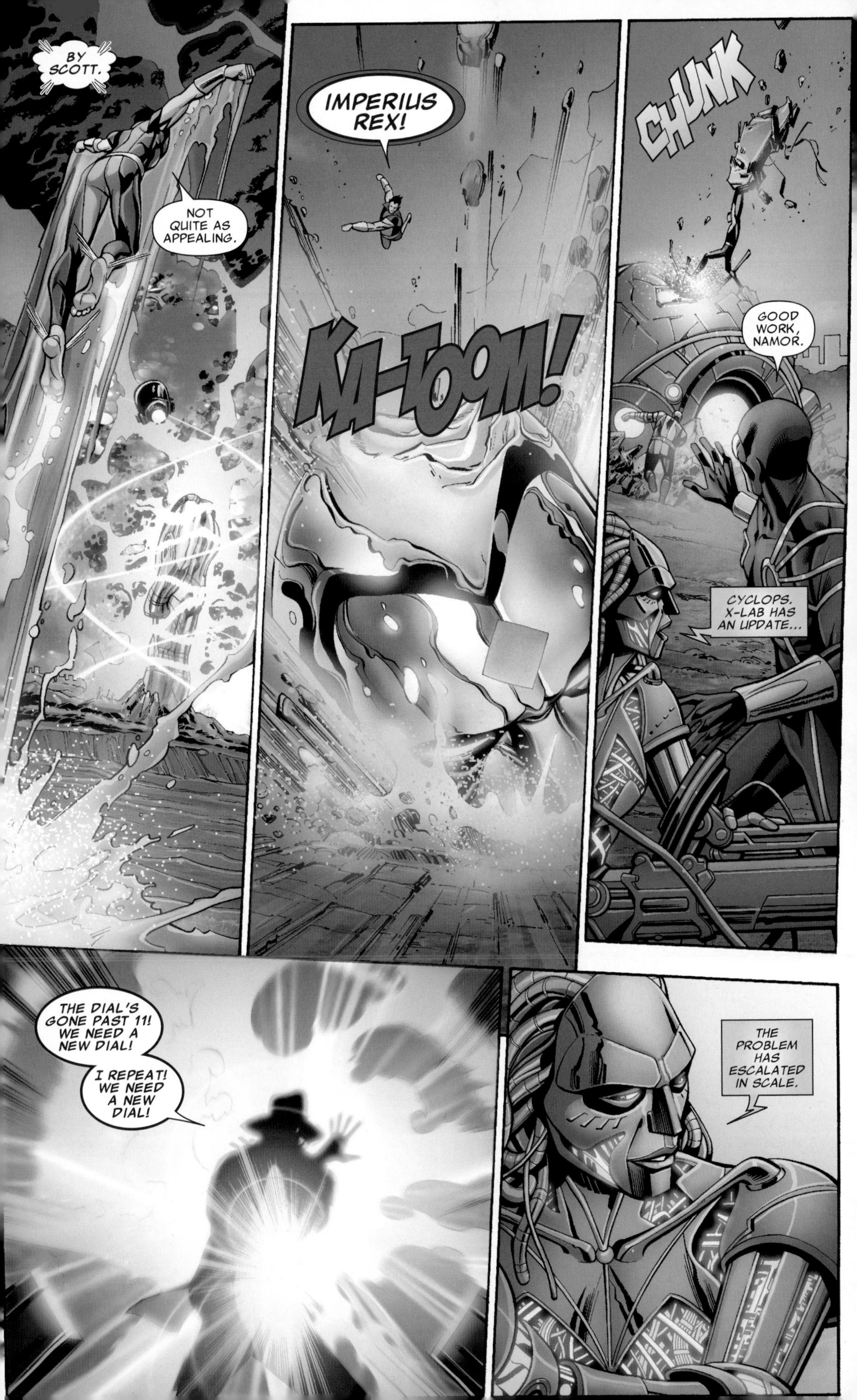

BY SCOTT.
NOT QUITE AS APPEALING.
IMPERIUS REX!
KA-TOOM!
CHUNK
GOOD WORK, NAMOR.
CYCLOPS. X-LAB HAS AN UPDATE...
THE DIAL'S GONE PAST 11! WE NEED A NEW DIAL!
I REPEAT! WE NEED A NEW DIAL!
THE PROBLEM HAS ESCALATED IN SCALE.

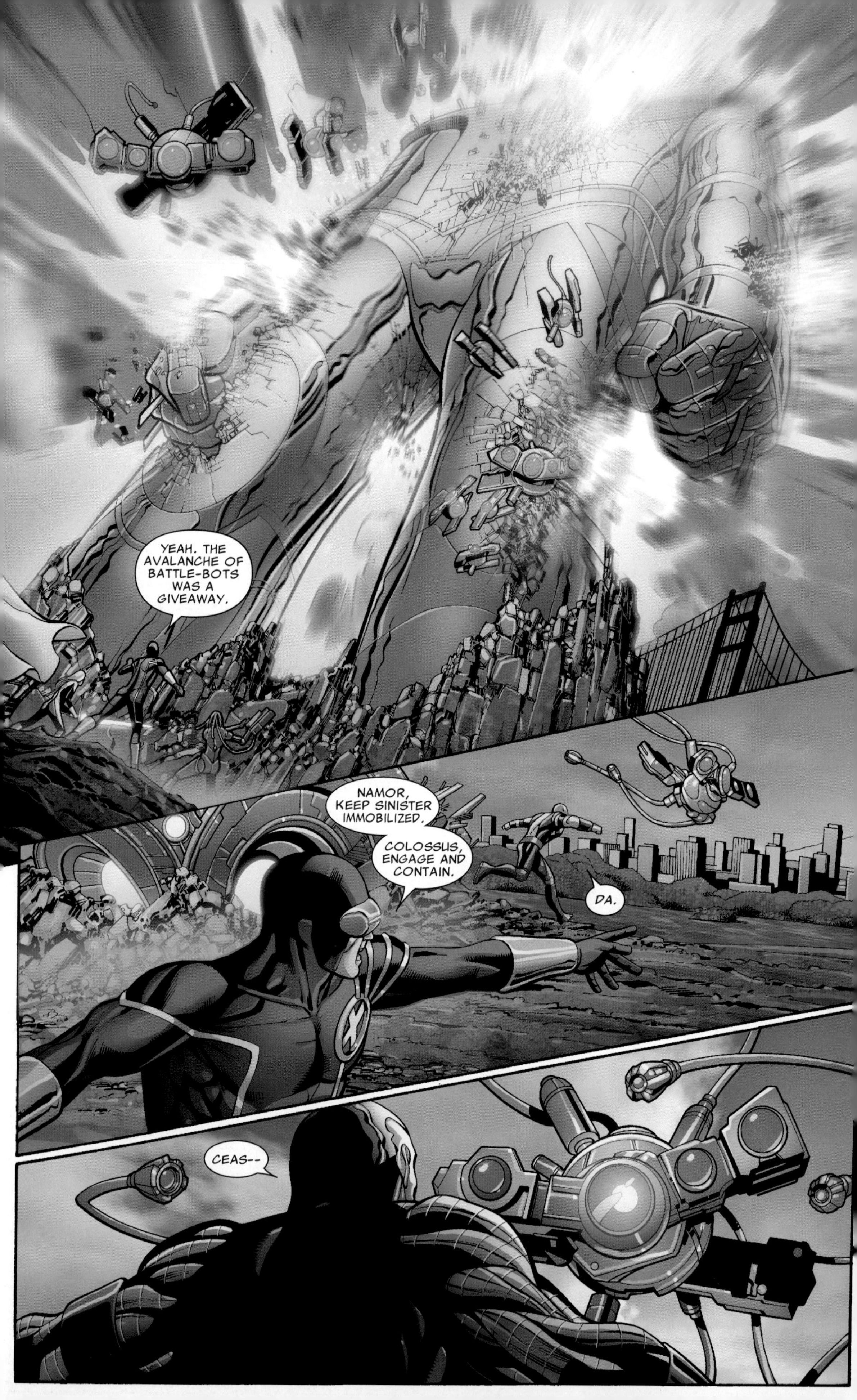
YEAH. THE AVALANCHE OF BATTLE-BOTS WAS A GIVEAWAY.
NAMOR, KEEP SINISTER IMMOBILIZED.
COLOSSUS, ENGAGE AND CONTAIN.
DA.
CEAS--

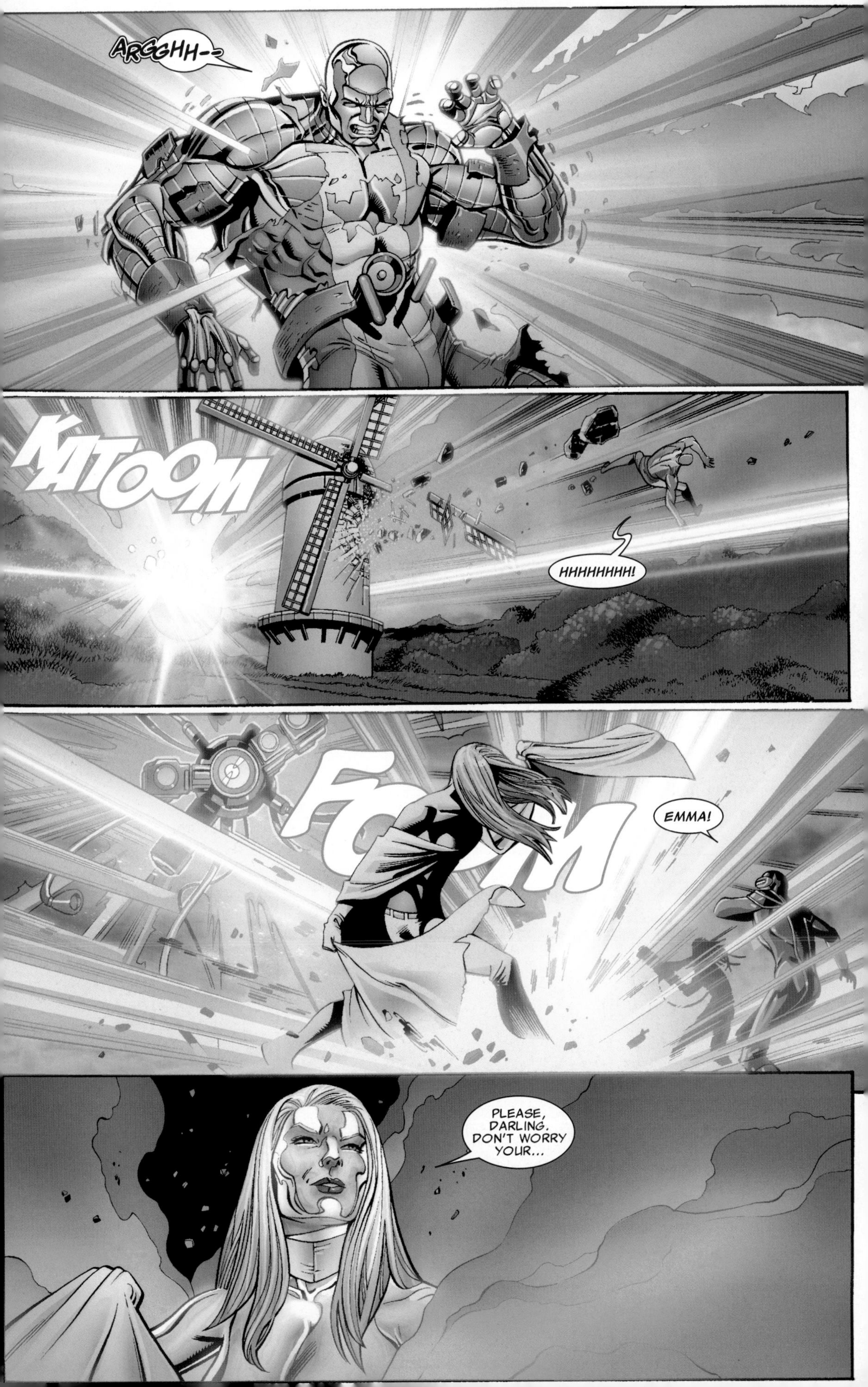
ARGGHH--
KATOOM
HHHHHHHH!
FOOM
EMMA!
PLEASE, DARLING, DON'T WORRY YOUR...

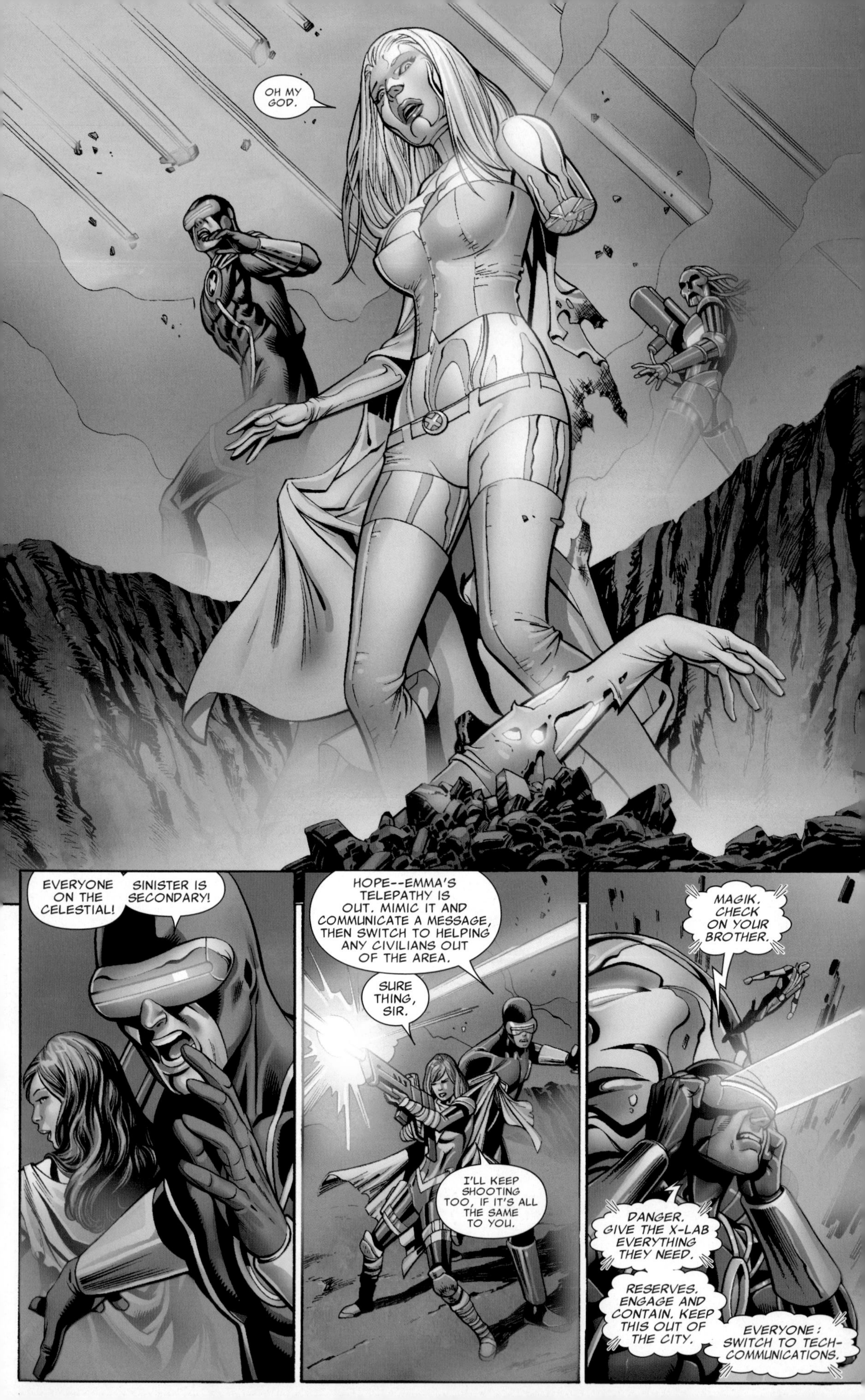
OH MY GOD.
EVERYONE ON THE CELESTIAL!
SINISTER IS SECONDARY!
HOPE--EMMA'S TELEPATHY IS OUT. MIMIC IT AND COMMUNICATE A MESSAGE, THEN SWITCH TO HELPING ANY CIVILIANS OUT OF THE AREA.
SURE THING, SIR.
I'LL KEEP SHOOTING TOO, IF IT'S ALL THE SAME TO YOU.
MAGIK, CHECK ON YOUR BROTHER.
DANGER. GIVE THE X-LAB EVERYTHING THEY NEED.
RESERVES. ENGAGE AND CONTAIN. KEEP THIS OUT OF THE CITY.
EVERYONE: SWITCH TO TECH-COMMUNICATIONS.

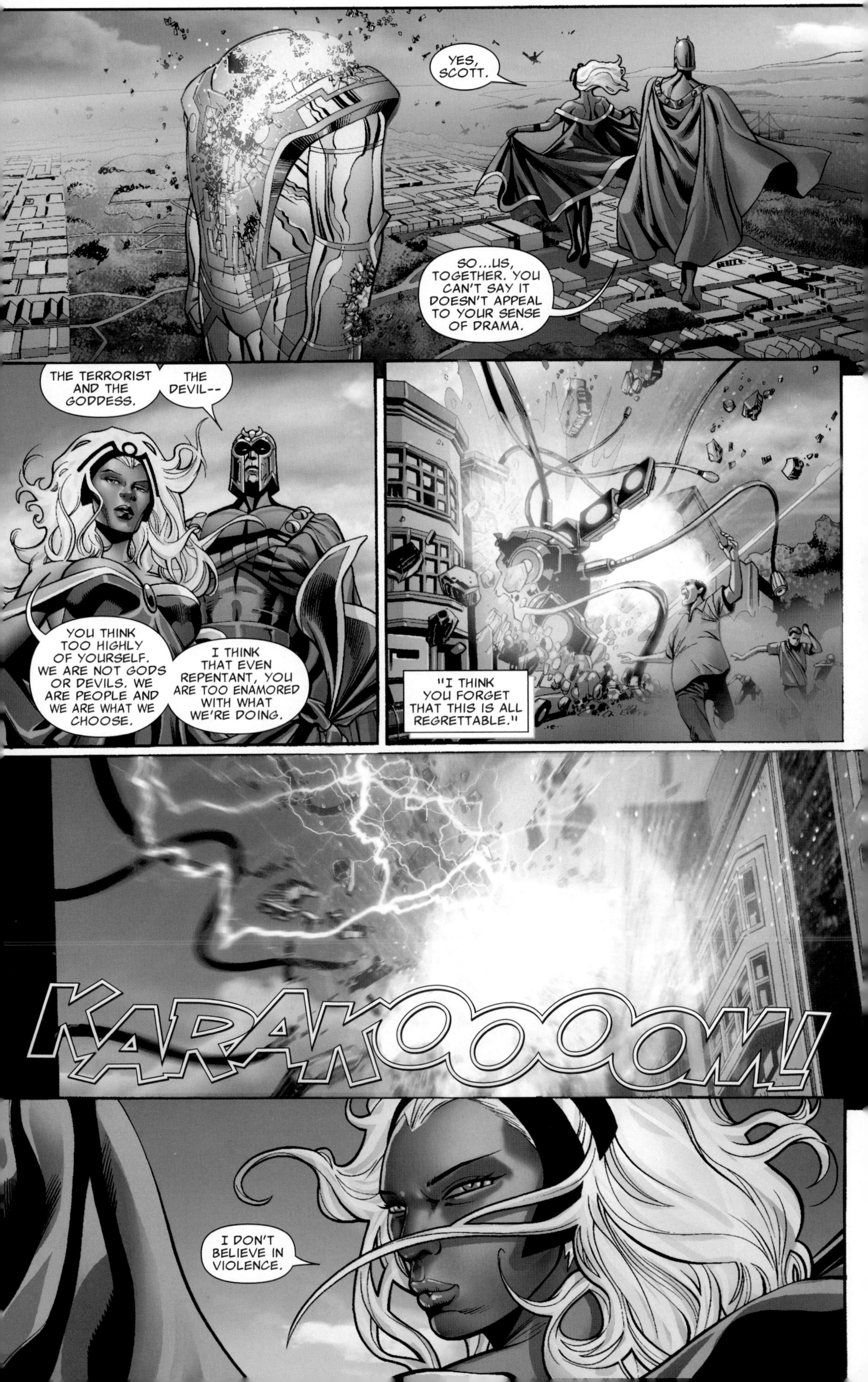

YES, SCOTT.
SO...US, TOGETHER. YOU CAN'T SAY IT DOESN'T APPEAL TO YOUR SENSE OF DRAMA.
THE TERRORIST AND THE GODDESS.
THE DEVIL--
YOU THINK TOO HIGHLY OF YOURSELF. WE ARE NOT GODS OR DEVILS. WE ARE PEOPLE AND WE ARE WHAT WE CHOOSE.
I THINK THAT EVEN REPENTANT, YOU ARE TOO ENAMORED WITH WHAT WE'RE DOING.
"I THINK YOU FORGET THAT THIS IS ALL REGRETTABLE."
KARAKOOOOM!
I DON'T BELIEVE IN VIOLENCE.

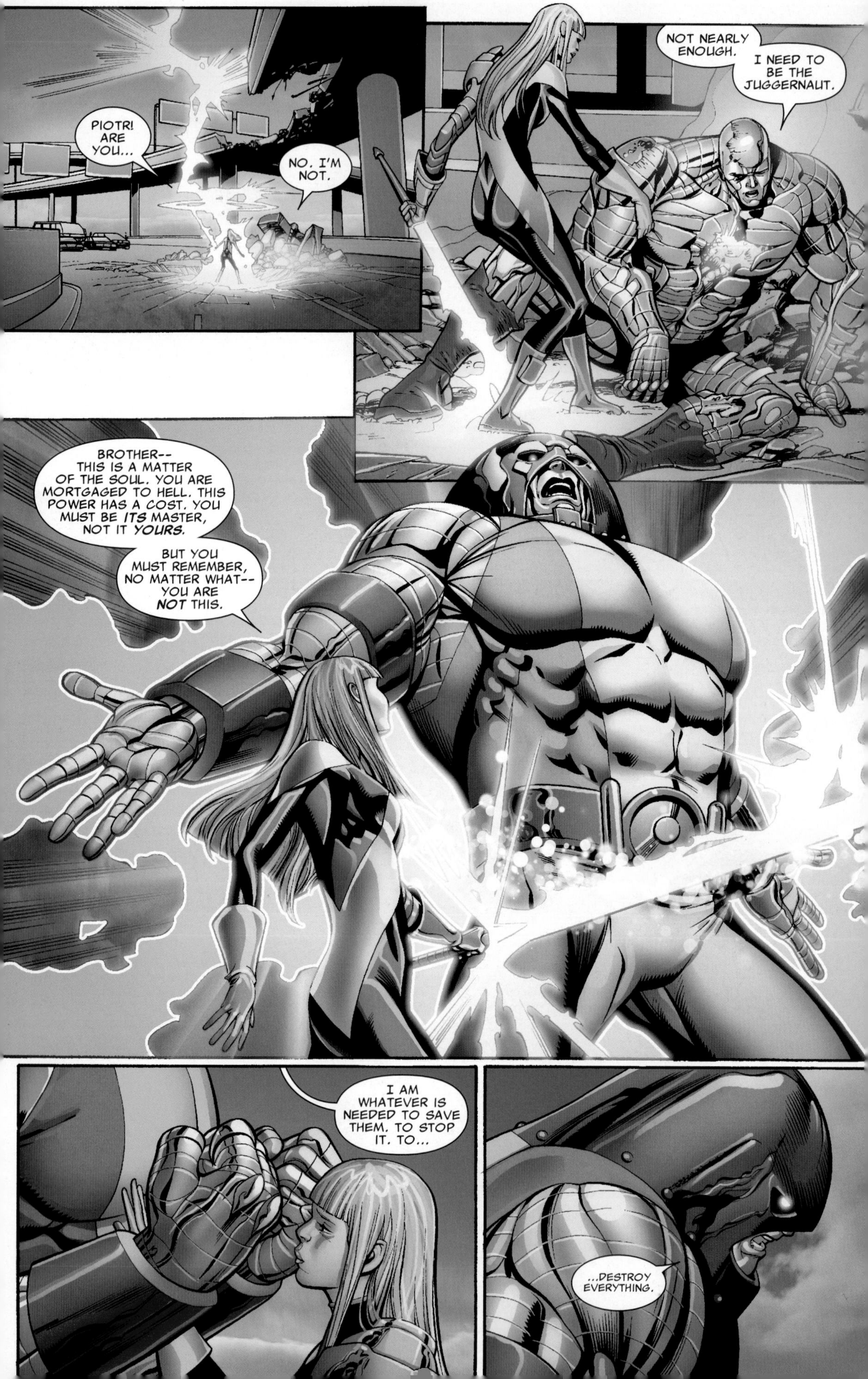
PIOTR! ARE YOU...
NO. I'M NOT.
NOT NEARLY ENOUGH.
I NEED TO BE THE JUGGERNAUT.
BROTHER-- THIS IS A MATTER OF THE SOUL. YOU ARE MORTGAGED TO HELL. THIS POWER HAS A COST. YOU MUST BE *ITS* MASTER, NOT IT *YOURS*.
BUT YOU MUST REMEMBER, NO MATTER WHAT-- YOU ARE *NOT* THIS.
I AM WHATEVER IS NEEDED TO SAVE THEM. TO STOP IT. TO...
...DESTROY EVERYTHING.

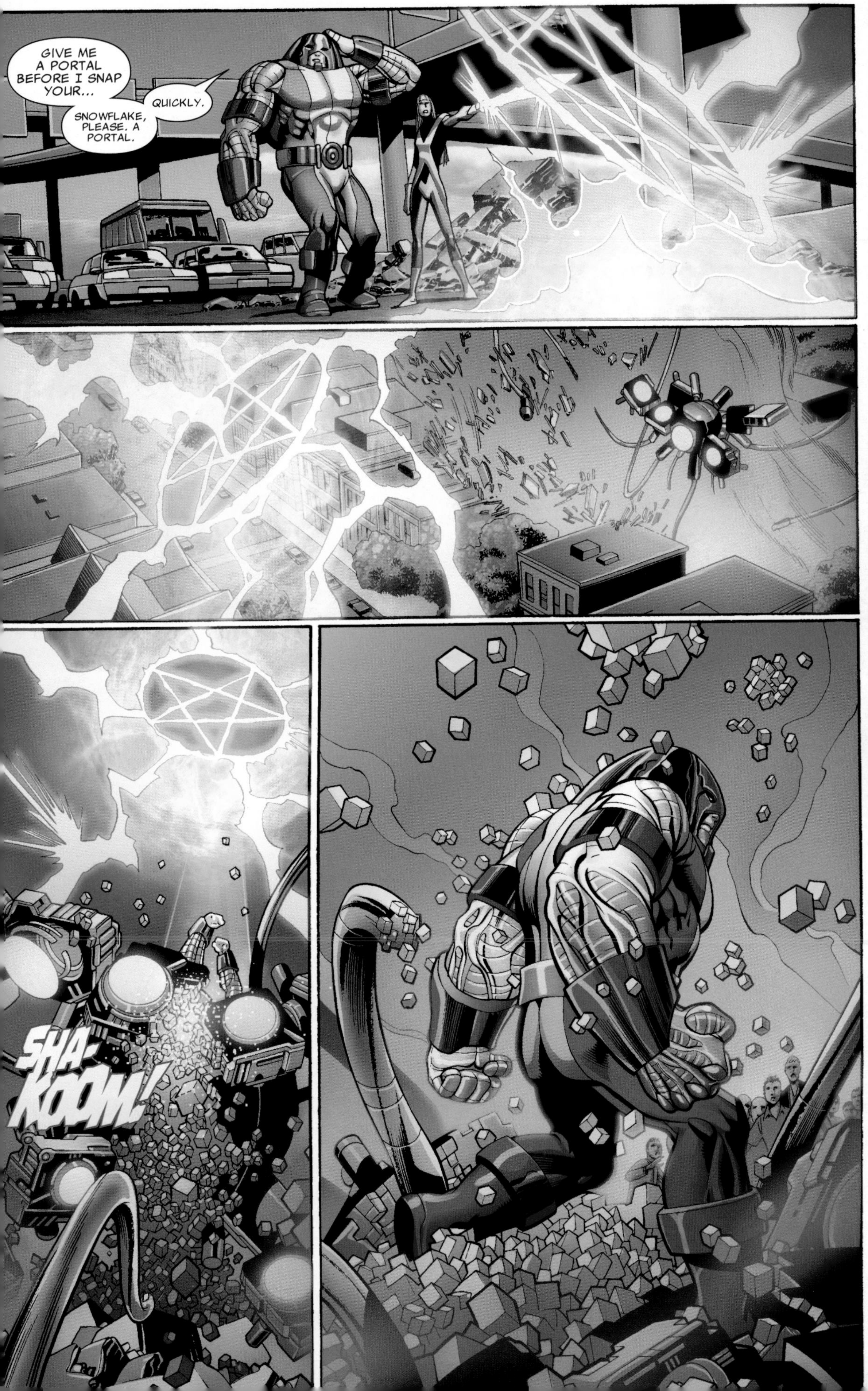
GIVE ME A PORTAL BEFORE I SNAP YOUR...
QUICKLY.
SNOWFLAKE, PLEASE. A PORTAL.
SHA-KOOM!

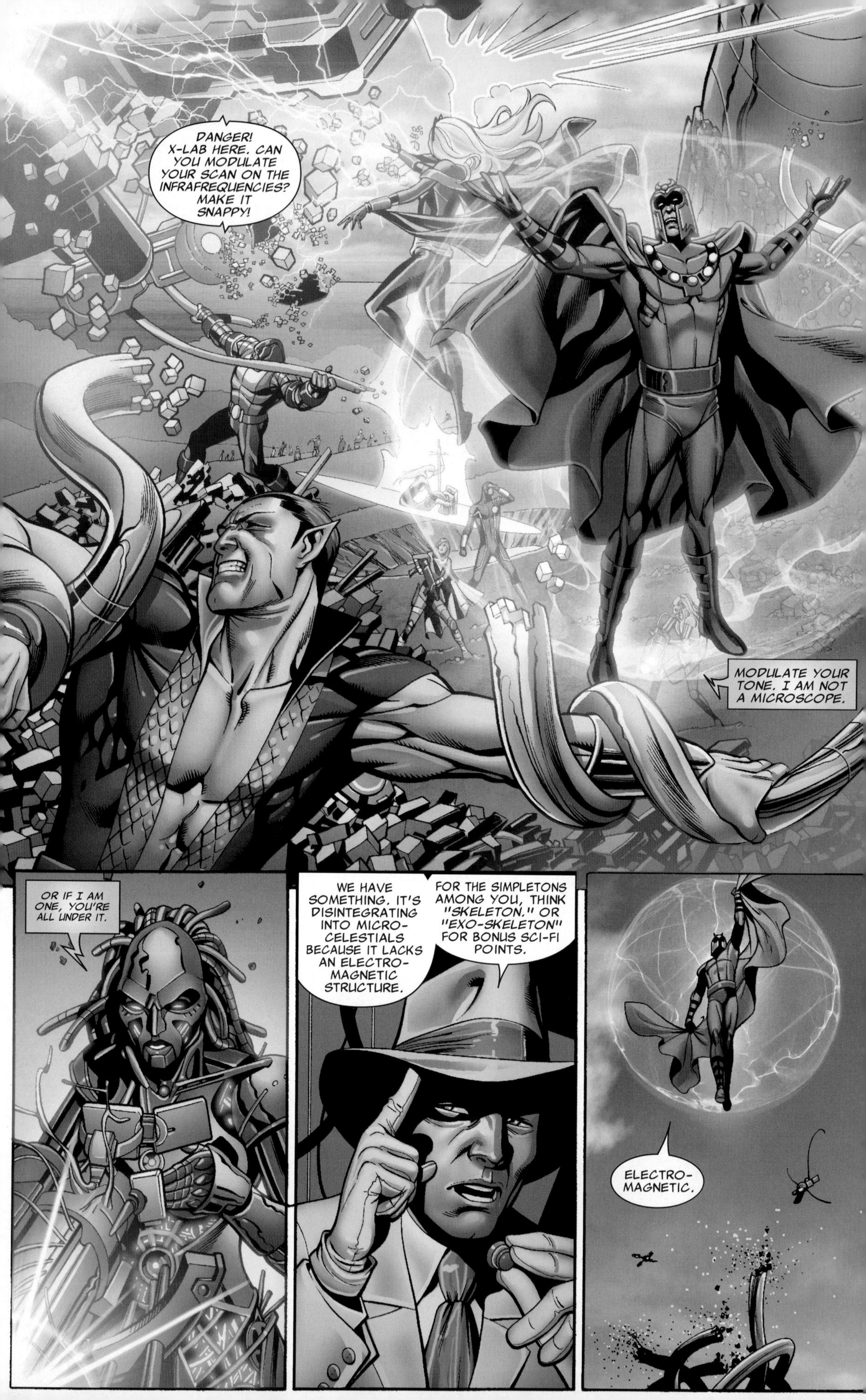
DANGER! X-LAB HERE. CAN YOU MODULATE YOUR SCAN ON THE INFRAFREQUENCIES? MAKE IT SNAPPY!
MODULATE YOUR TONE. I AM NOT A MICROSCOPE.
OR IF I AM ONE, YOU'RE ALL UNDER IT.
WE HAVE SOMETHING. IT'S DISINTEGRATING INTO MICRO-CELESTIALS BECAUSE IT LACKS AN ELECTRO-MAGNETIC STRUCTURE.
FOR THE SIMPLETONS AMONG YOU, THINK "SKELETON." OR "EXO-SKELETON" FOR BONUS SCI-FI POINTS.
ELECTRO-MAGNETIC.

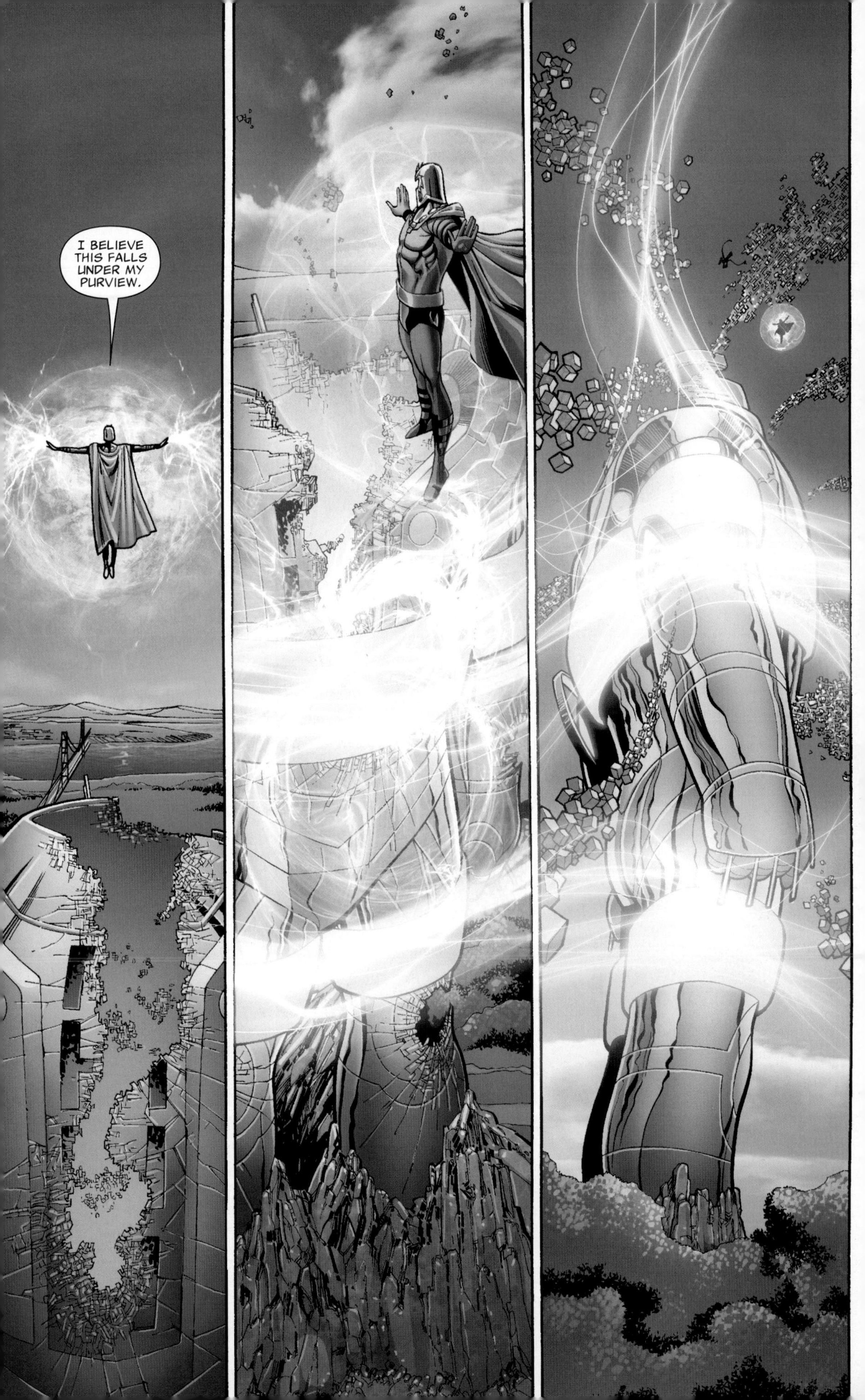
I BELIEVE THIS FALLS UNDER MY PURVIEW.

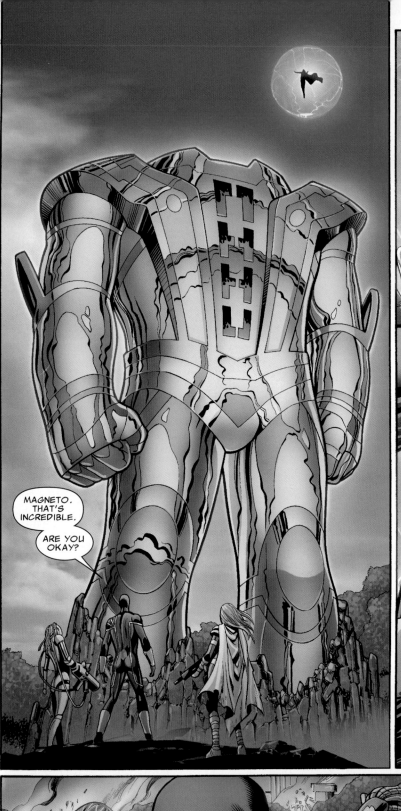

MAGNETO. THAT'S INCREDIBLE.

ARE YOU OKAY?

I'M ACTING AS SURROGATE NERVOUS SYSTEM FOR A COSMIC DEITY.

IF YOU DON'T RESOLVE THIS SITUATION WITH HASTE, EXPECT MY BRAINS TO LEAK FROM MY EYE SOCKETS.

DANGER: TAP SATELLITES AND TRACE. ANY IDEA WHERE SINISTER TOOK THE HEAD? IS THERE ANY CHANCE OF LOCATING HIM?

NO NEED FOR SATELLITES.

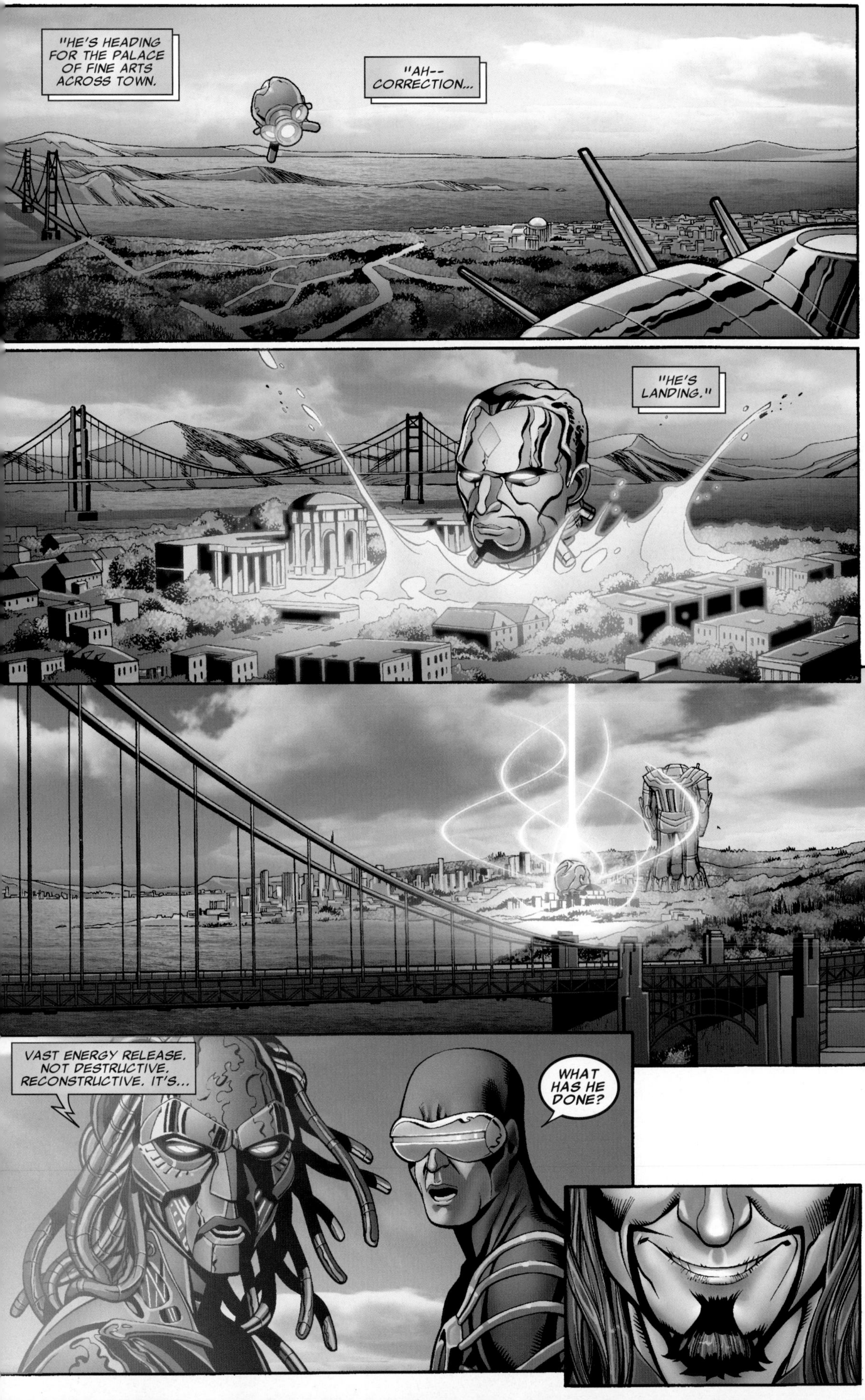
"HE'S HEADING FOR THE PALACE OF FINE ARTS ACROSS TOWN.
"AH-- CORRECTION...
"HE'S LANDING."
VAST ENERGY RELEASE. NOT DESTRUCTIVE. RECONSTRUCTIVE. IT'S...
WHAT HAS HE DONE?

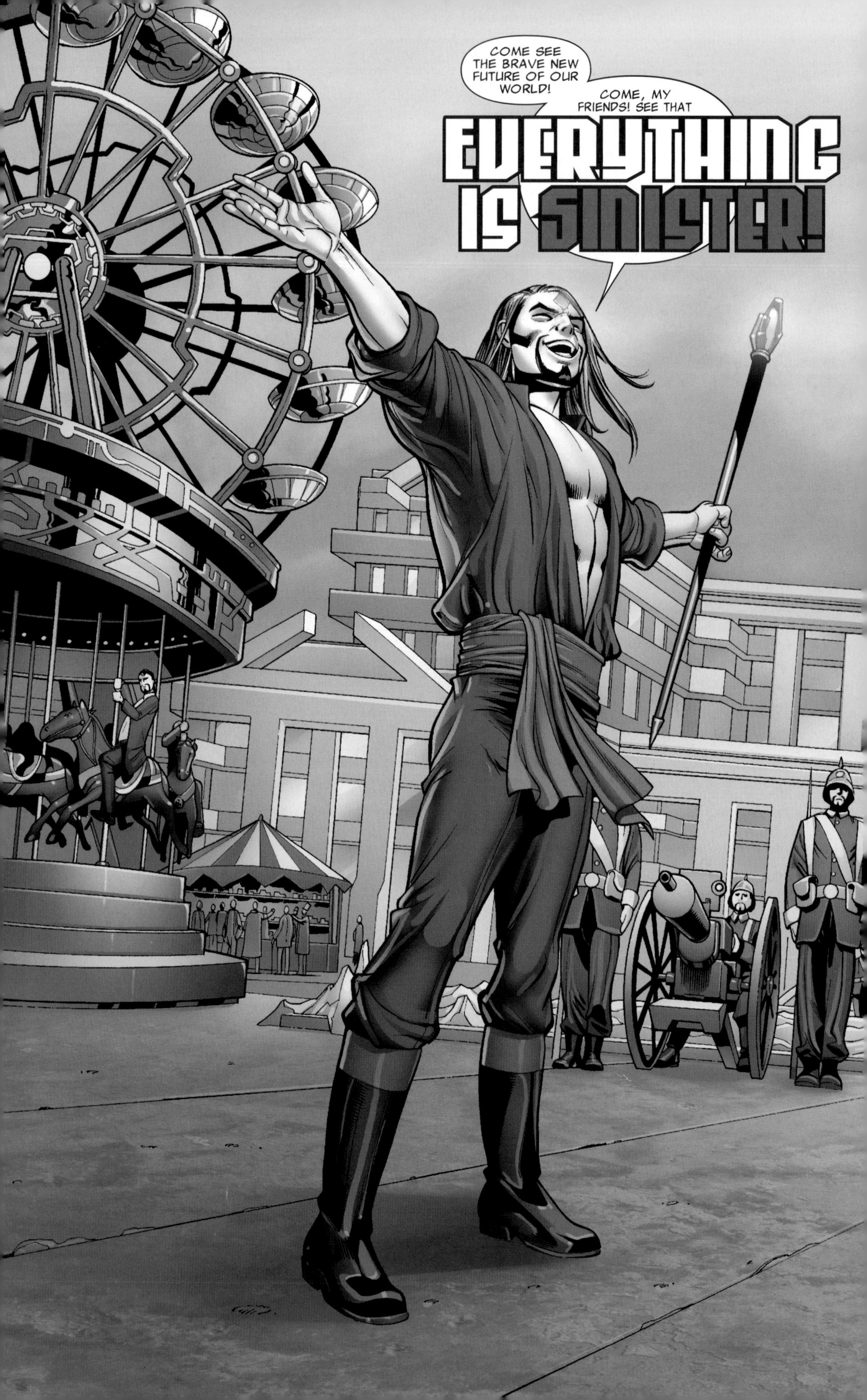
COME SEE THE BRAVE NEW FUTURE OF OUR WORLD!
COME, MY FRIENDS! SEE THAT
EVERYTHING IS SINISTER!

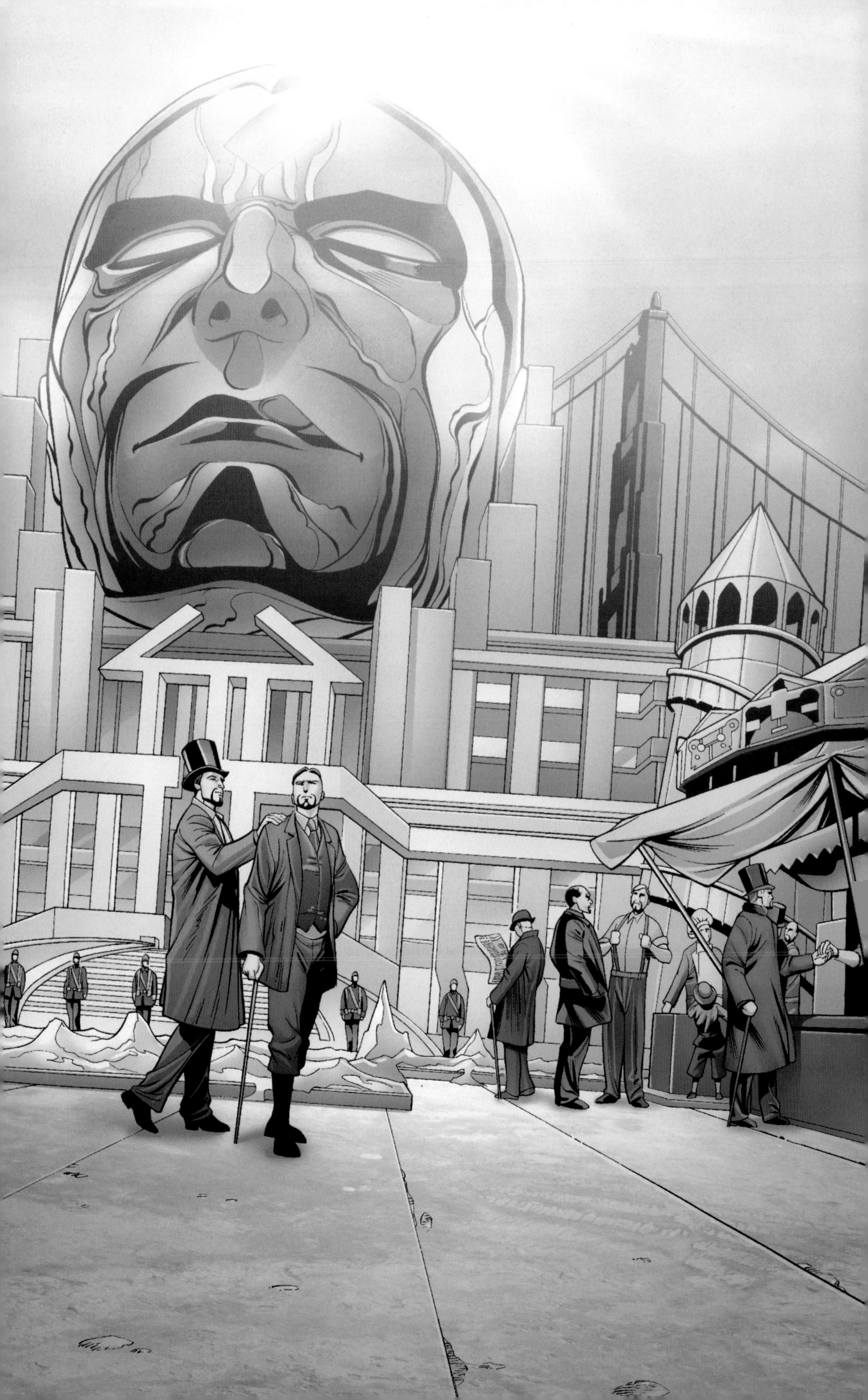

2

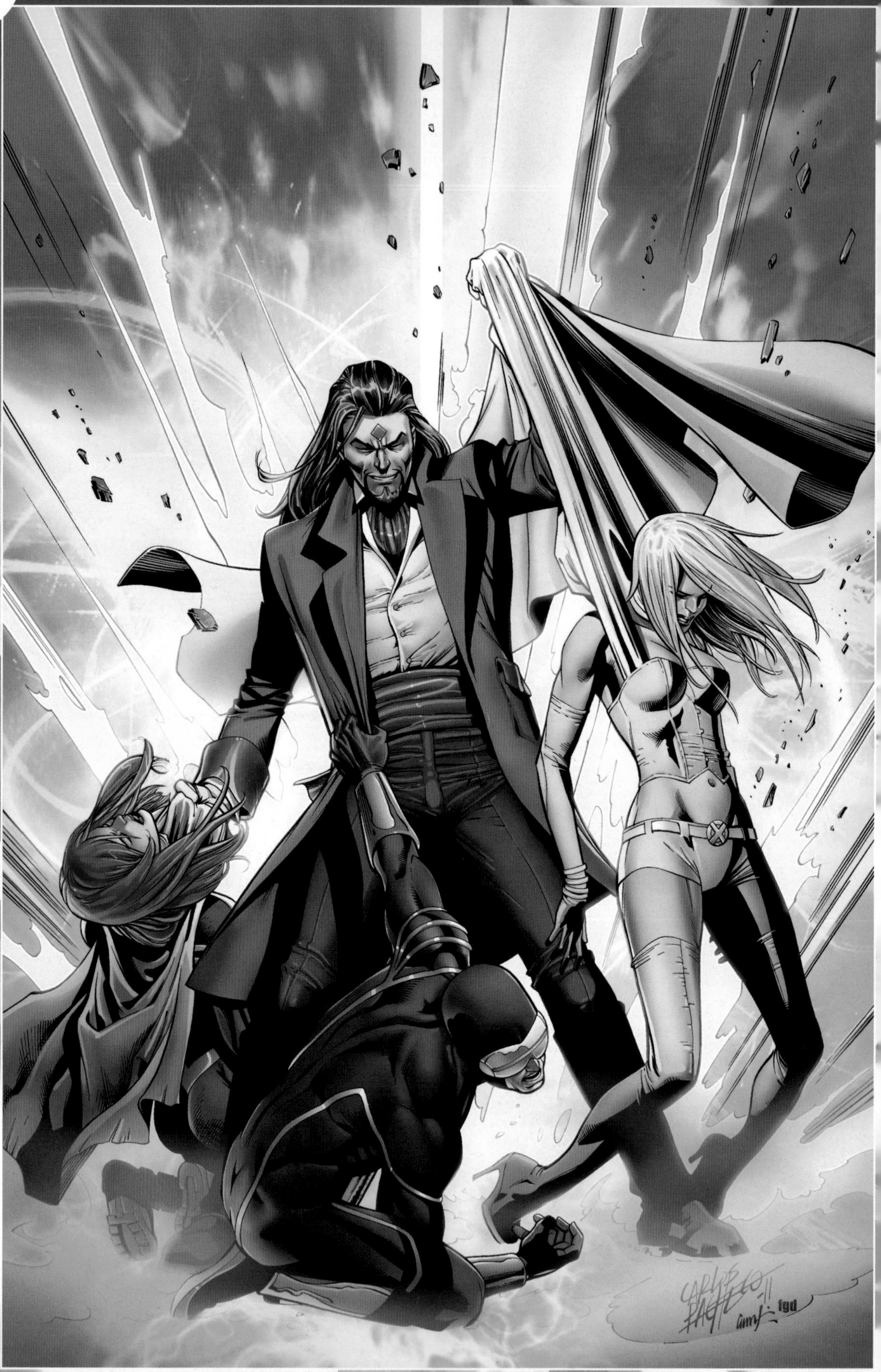

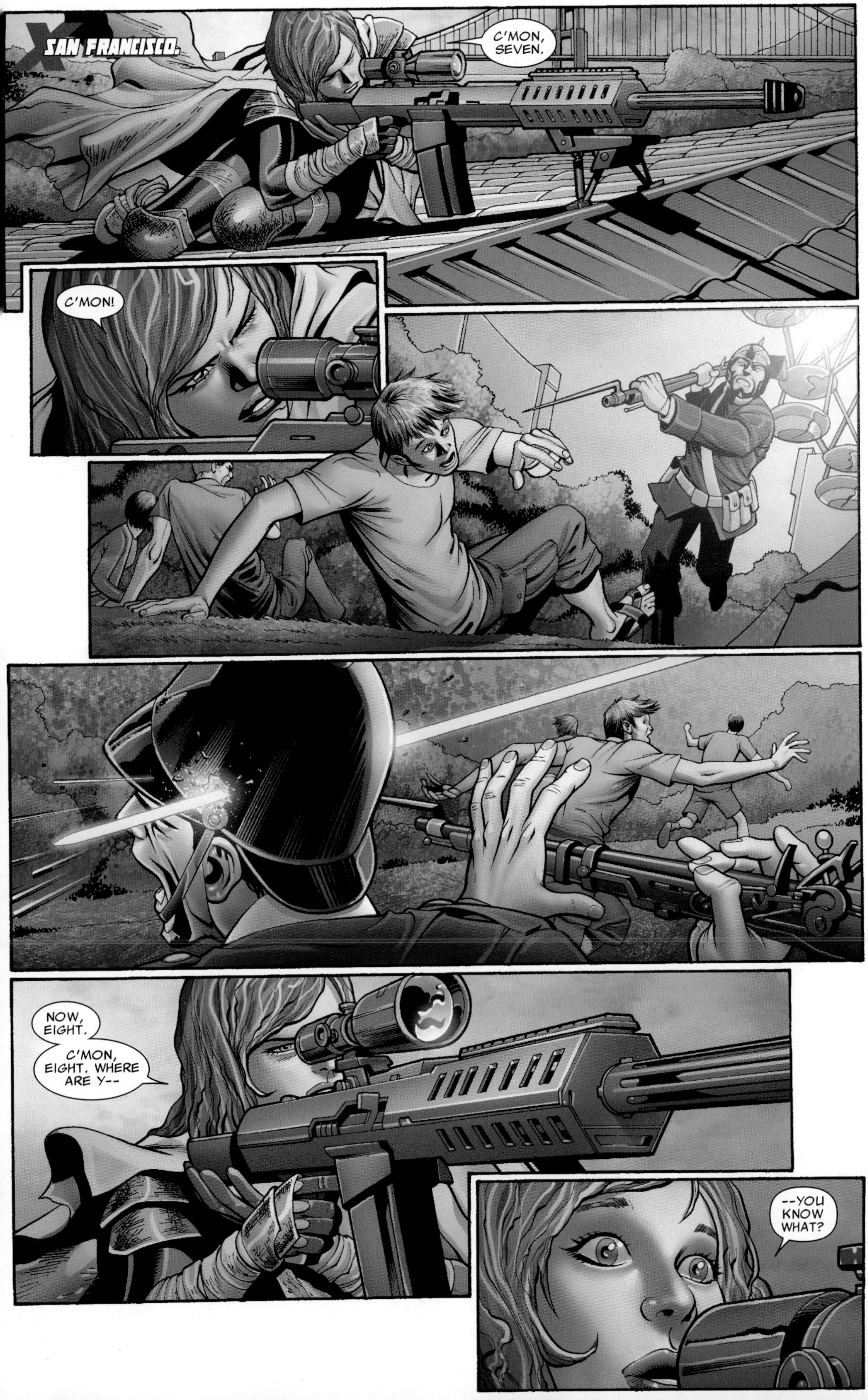
SAN FRANCISCO.
C'MON, SEVEN.
C'MON!
NOW, EIGHT.
C'MON, EIGHT. WHERE ARE Y--
--YOU KNOW WHAT?

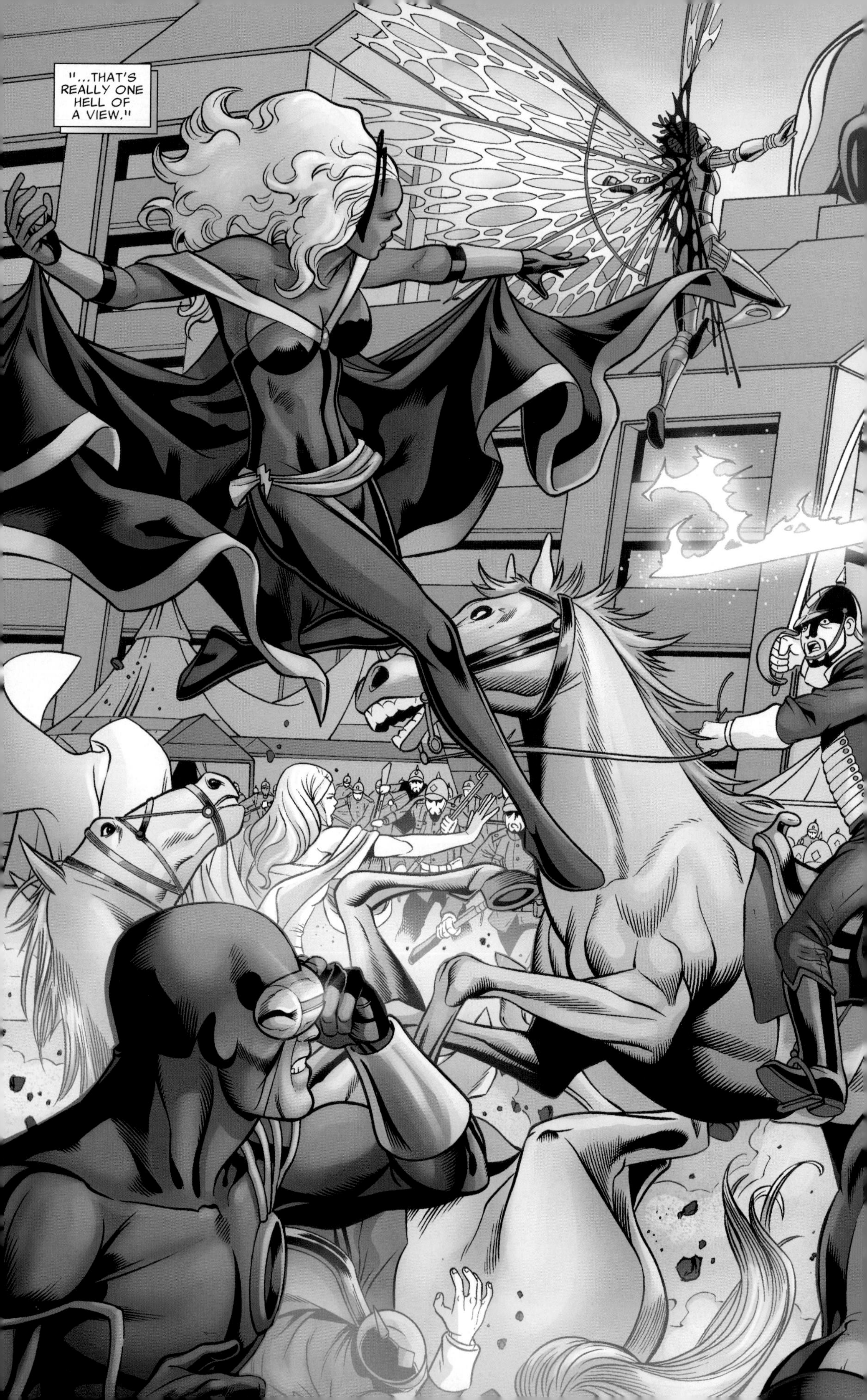
"...THAT'S REALLY ONE HELL OF A VIEW."

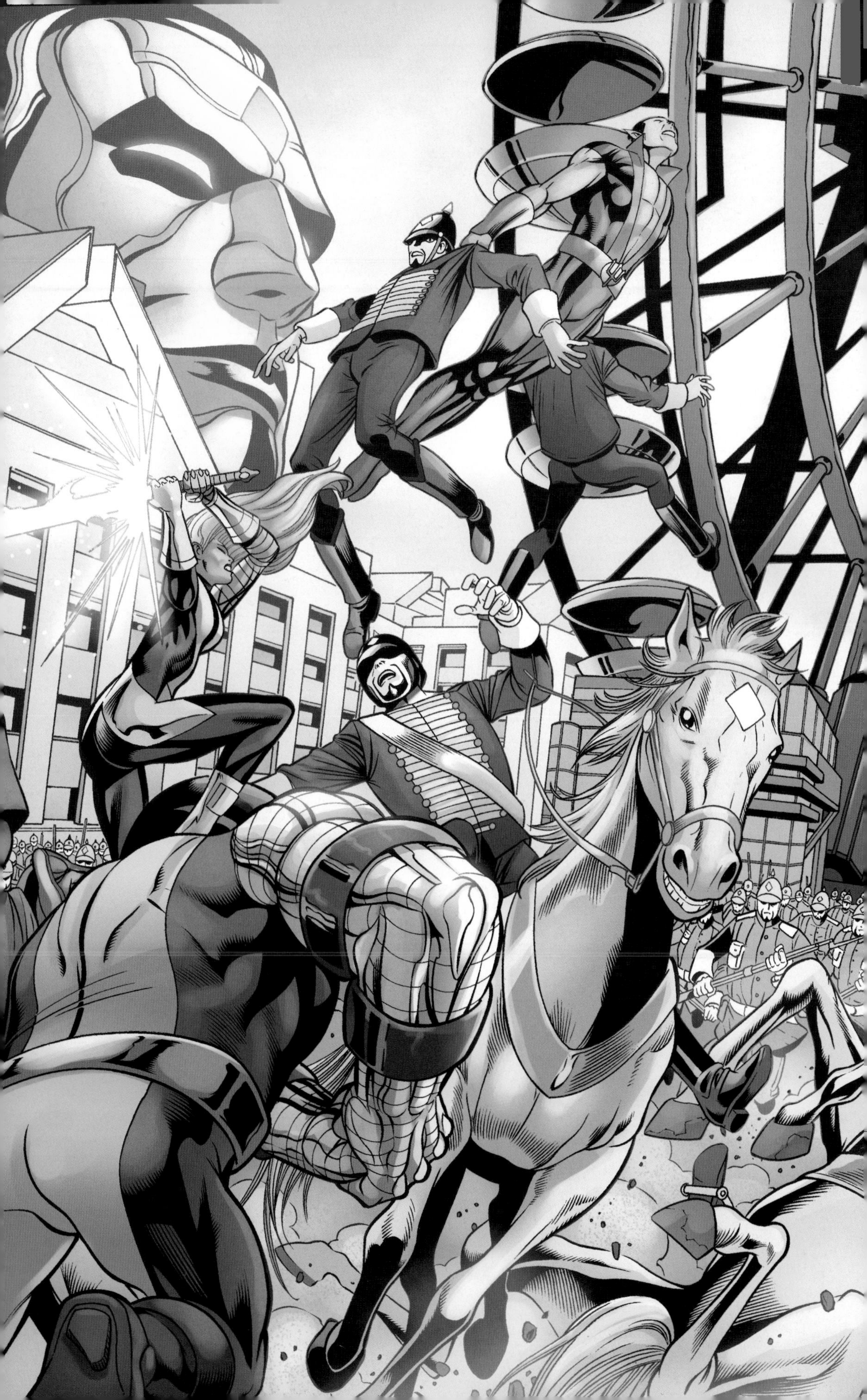

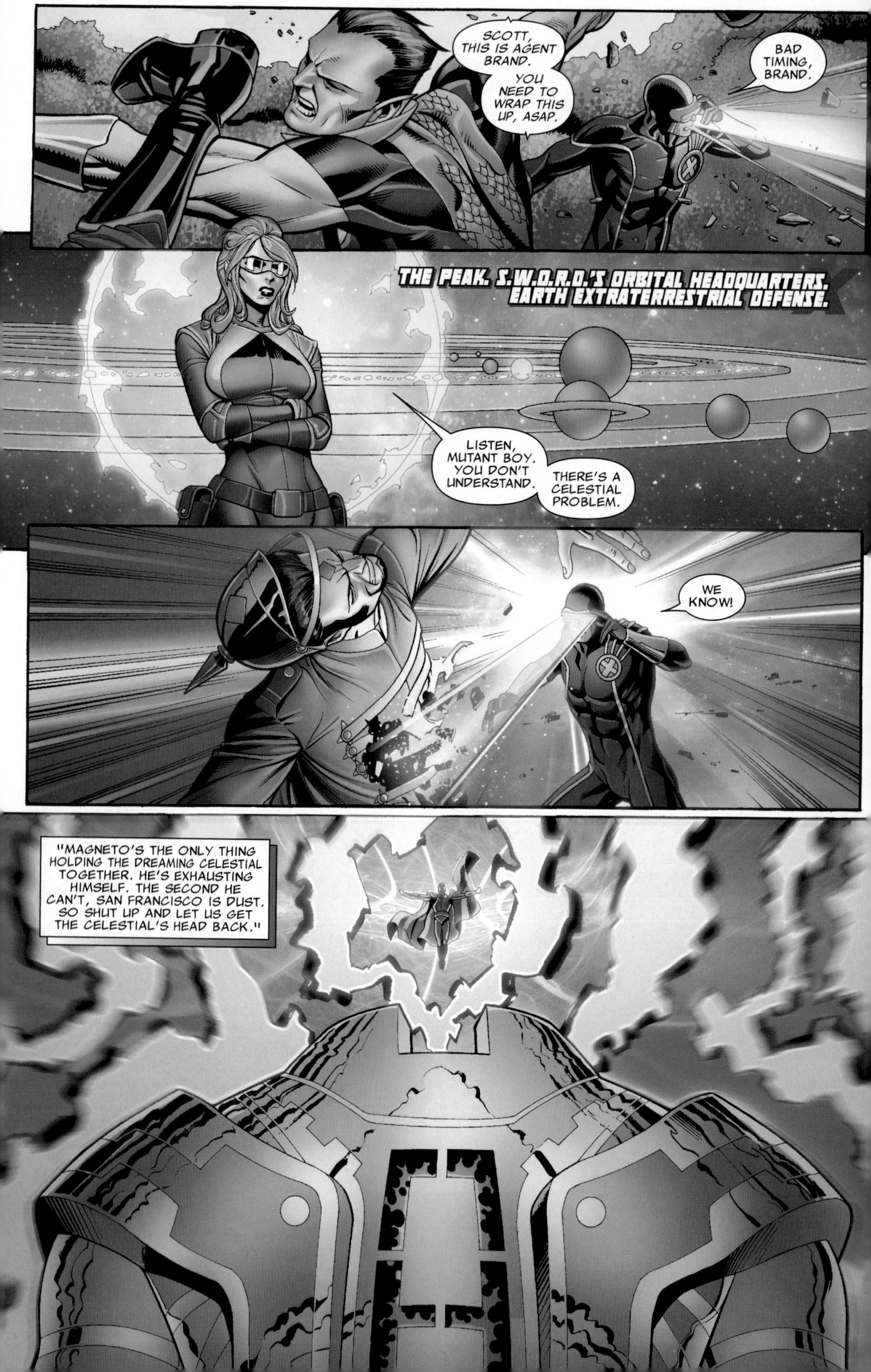
SCOTT, THIS IS AGENT BRAND.
YOU NEED TO WRAP THIS UP, ASAP.
BAD TIMING, BRAND.
THE PEAK. S.W.O.R.D.'S ORBITAL HEADQUARTERS. EARTH EXTRATERRESTRIAL DEFENSE.
LISTEN, MUTANT BOY. YOU DON'T UNDERSTAND.
THERE'S A CELESTIAL PROBLEM.
WE KNOW!
"MAGNETO'S THE ONLY THING HOLDING THE DREAMING CELESTIAL TOGETHER. HE'S EXHAUSTING HIMSELF. THE SECOND HE CAN'T, SAN FRANCISCO IS DUST. SO SHUT UP AND LET US GET THE CELESTIAL'S HEAD BACK."

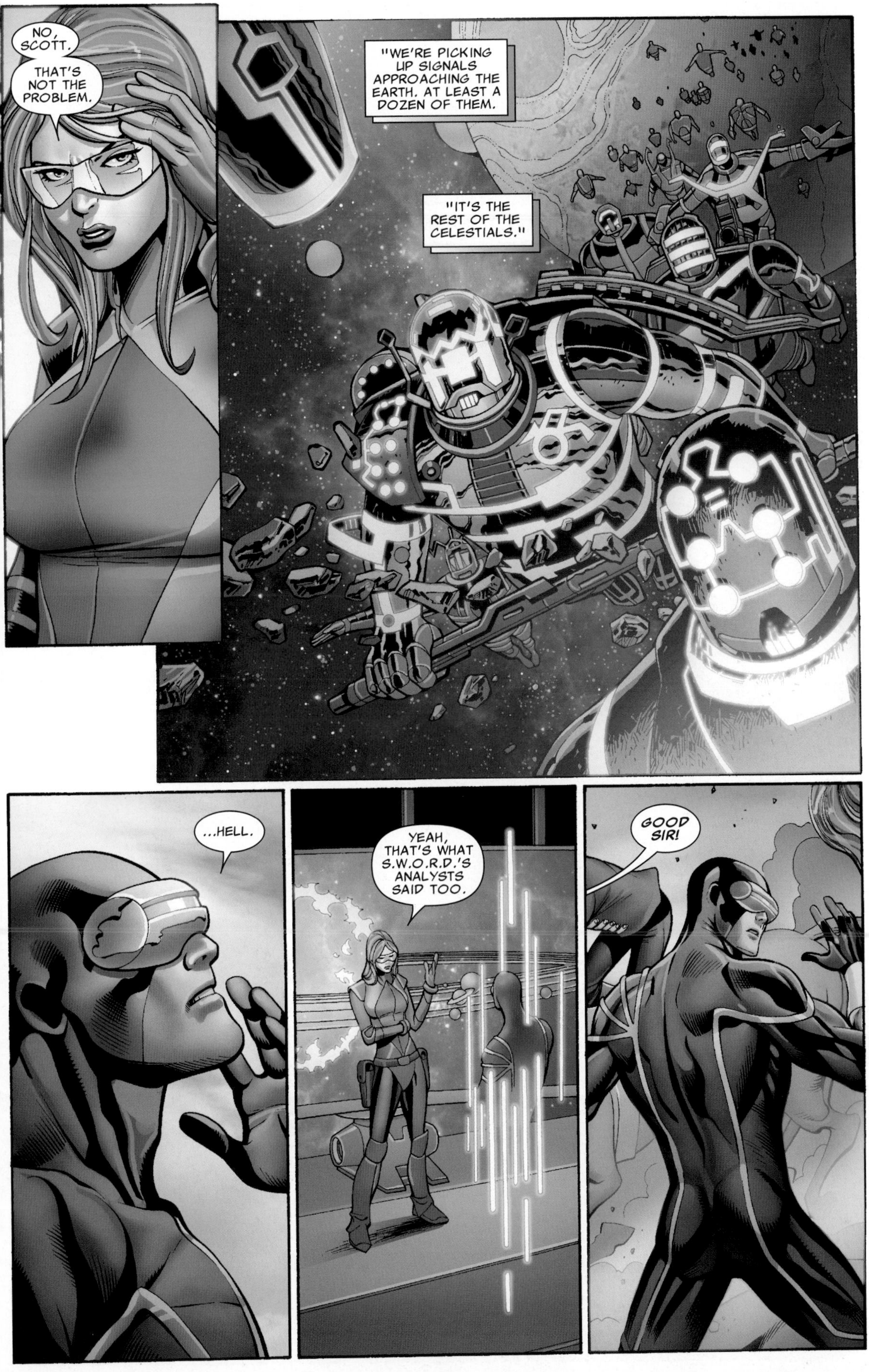
NO, SCOTT.
THAT'S NOT THE PROBLEM.
"WE'RE PICKING UP SIGNALS APPROACHING THE EARTH. AT LEAST A DOZEN OF THEM.
"IT'S THE REST OF THE CELESTIALS."
...HELL.
YEAH, THAT'S WHAT S.W.O.R.D.'S ANALYSTS SAID TOO.
GOOD SIR!

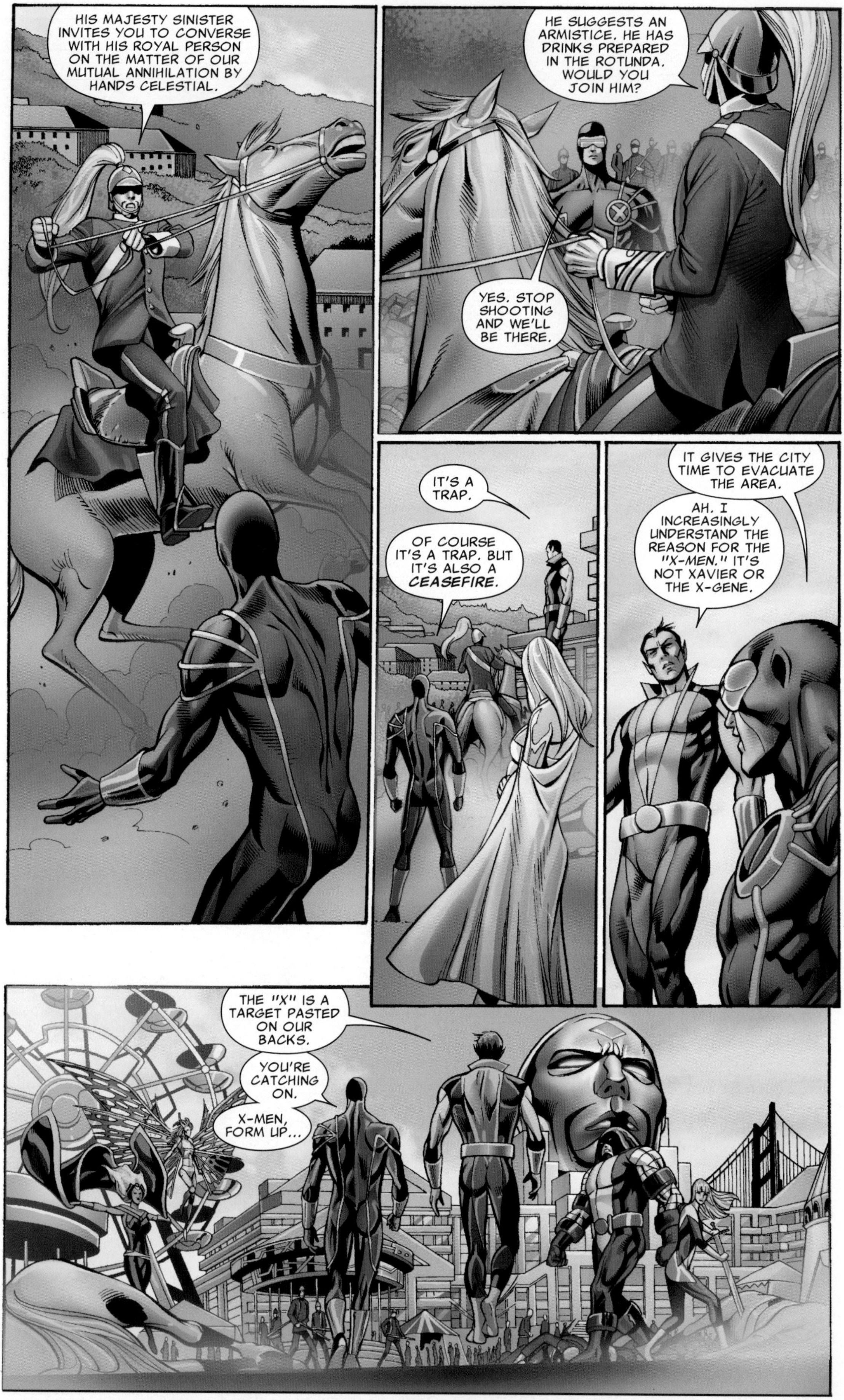
HIS MAJESTY SINISTER INVITES YOU TO CONVERSE WITH HIS ROYAL PERSON ON THE MATTER OF OUR MUTUAL ANNIHILATION BY HANDS CELESTIAL.
HE SUGGESTS AN ARMISTICE. HE HAS DRINKS PREPARED IN THE ROTUNDA. WOULD YOU JOIN HIM?
YES. STOP SHOOTING AND WE'LL BE THERE.
IT'S A TRAP.
OF COURSE IT'S A TRAP. BUT IT'S ALSO A *CEASEFIRE*.
IT GIVES THE CITY TIME TO EVACUATE THE AREA.
AH. I INCREASINGLY UNDERSTAND THE REASON FOR THE "X-MEN." IT'S NOT XAVIER OR THE X-GENE.
THE "X" IS A TARGET PASTED ON OUR BACKS.
YOU'RE CATCHING ON.
X-MEN, FORM UP...

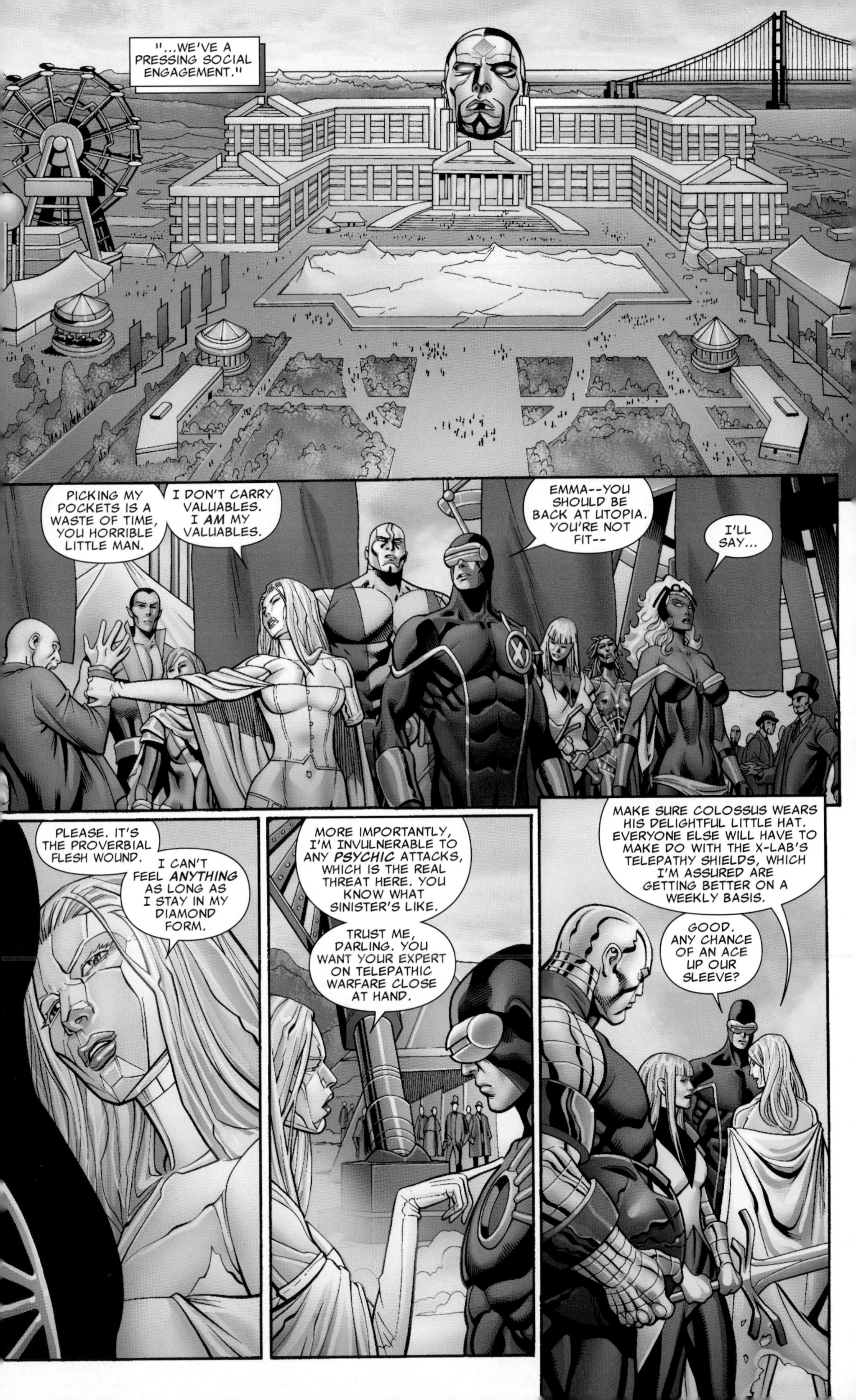

"...WE'VE A PRESSING SOCIAL ENGAGEMENT."
PICKING MY POCKETS IS A WASTE OF TIME, YOU HORRIBLE LITTLE MAN.
I DON'T CARRY VALUABLES. I AM MY VALUABLES.
EMMA--YOU SHOULD BE BACK AT UTOPIA. YOU'RE NOT FIT--
I'LL SAY...
PLEASE. IT'S THE PROVERBIAL FLESH WOUND.
I CAN'T FEEL ANYTHING AS LONG AS I STAY IN MY DIAMOND FORM.
MORE IMPORTANTLY, I'M INVULNERABLE TO ANY PSYCHIC ATTACKS, WHICH IS THE REAL THREAT HERE. YOU KNOW WHAT SINISTER'S LIKE.
TRUST ME, DARLING. YOU WANT YOUR EXPERT ON TELEPATHIC WARFARE CLOSE AT HAND.
MAKE SURE COLOSSUS WEARS HIS DELIGHTFUL LITTLE HAT. EVERYONE ELSE WILL HAVE TO MAKE DO WITH THE X-LAB'S TELEPATHY SHIELDS, WHICH I'M ASSURED ARE GETTING BETTER ON A WEEKLY BASIS.
GOOD. ANY CHANCE OF AN ACE UP OUR SLEEVE?

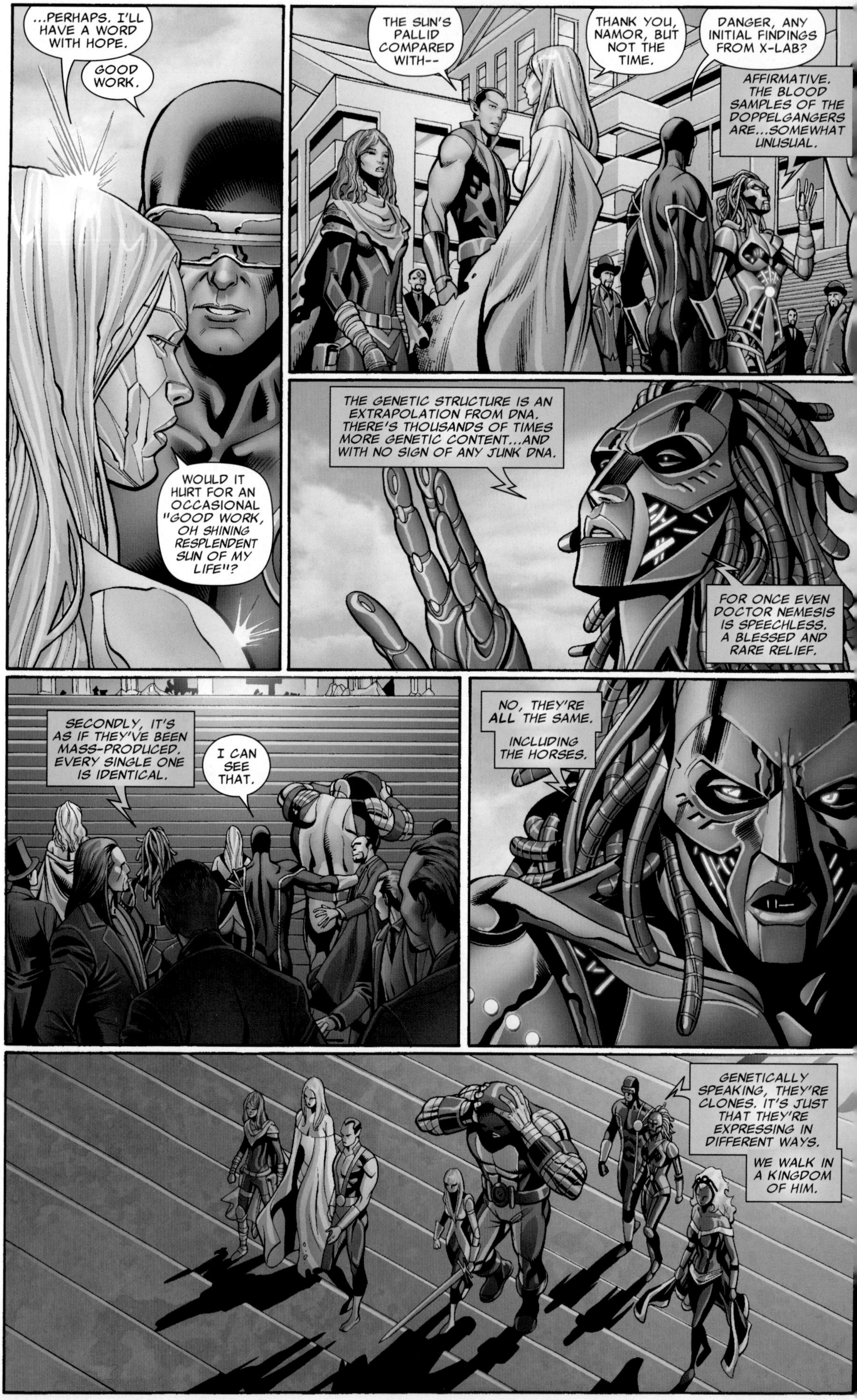
...PERHAPS. I'LL HAVE A WORD WITH HOPE.
GOOD WORK.
WOULD IT HURT FOR AN OCCASIONAL "GOOD WORK, OH SHINING RESPLENDENT SUN OF MY LIFE"?
THE SUN'S PALLID COMPARED WITH--
THANK YOU, NAMOR, BUT NOT THE TIME.
DANGER, ANY INITIAL FINDINGS FROM X-LAB?
AFFIRMATIVE. THE BLOOD SAMPLES OF THE DOPPELGANGERS ARE...SOMEWHAT UNUSUAL.
THE GENETIC STRUCTURE IS AN EXTRAPOLATION FROM DNA. THERE'S THOUSANDS OF TIMES MORE GENETIC CONTENT...AND WITH NO SIGN OF ANY JUNK DNA.
FOR ONCE EVEN DOCTOR NEMESIS IS SPEECHLESS. A BLESSED AND RARE RELIEF.
SECONDLY, IT'S AS IF THEY'VE BEEN MASS-PRODUCED. EVERY SINGLE ONE IS IDENTICAL.
I CAN SEE THAT.
NO, THEY'RE ALL THE SAME.
INCLUDING THE HORSES.
GENETICALLY SPEAKING, THEY'RE CLONES. IT'S JUST THAT THEY'RE EXPRESSING IN DIFFERENT WAYS.
WE WALK IN A KINGDOM OF HIM.

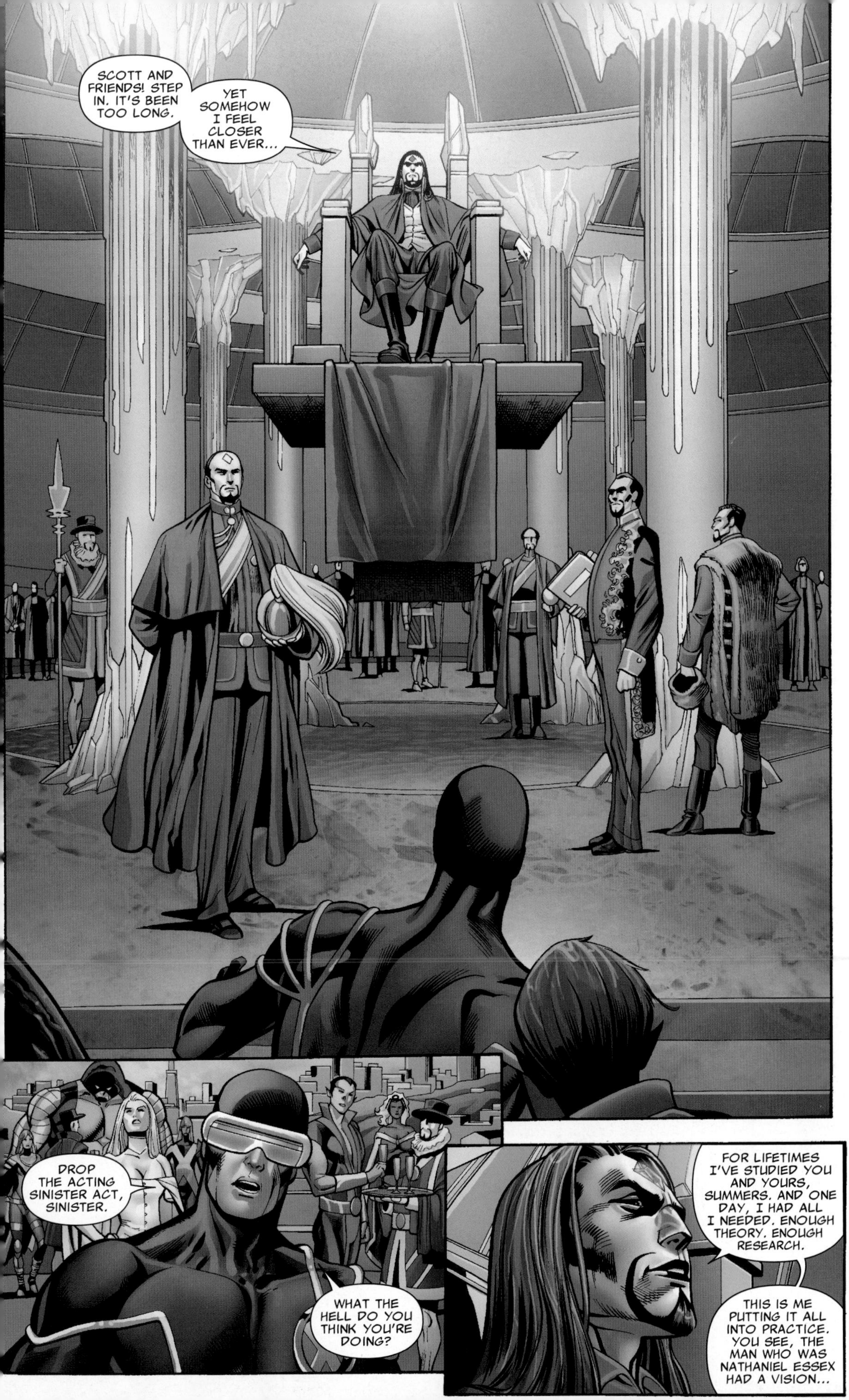
SCOTT AND FRIENDS! STEP IN. IT'S BEEN TOO LONG.
YET SOMEHOW I FEEL CLOSER THAN EVER...
DROP THE ACTING SINISTER ACT, SINISTER.
WHAT THE HELL DO YOU THINK YOU'RE DOING?
FOR LIFETIMES I'VE STUDIED YOU AND YOURS, SUMMERS. AND ONE DAY, I HAD ALL I NEEDED. ENOUGH THEORY. ENOUGH RESEARCH.
THIS IS ME PUTTING IT ALL INTO PRACTICE. YOU SEE, THE MAN WHO WAS NATHANIEL ESSEX HAD A VISION...

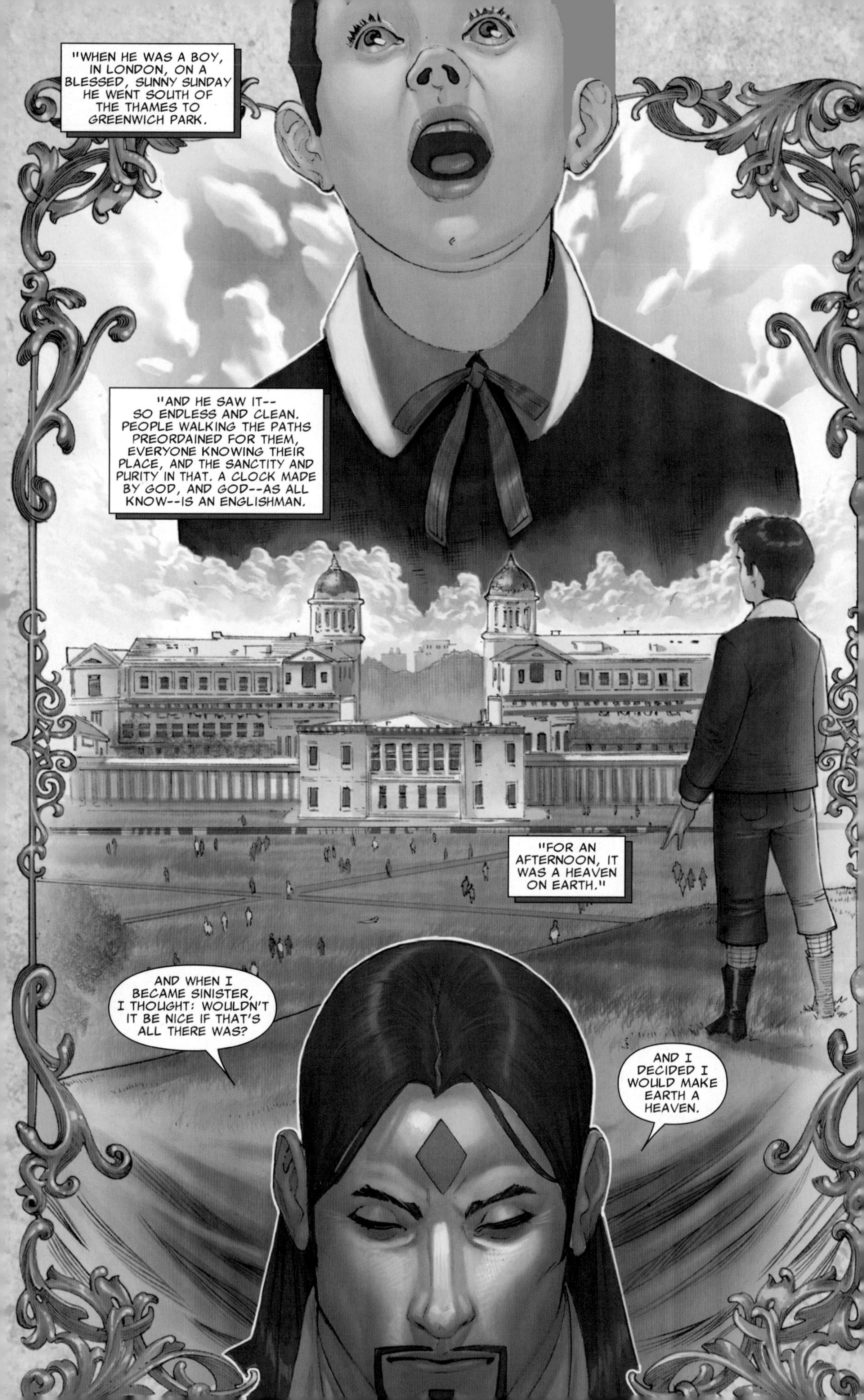
"WHEN HE WAS A BOY, IN LONDON, ON A BLESSED, SUNNY SUNDAY HE WENT SOUTH OF THE THAMES TO GREENWICH PARK.
"AND HE SAW IT-- SO ENDLESS AND CLEAN. PEOPLE WALKING THE PATHS PREORDAINED FOR THEM, EVERYONE KNOWING THEIR PLACE, AND THE SANCTITY AND PURITY IN THAT. A CLOCK MADE BY GOD, AND GOD--AS ALL KNOW--IS AN ENGLISHMAN.
"FOR AN AFTERNOON, IT WAS A HEAVEN ON EARTH."
AND WHEN I BECAME SINISTER, I THOUGHT: WOULDN'T IT BE NICE IF THAT'S ALL THERE WAS?
AND I DECIDED I WOULD MAKE EARTH A HEAVEN.

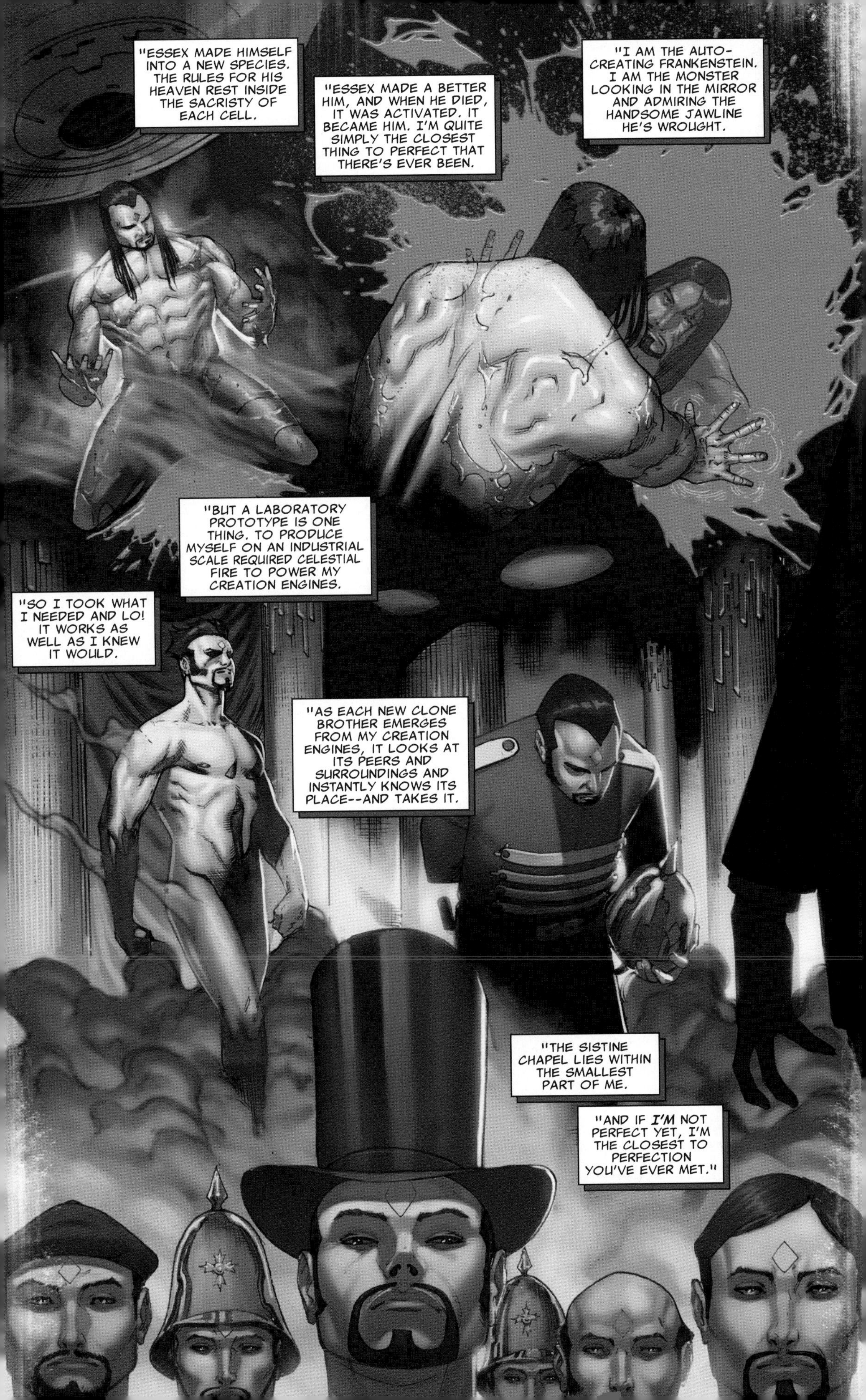
"ESSEX MADE HIMSELF INTO A NEW SPECIES. THE RULES FOR HIS HEAVEN REST INSIDE THE SACRISTY OF EACH CELL.
"ESSEX MADE A BETTER HIM, AND WHEN HE DIED, IT WAS ACTIVATED. IT BECAME HIM. I'M QUITE SIMPLY THE CLOSEST THING TO PERFECT THAT THERE'S EVER BEEN.
"I AM THE AUTO-CREATING FRANKENSTEIN. I AM THE MONSTER LOOKING IN THE MIRROR AND ADMIRING THE HANDSOME JAWLINE HE'S WROUGHT.
"BUT A LABORATORY PROTOTYPE IS ONE THING. TO PRODUCE MYSELF ON AN INDUSTRIAL SCALE REQUIRED CELESTIAL FIRE TO POWER MY CREATION ENGINES.
"SO I TOOK WHAT I NEEDED AND LO! IT WORKS AS WELL AS I KNEW IT WOULD.
"AS EACH NEW CLONE BROTHER EMERGES FROM MY CREATION ENGINES, IT LOOKS AT ITS PEERS AND SURROUNDINGS AND INSTANTLY KNOWS ITS PLACE--AND TAKES IT.
"THE SISTINE CHAPEL LIES WITHIN THE SMALLEST PART OF ME.
"AND IF *I'M* NOT PERFECT YET, I'M THE CLOSEST TO PERFECTION YOU'VE EVER MET."

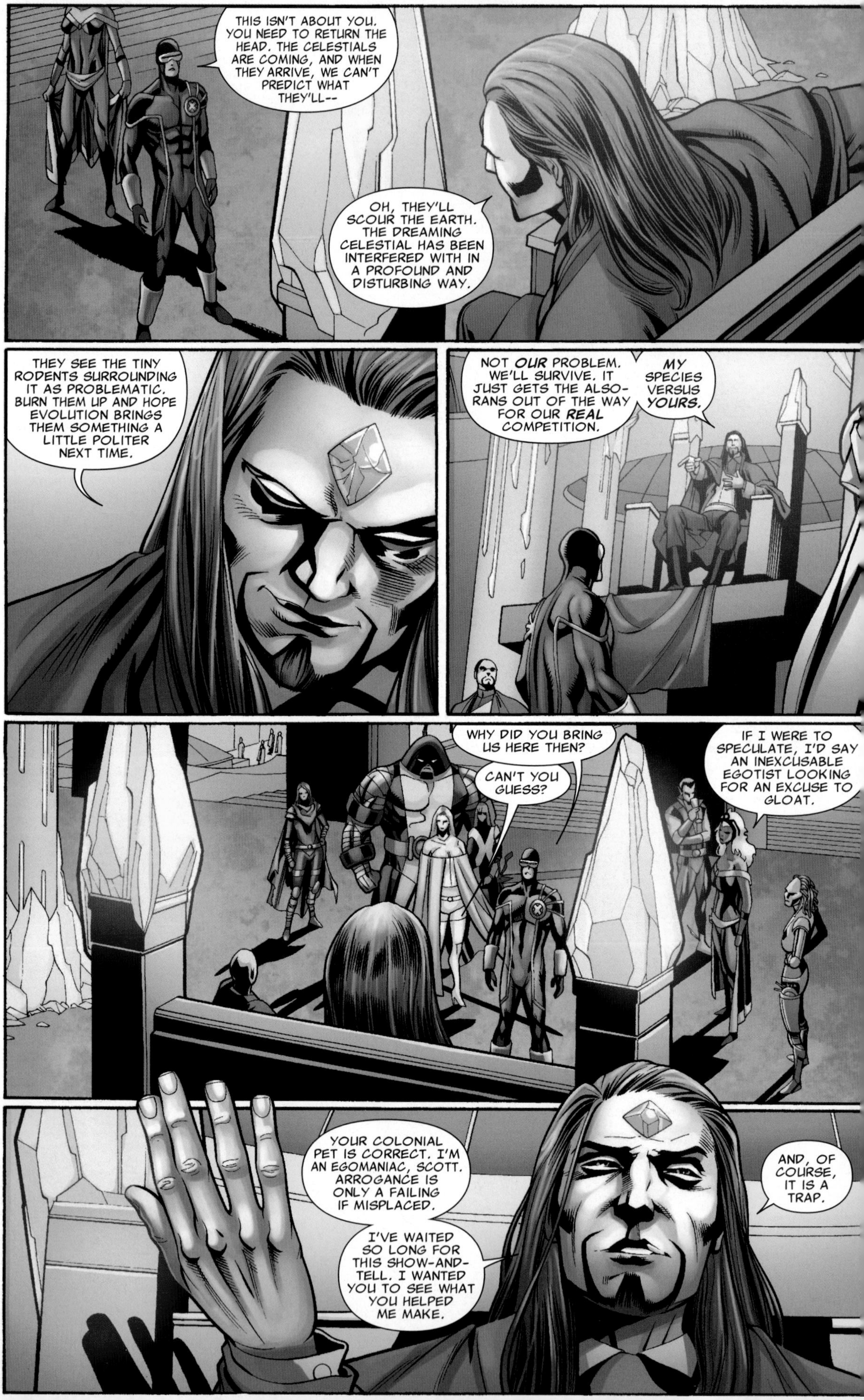

THIS ISN'T ABOUT YOU. YOU NEED TO RETURN THE HEAD. THE CELESTIALS ARE COMING, AND WHEN THEY ARRIVE, WE CAN'T PREDICT WHAT THEY'LL--
OH, THEY'LL SCOUR THE EARTH. THE DREAMING CELESTIAL HAS BEEN INTERFERED WITH IN A PROFOUND AND DISTURBING WAY.
THEY SEE THE TINY RODENTS SURROUNDING IT AS PROBLEMATIC. BURN THEM UP AND HOPE EVOLUTION BRINGS THEM SOMETHING A LITTLE POLITER NEXT TIME.
NOT OUR PROBLEM. WE'LL SURVIVE. IT JUST GETS THE ALSO-RANS OUT OF THE WAY FOR OUR REAL COMPETITION.
MY SPECIES VERSUS YOURS.
WHY DID YOU BRING US HERE THEN?
CAN'T YOU GUESS?
IF I WERE TO SPECULATE, I'D SAY AN INEXCUSABLE EGOTIST LOOKING FOR AN EXCUSE TO GLOAT.
YOUR COLONIAL PET IS CORRECT. I'M AN EGOMANIAC, SCOTT. ARROGANCE IS ONLY A FAILING IF MISPLACED.
I'VE WAITED SO LONG FOR THIS SHOW-AND-TELL. I WANTED YOU TO SEE WHAT YOU HELPED ME MAKE.
AND, OF COURSE, IT IS A TRAP.

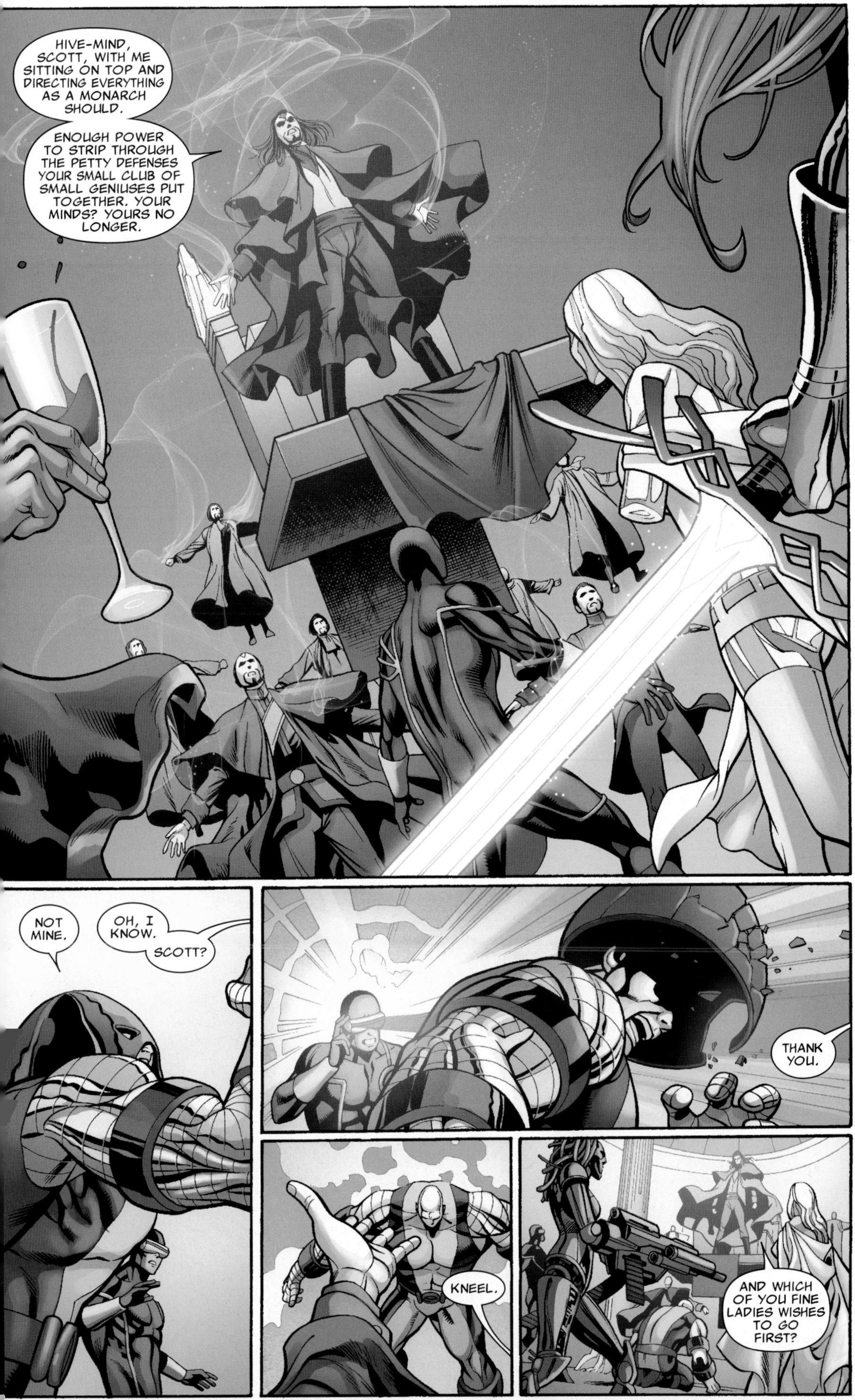
HIVE-MIND, SCOTT, WITH ME SITTING ON TOP AND DIRECTING EVERYTHING AS A MONARCH SHOULD.
ENOUGH POWER TO STRIP THROUGH THE PETTY DEFENSES YOUR SMALL CLUB OF SMALL GENIUSES PUT TOGETHER. YOUR MINDS? YOURS NO LONGER.
NOT MINE.
OH, I KNOW.
SCOTT?
THANK YOU.
KNEEL.
AND WHICH OF YOU FINE LADIES WISHES TO GO FIRST?

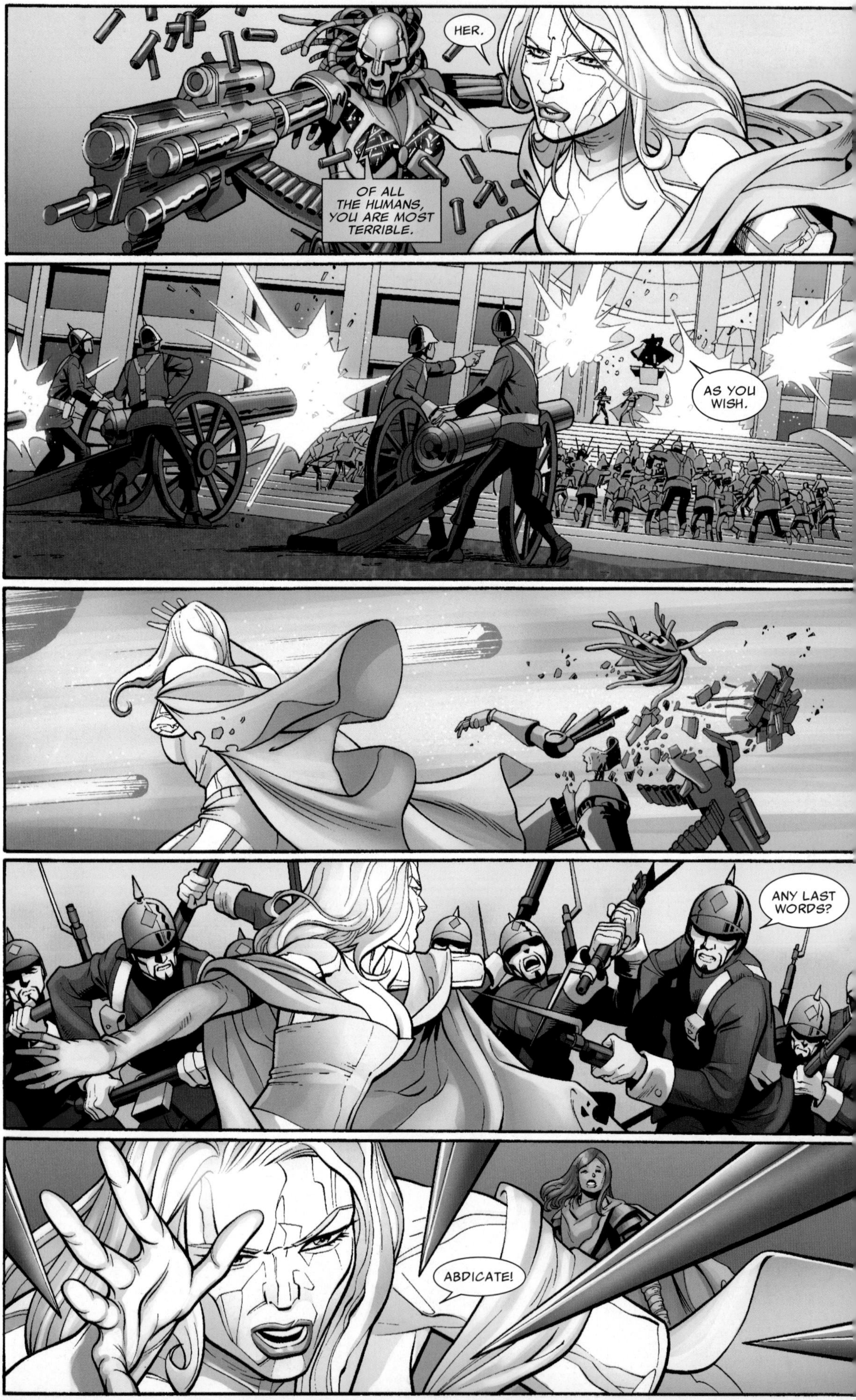
HER.
OF ALL THE HUMANS, YOU ARE MOST TERRIBLE.
AS YOU WISH.
ANY LAST WORDS?
ABDICATE!

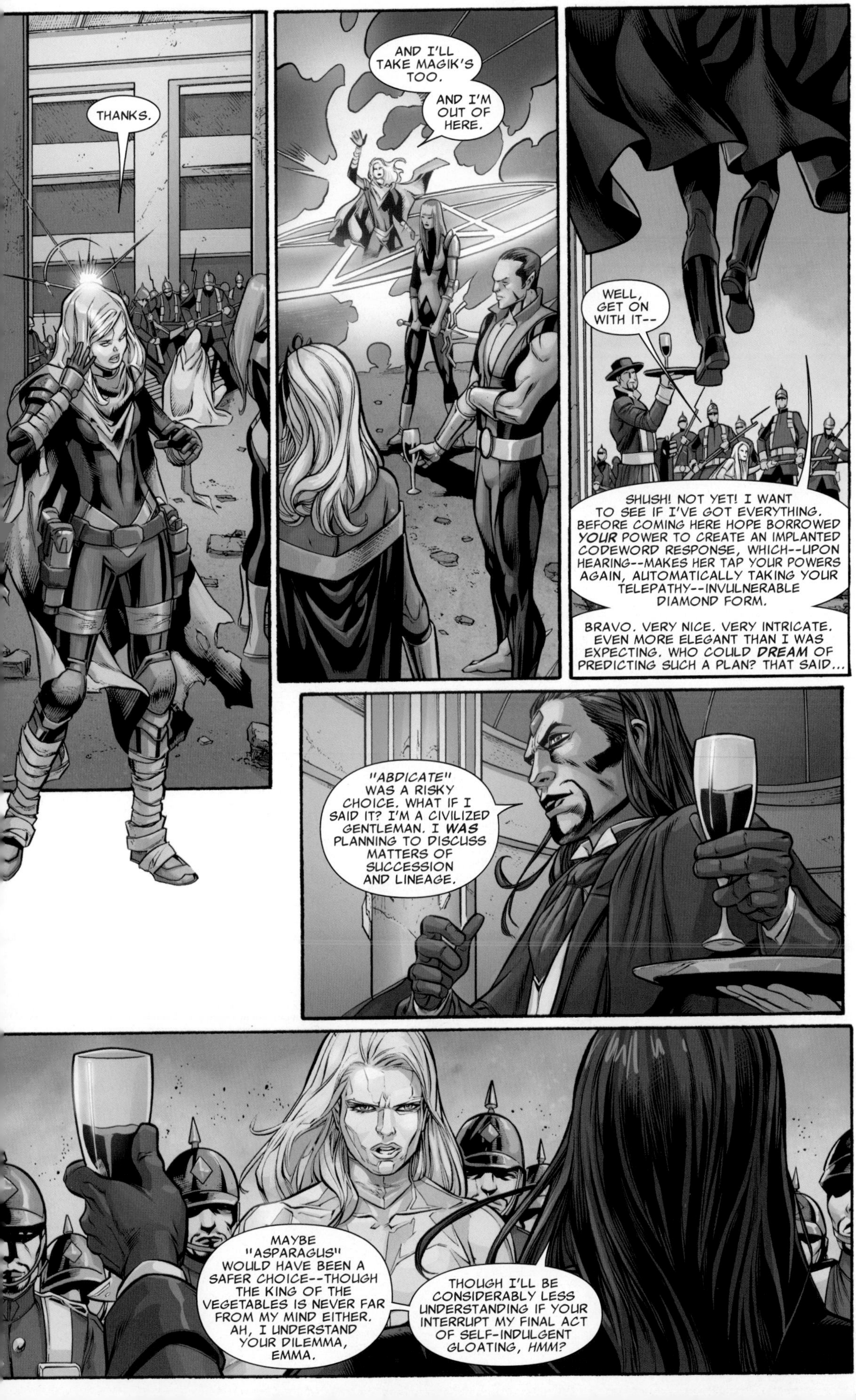
THANKS.
AND I'LL TAKE MAGIK'S TOO.
AND I'M OUT OF HERE.
WELL, GET ON WITH IT--
SHUSH! NOT YET! I WANT TO SEE IF I'VE GOT EVERYTHING. BEFORE COMING HERE HOPE BORROWED YOUR POWER TO CREATE AN IMPLANTED CODEWORD RESPONSE, WHICH--UPON HEARING--MAKES HER TAP YOUR POWERS AGAIN, AUTOMATICALLY TAKING YOUR TELEPATHY--INVULNERABLE DIAMOND FORM.
BRAVO. VERY NICE. VERY INTRICATE. EVEN MORE ELEGANT THAN I WAS EXPECTING. WHO COULD DREAM OF PREDICTING SUCH A PLAN? THAT SAID...
"ABDICATE" WAS A RISKY CHOICE. WHAT IF I SAID IT? I'M A CIVILIZED GENTLEMAN. I WAS PLANNING TO DISCUSS MATTERS OF SUCCESSION AND LINEAGE.
MAYBE "ASPARAGUS" WOULD HAVE BEEN A SAFER CHOICE--THOUGH THE KING OF THE VEGETABLES IS NEVER FAR FROM MY MIND EITHER. AH, I UNDERSTAND YOUR DILEMMA, EMMA.
THOUGH I'LL BE CONSIDERABLY LESS UNDERSTANDING IF YOUR INTERRUPT MY FINAL ACT OF SELF-INDULGENT GLOATING, HMM?

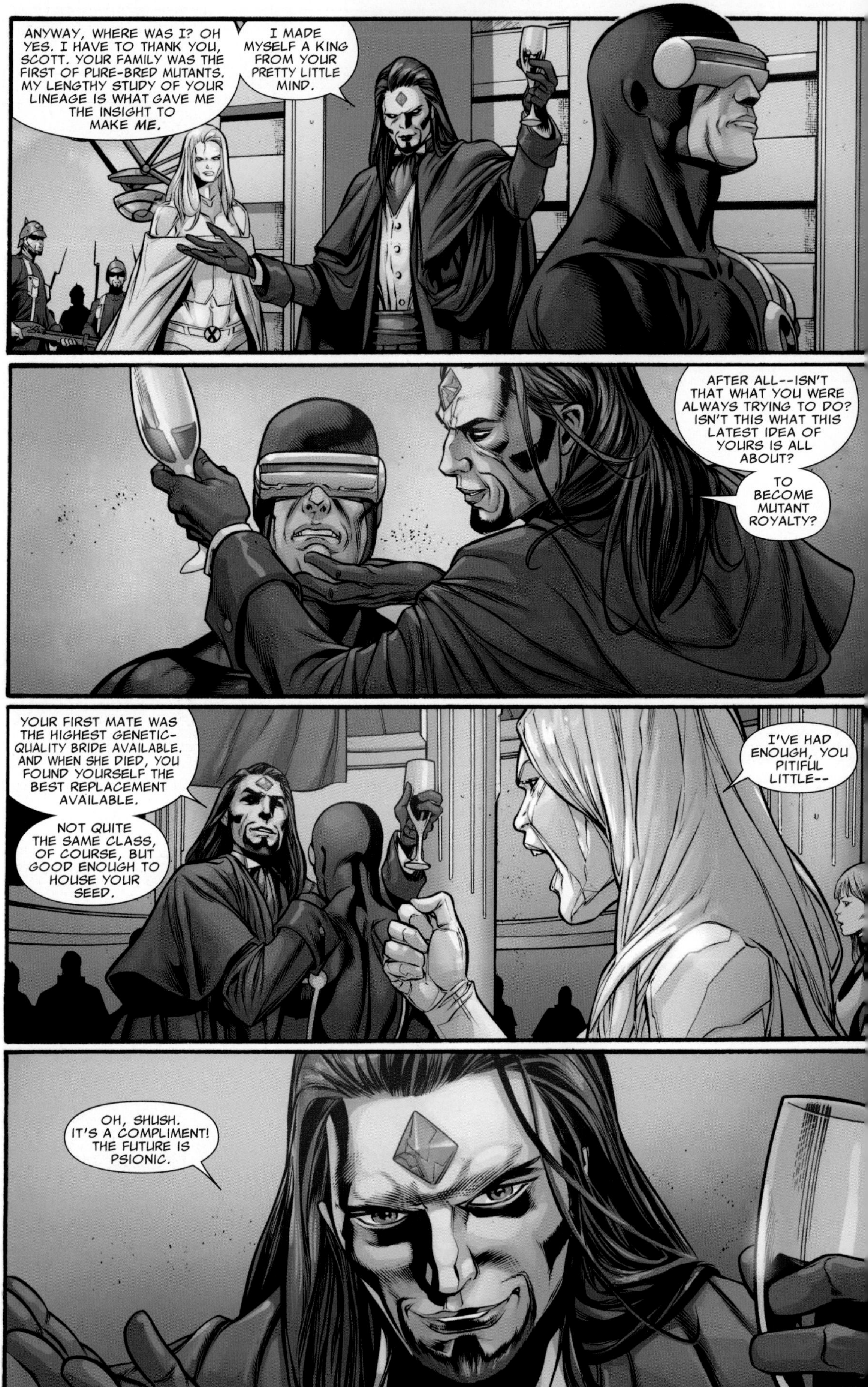
ANYWAY, WHERE WAS I? OH YES. I HAVE TO THANK YOU, SCOTT. YOUR FAMILY WAS THE FIRST OF PURE-BRED MUTANTS. MY LENGTHY STUDY OF YOUR LINEAGE IS WHAT GAVE ME THE INSIGHT TO MAKE *ME.*
I MADE MYSELF A KING FROM YOUR PRETTY LITTLE MIND.
AFTER ALL--ISN'T THAT WHAT YOU WERE ALWAYS TRYING TO DO? ISN'T THIS WHAT THIS LATEST IDEA OF YOURS IS ALL ABOUT?
TO BECOME MUTANT ROYALTY?
YOUR FIRST MATE WAS THE HIGHEST GENETIC-QUALITY BRIDE AVAILABLE. AND WHEN SHE DIED, YOU FOUND YOURSELF THE BEST REPLACEMENT AVAILABLE.
NOT QUITE THE SAME CLASS, OF COURSE, BUT GOOD ENOUGH TO HOUSE YOUR SEED.
I'VE HAD ENOUGH, YOU PITIFUL LITTLE--
OH, SHUSH. IT'S A COMPLIMENT! THE FUTURE IS PSIONIC.

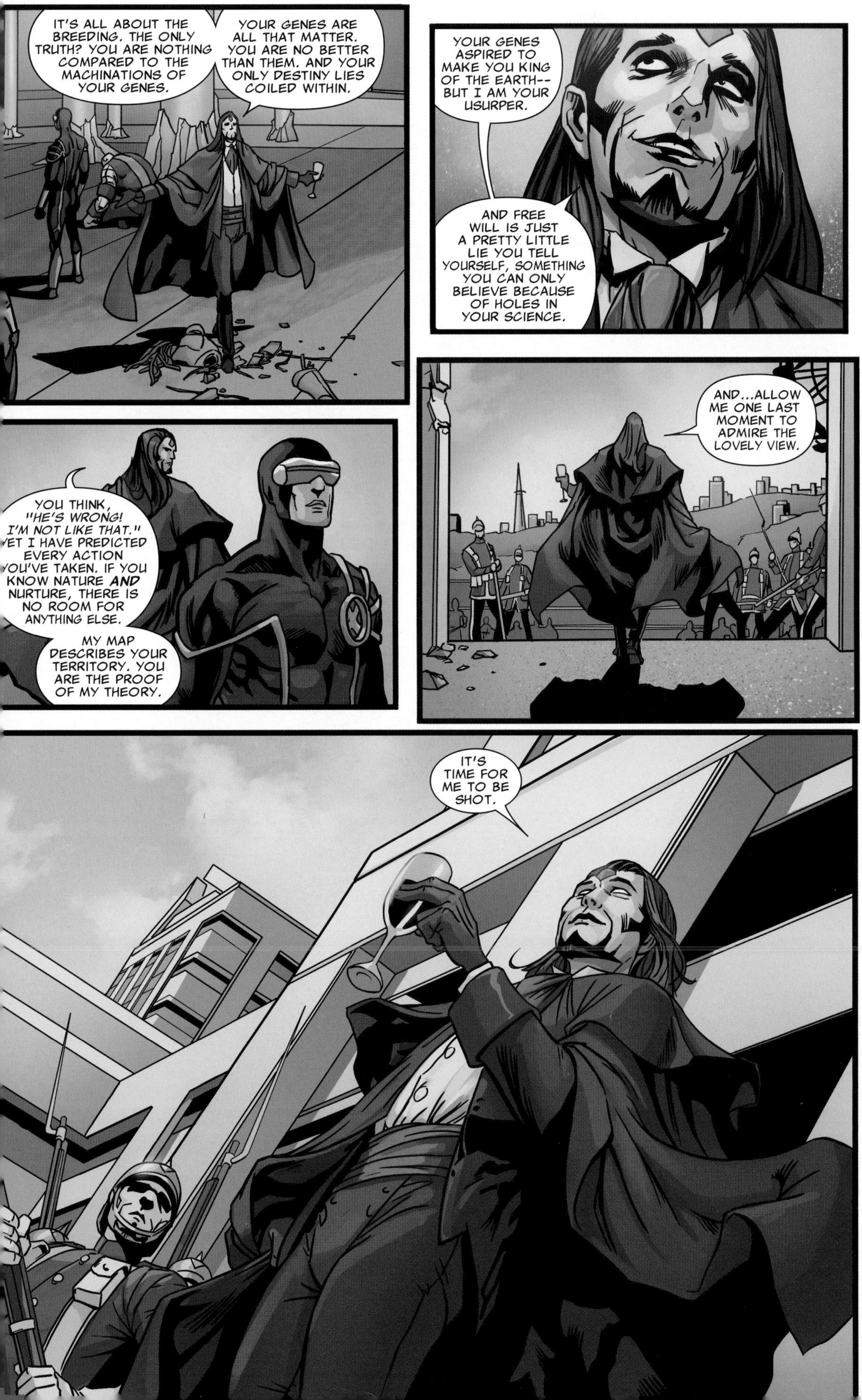
IT'S ALL ABOUT THE BREEDING. THE ONLY TRUTH? YOU ARE NOTHING COMPARED TO THE MACHINATIONS OF YOUR GENES.
YOUR GENES ARE ALL THAT MATTER. YOU ARE NO BETTER THAN THEM. AND YOUR ONLY DESTINY LIES COILED WITHIN.
YOUR GENES ASPIRED TO MAKE YOU KING OF THE EARTH--BUT I AM YOUR USURPER.
AND FREE WILL IS JUST A PRETTY LITTLE LIE YOU TELL YOURSELF, SOMETHING YOU CAN ONLY BELIEVE BECAUSE OF HOLES IN YOUR SCIENCE.
YOU THINK, "HE'S WRONG! I'M NOT LIKE THAT." YET I HAVE PREDICTED EVERY ACTION YOU'VE TAKEN. IF YOU KNOW NATURE AND NURTURE, THERE IS NO ROOM FOR ANYTHING ELSE.
MY MAP DESCRIBES YOUR TERRITORY. YOU ARE THE PROOF OF MY THEORY.
AND...ALLOW ME ONE LAST MOMENT TO ADMIRE THE LOVELY VIEW.
IT'S TIME FOR ME TO BE SHOT.

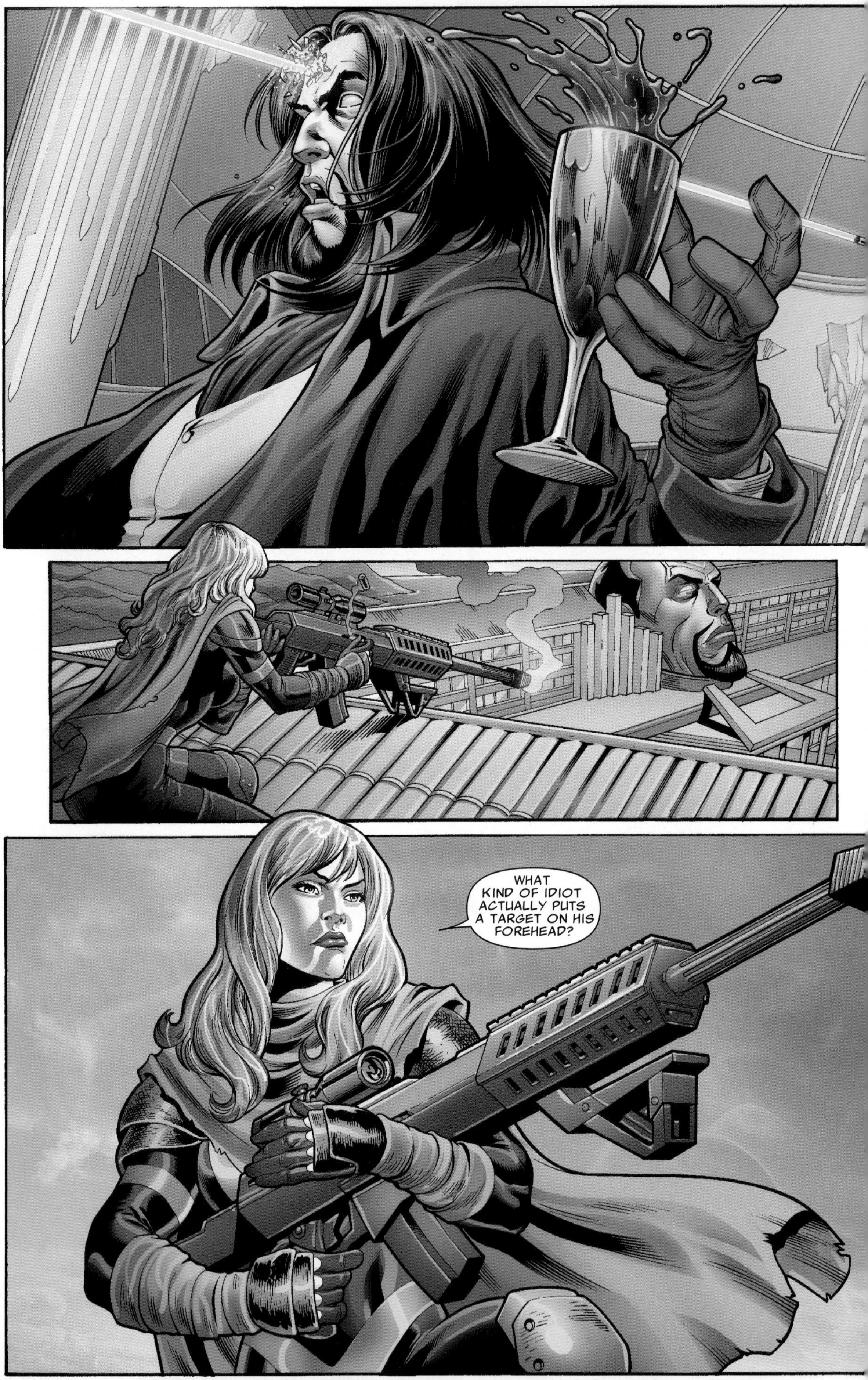
WHAT KIND OF IDIOT ACTUALLY PUTS A TARGET ON HIS FOREHEAD?

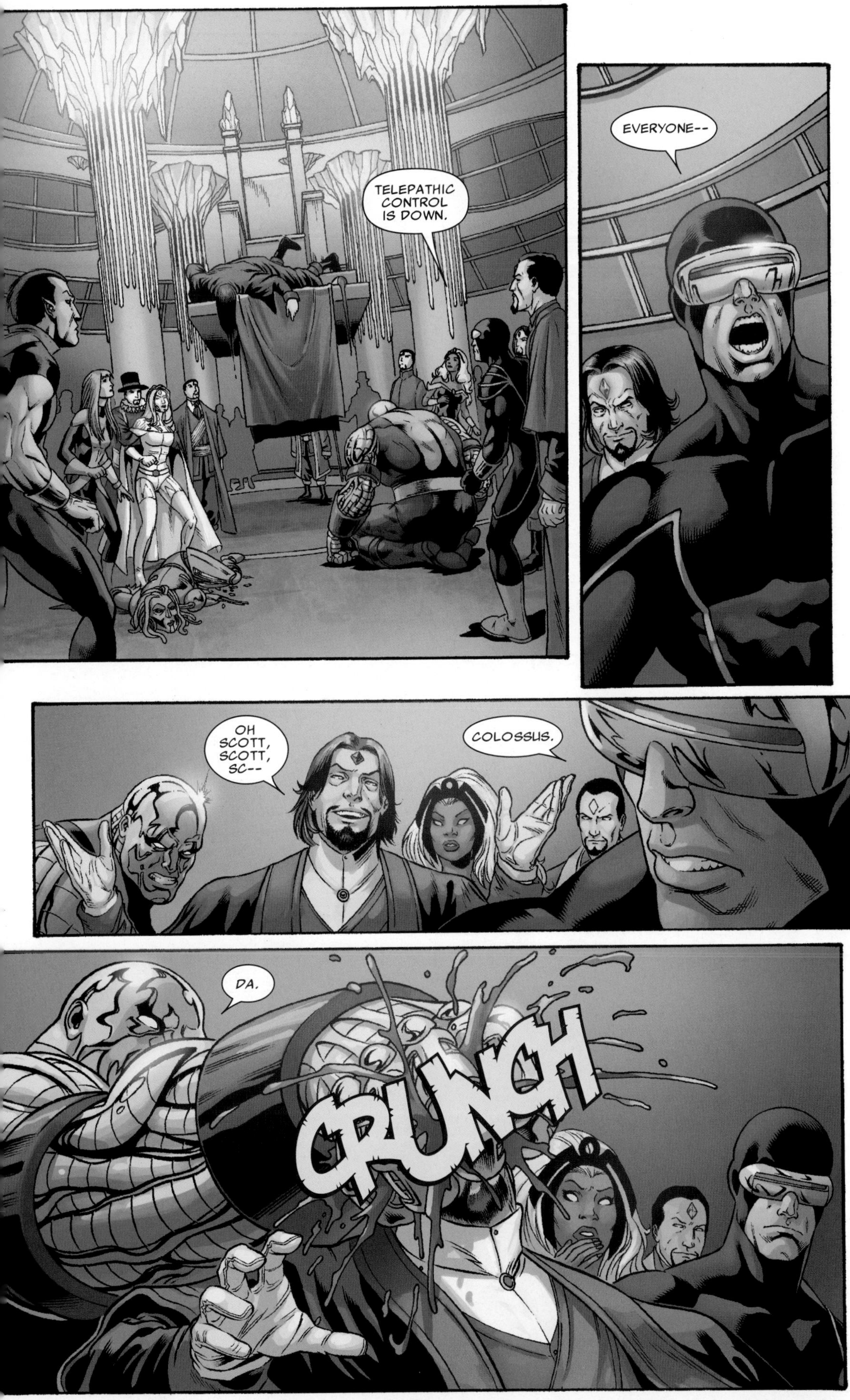

TELEPATHIC CONTROL IS DOWN.
EVERYONE--
OH SCOTT, SCOTT, SC--
COLOSSUS.
DA.
CRUNCH

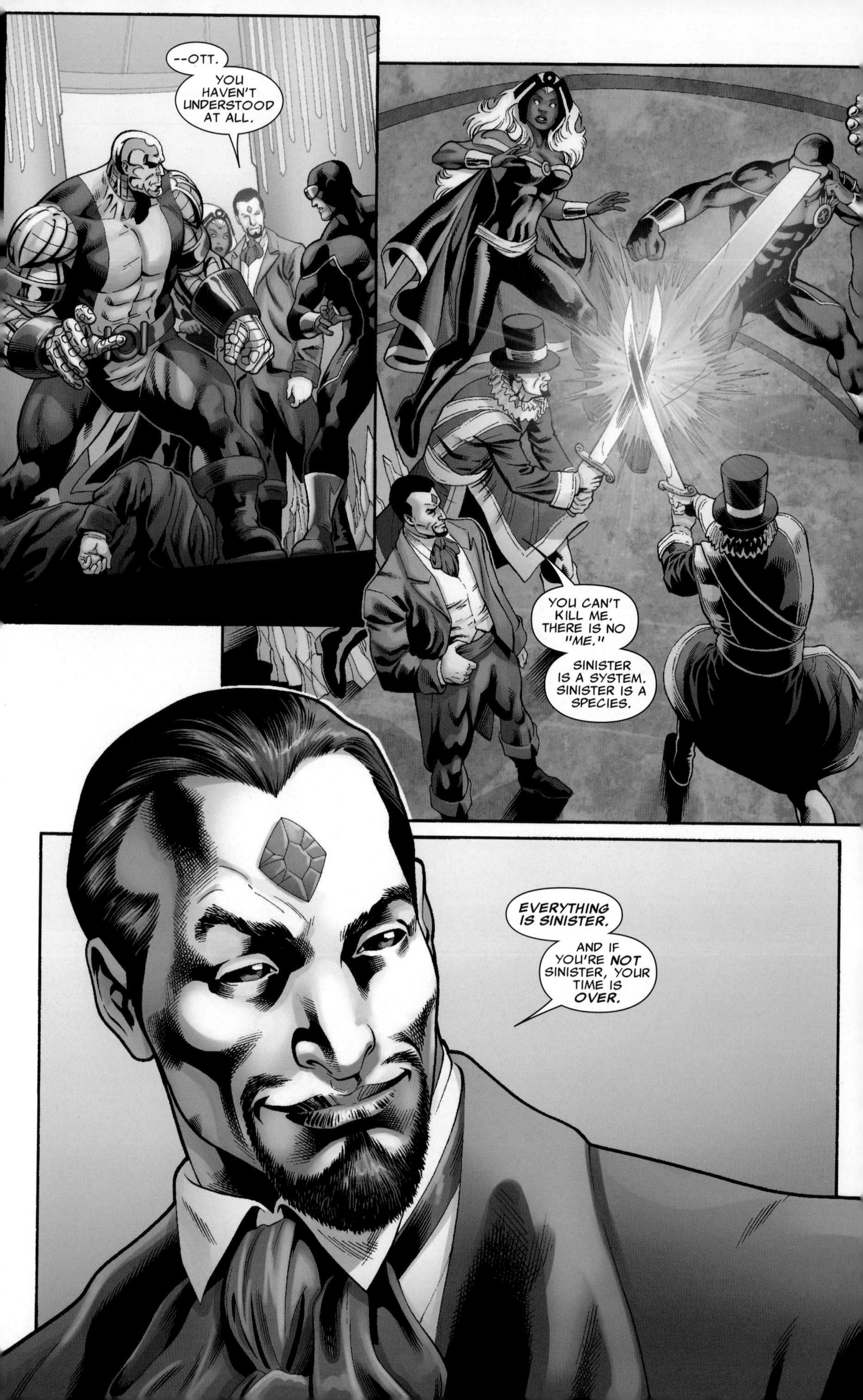

--OTT.
YOU HAVEN'T UNDERSTOOD AT ALL.
YOU CAN'T KILL ME. THERE IS NO "ME."
SINISTER IS A SYSTEM. SINISTER IS A SPECIES.
EVERYTHING IS SINISTER.
AND IF YOU'RE NOT SINISTER, YOUR TIME IS OVER.

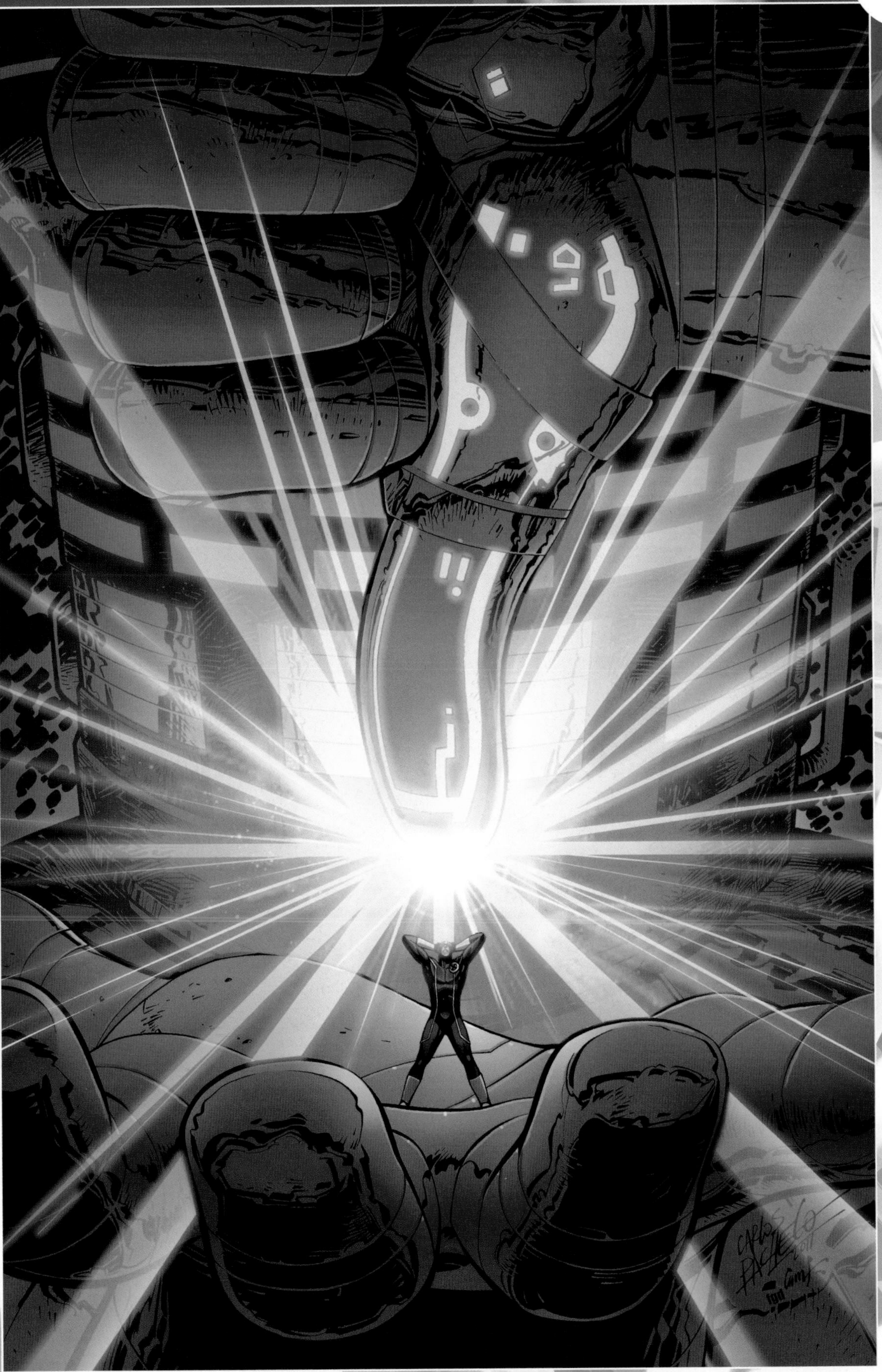

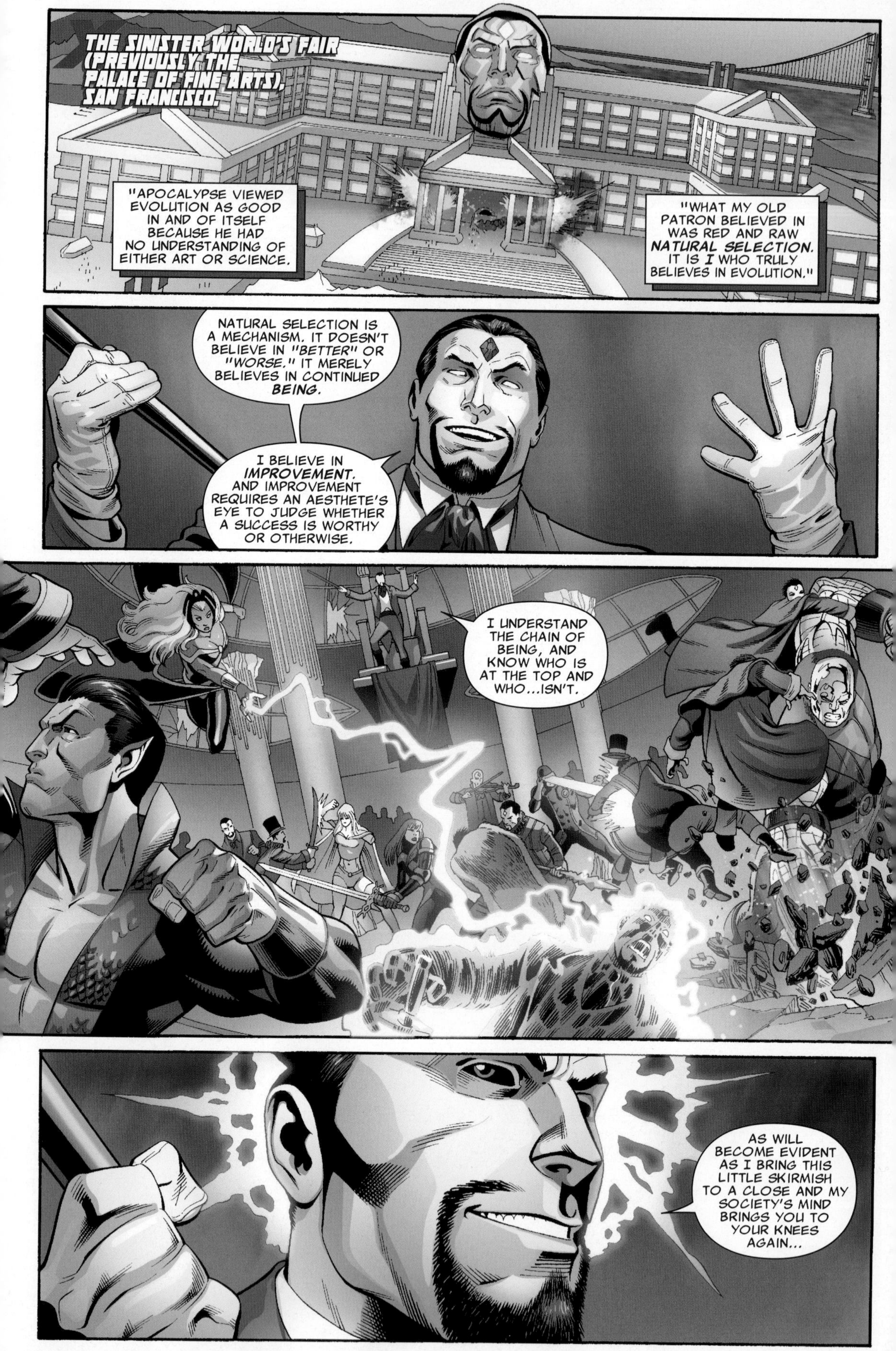
THE SINISTER WORLD'S FAIR (PREVIOUSLY THE PALACE OF FINE ARTS), SAN FRANCISCO.
"APOCALYPSE VIEWED EVOLUTION AS GOOD IN AND OF ITSELF BECAUSE HE HAD NO UNDERSTANDING OF EITHER ART OR SCIENCE.
"WHAT MY OLD PATRON BELIEVED IN WAS RED AND RAW NATURAL SELECTION. IT IS I WHO TRULY BELIEVES IN EVOLUTION."
NATURAL SELECTION IS A MECHANISM. IT DOESN'T BELIEVE IN "BETTER" OR "WORSE." IT MERELY BELIEVES IN CONTINUED BEING.
I BELIEVE IN IMPROVEMENT. AND IMPROVEMENT REQUIRES AN AESTHETE'S EYE TO JUDGE WHETHER A SUCCESS IS WORTHY OR OTHERWISE.
I UNDERSTAND THE CHAIN OF BEING, AND KNOW WHO IS AT THE TOP AND WHO...ISN'T.
AS WILL BECOME EVIDENT AS I BRING THIS LITTLE SKIRMISH TO A CLOSE AND MY SOCIETY'S MIND BRINGS YOU TO YOUR KNEES AGAIN...

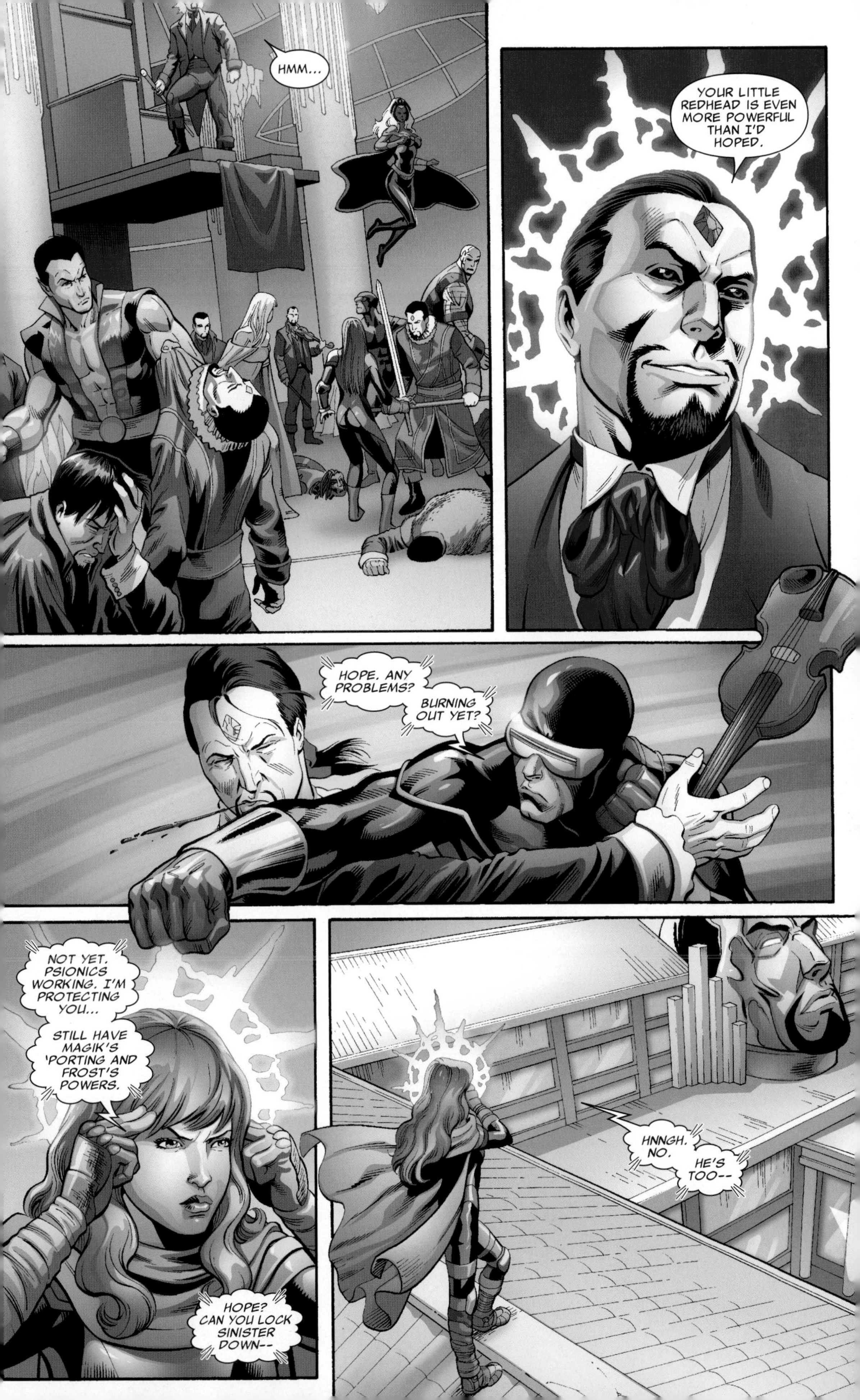
HMM...
YOUR LITTLE REDHEAD IS EVEN MORE POWERFUL THAN I'D HOPED.
HOPE. ANY PROBLEMS?
BURNING OUT YET?
NOT YET. PSIONICS WORKING. I'M PROTECTING YOU...
STILL HAVE MAGIK'S 'PORTING AND FROST'S POWERS.
HOPE? CAN YOU LOCK SINISTER DOWN--
HNNGH. NO.
HE'S TOO--

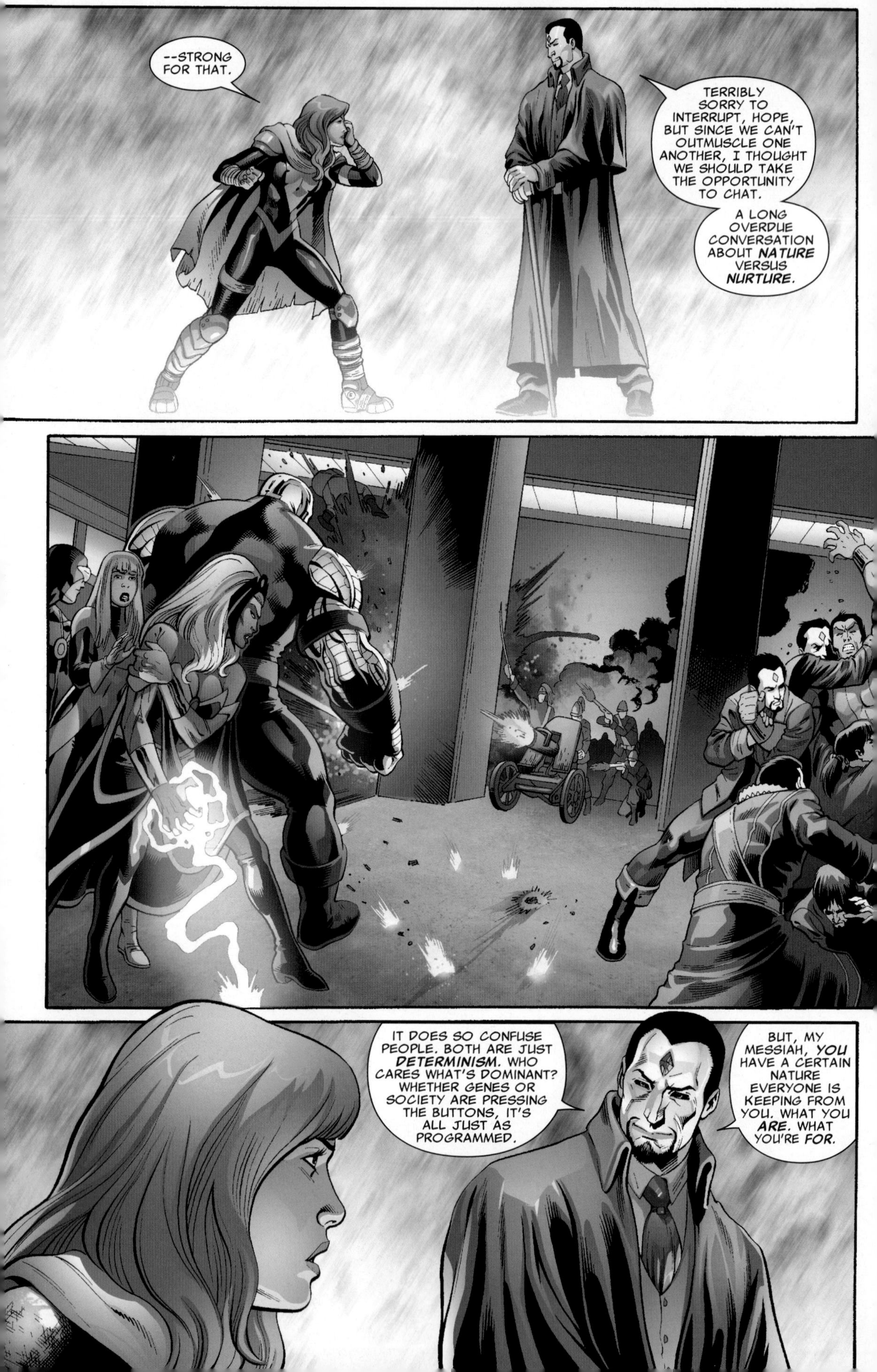
--STRONG FOR THAT.
TERRIBLY SORRY TO INTERRUPT, HOPE, BUT SINCE WE CAN'T OUTMUSCLE ONE ANOTHER, I THOUGHT WE SHOULD TAKE THE OPPORTUNITY TO CHAT.
A LONG OVERDUE CONVERSATION ABOUT NATURE VERSUS NURTURE.
IT DOES SO CONFUSE PEOPLE. BOTH ARE JUST DETERMINISM. WHO CARES WHAT'S DOMINANT? WHETHER GENES OR SOCIETY ARE PRESSING THE BUTTONS, IT'S ALL JUST AS PROGRAMMED.
BUT, MY MESSIAH, YOU HAVE A CERTAIN NATURE EVERYONE IS KEEPING FROM YOU. WHAT YOU ARE. WHAT YOU'RE FOR.

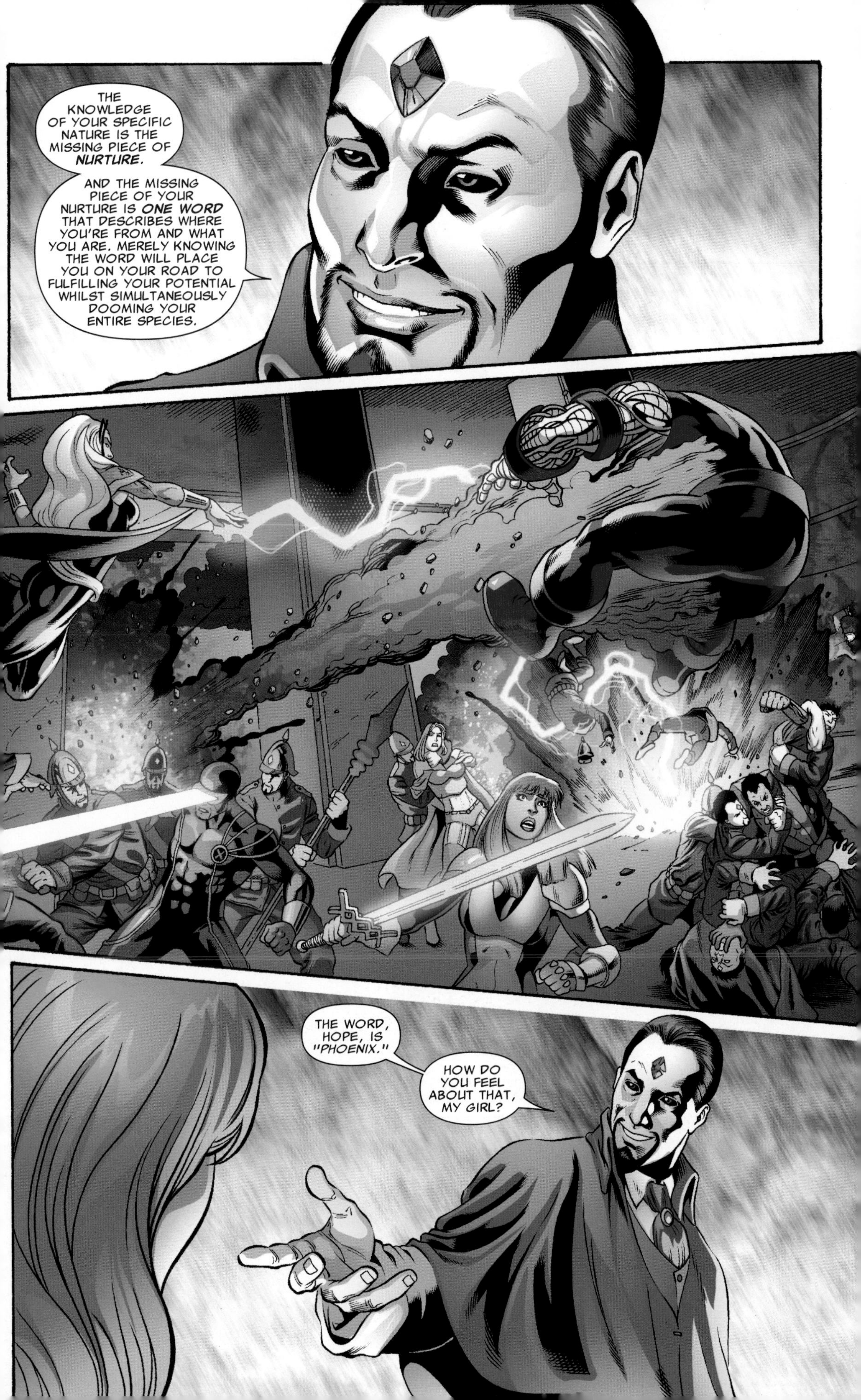
THE KNOWLEDGE OF YOUR SPECIFIC NATURE IS THE MISSING PIECE OF *NURTURE*.
AND THE MISSING PIECE OF YOUR NURTURE IS *ONE WORD* THAT DESCRIBES WHERE YOU'RE FROM AND WHAT YOU ARE. MERELY KNOWING THE WORD WILL PLACE YOU ON YOUR ROAD TO FULFILLING YOUR POTENTIAL WHILST SIMULTANEOUSLY DOOMING YOUR ENTIRE SPECIES.
THE WORD, HOPE, IS "*PHOENIX*."
HOW DO YOU FEEL ABOUT THAT, MY GIRL?

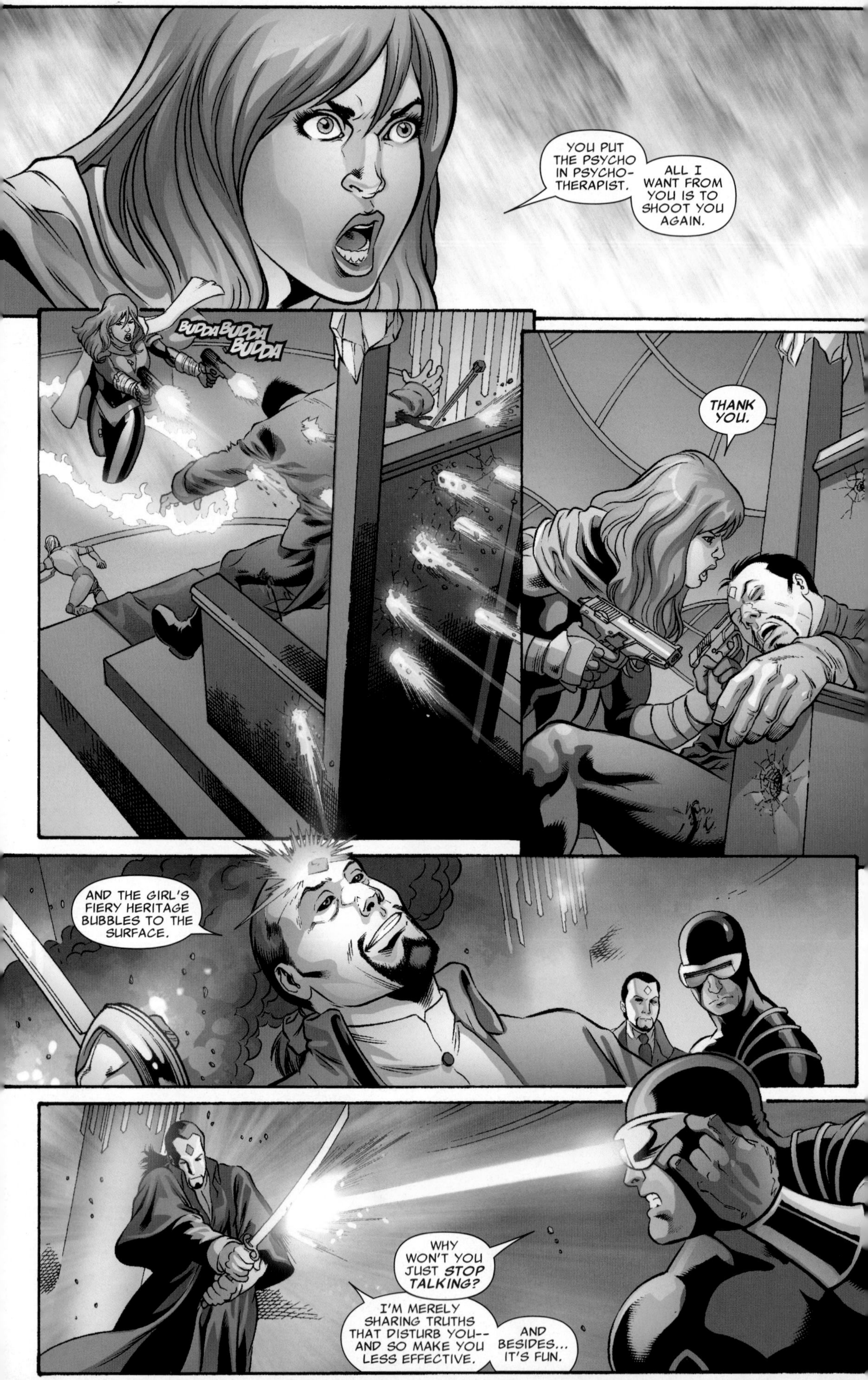
YOU PUT THE PSYCHO IN PSYCHO-THERAPIST.
ALL I WANT FROM YOU IS TO SHOOT YOU AGAIN.
BUDDA BUDDA BUDDA
THANK YOU.
AND THE GIRL'S FIERY HERITAGE BUBBLES TO THE SURFACE.
WHY WON'T YOU JUST STOP TALKING?
I'M MERELY SHARING TRUTHS THAT DISTURB YOU-- AND SO MAKE YOU LESS EFFECTIVE.
AND BESIDES... IT'S FUN.

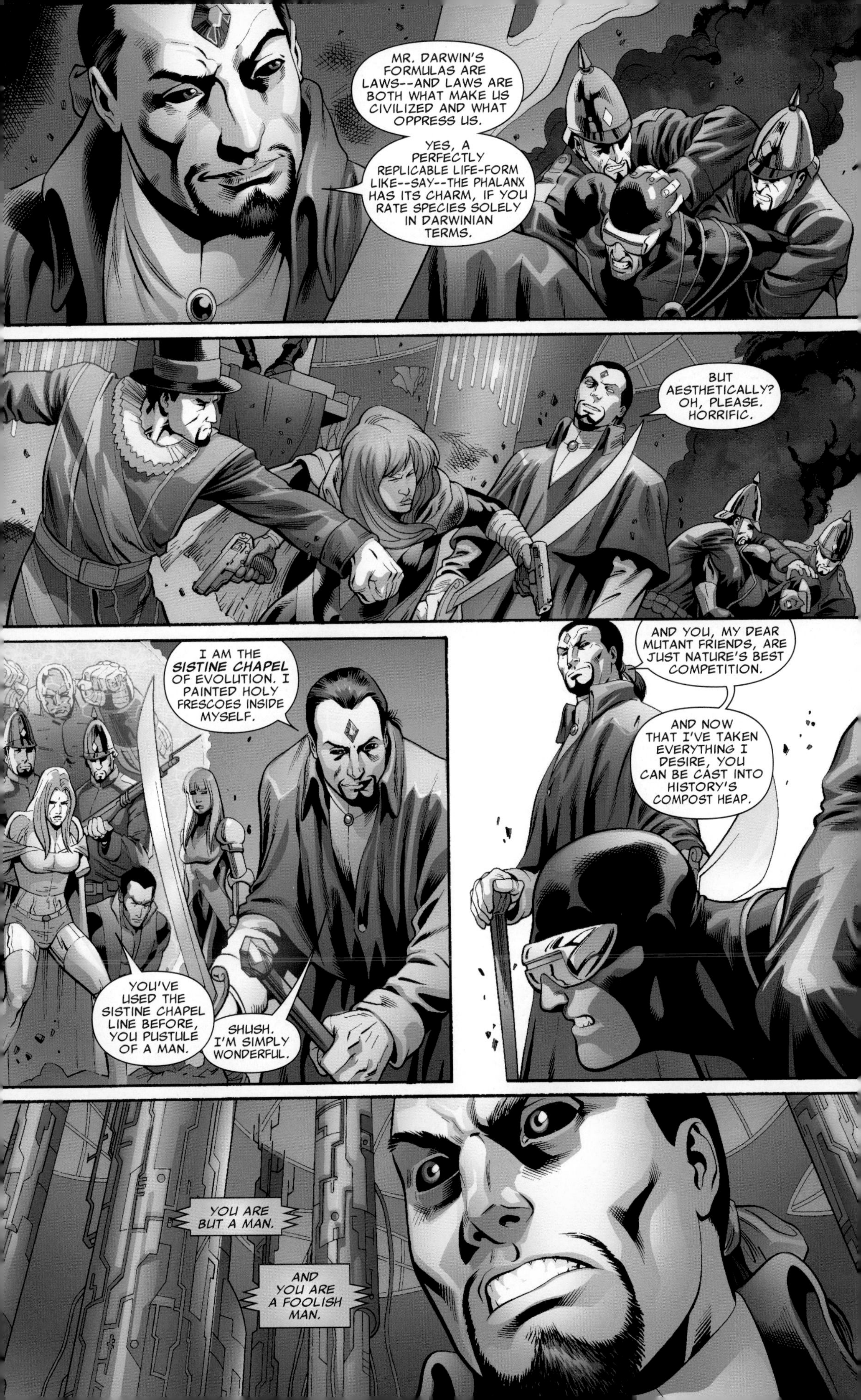
MR. DARWIN'S FORMULAS ARE LAWS--AND LAWS ARE BOTH WHAT MAKE US CIVILIZED AND WHAT OPPRESS US.
YES, A PERFECTLY REPLICABLE LIFE-FORM LIKE--SAY--THE PHALANX HAS ITS CHARM, IF YOU RATE SPECIES SOLELY IN DARWINIAN TERMS.
BUT AESTHETICALLY? OH, PLEASE. HORRIFIC.
I AM THE SISTINE CHAPEL OF EVOLUTION. I PAINTED HOLY FRESCOES INSIDE MYSELF.
YOU'VE USED THE SISTINE CHAPEL LINE BEFORE, YOU PUSTULE OF A MAN.
SHUSH. I'M SIMPLY WONDERFUL.
AND YOU, MY DEAR MUTANT FRIENDS, ARE JUST NATURE'S BEST COMPETITION.
AND NOW THAT I'VE TAKEN EVERYTHING I DESIRE, YOU CAN BE CAST INTO HISTORY'S COMPOST HEAP.
YOU ARE BUT A MAN.
AND YOU ARE A FOOLISH MAN.

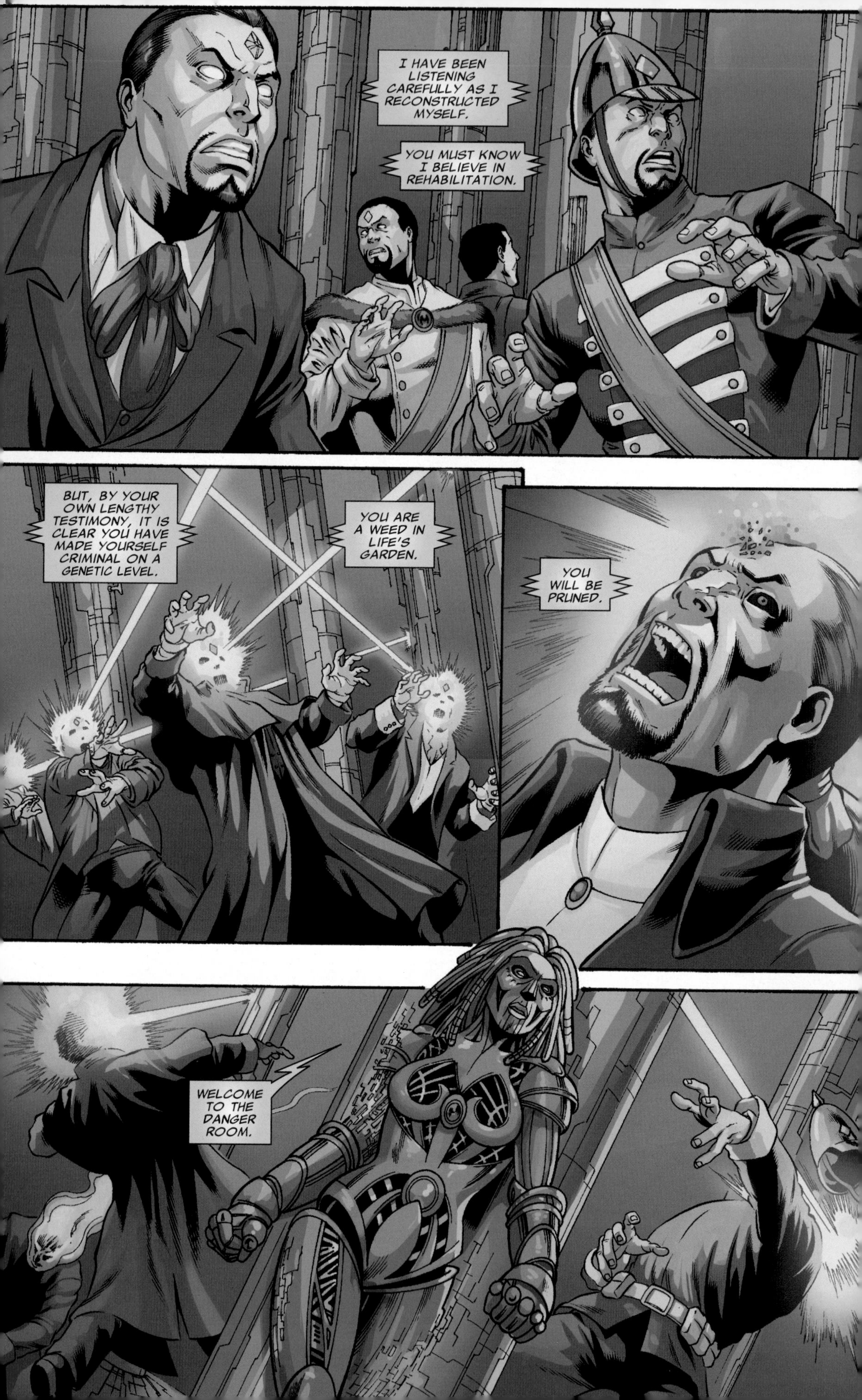
I HAVE BEEN LISTENING CAREFULLY AS I RECONSTRUCTED MYSELF.
YOU MUST KNOW I BELIEVE IN REHABILITATION.
BUT, BY YOUR OWN LENGTHY TESTIMONY, IT IS CLEAR YOU HAVE MADE YOURSELF CRIMINAL ON A GENETIC LEVEL.
YOU ARE A WEED IN LIFE'S GARDEN.
YOU WILL BE PRUNED.
WELCOME TO THE DANGER ROOM.

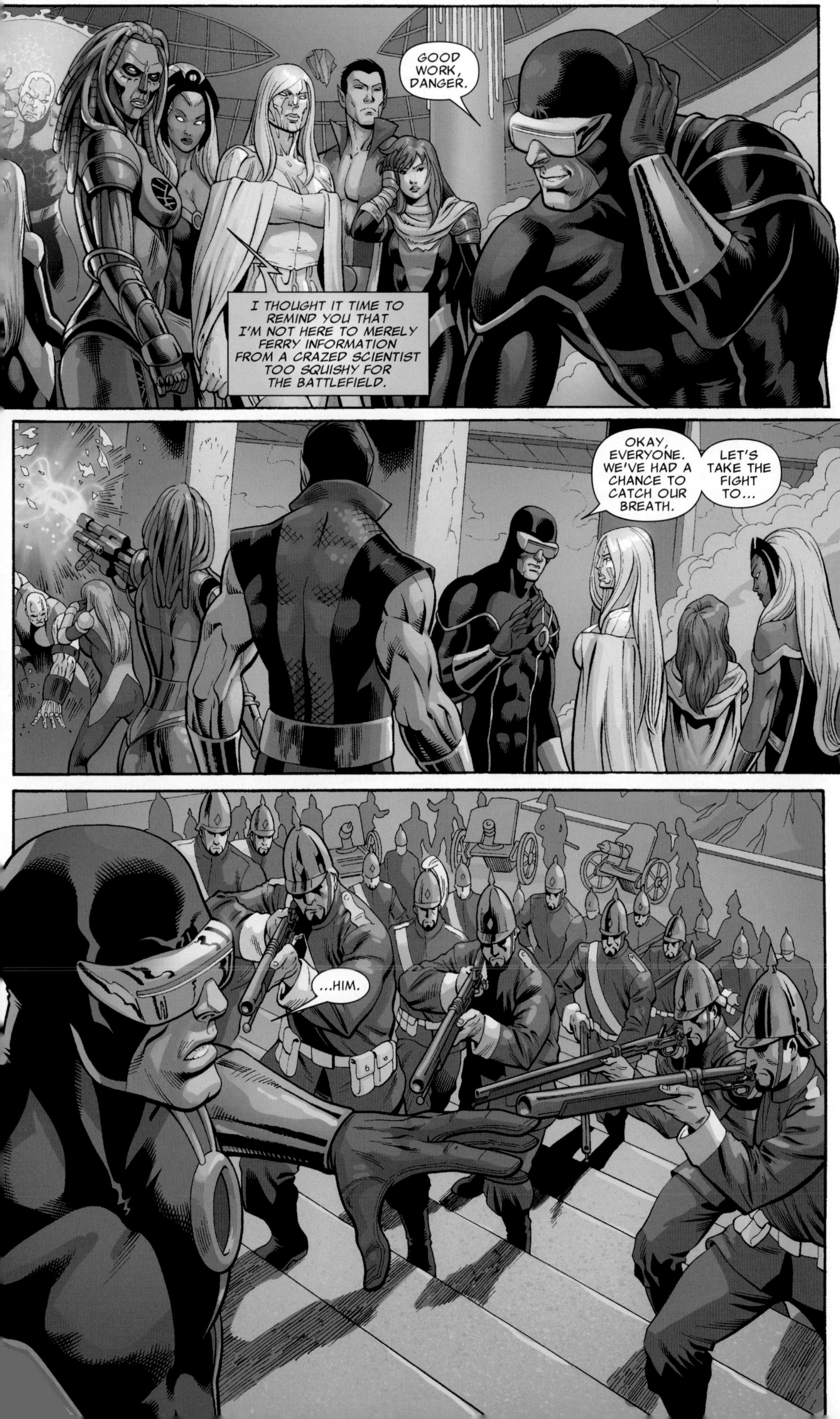
GOOD WORK, DANGER.
I THOUGHT IT TIME TO REMIND YOU THAT I'M NOT HERE TO MERELY FERRY INFORMATION FROM A CRAZED SCIENTIST TOO SQUISHY FOR THE BATTLEFIELD.
OKAY, EVERYONE. WE'VE HAD A CHANCE TO CATCH OUR BREATH.
LET'S TAKE THE FIGHT TO...
...HIM.

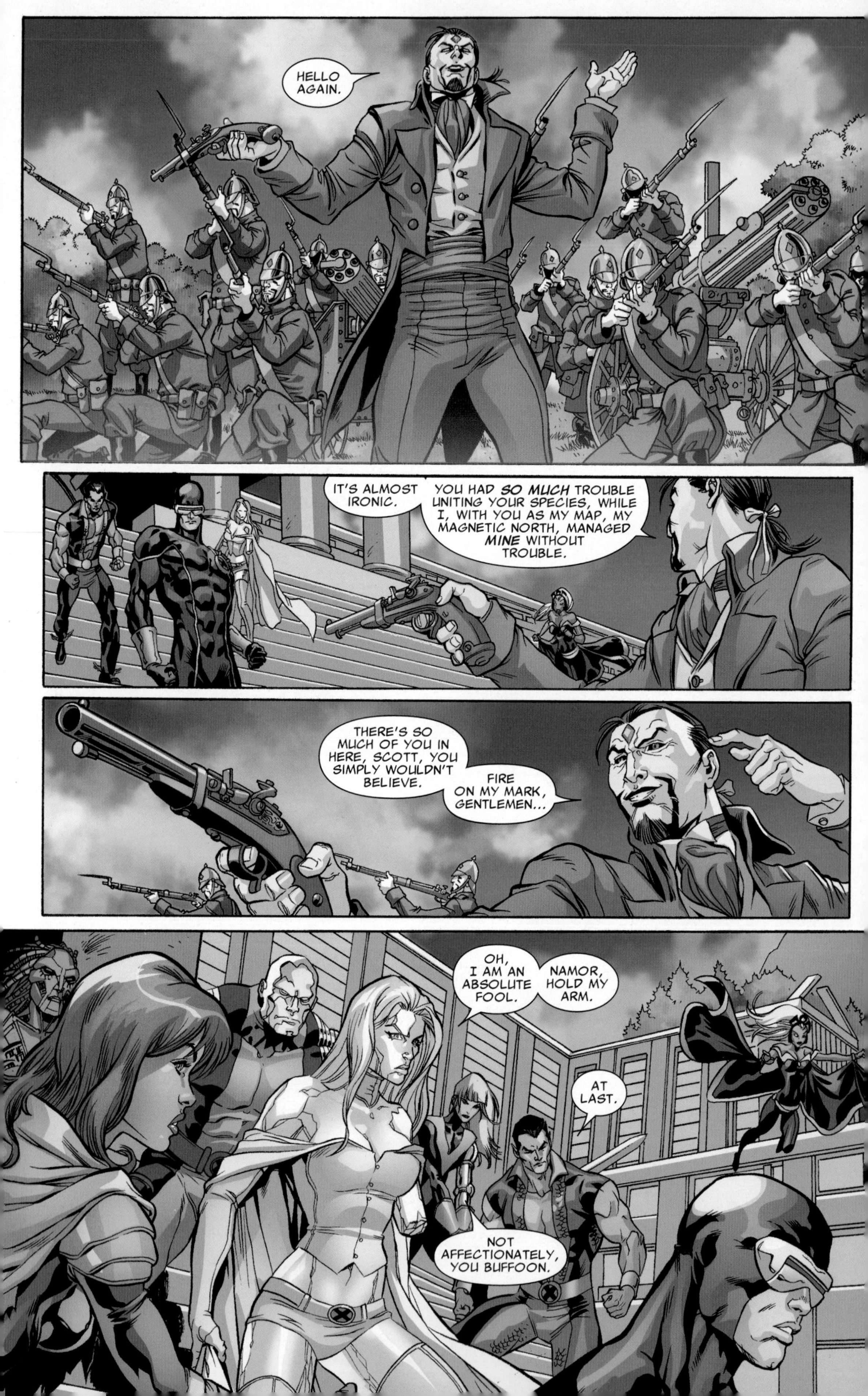
HELLO AGAIN.
IT'S ALMOST IRONIC.
YOU HAD SO MUCH TROUBLE UNITING YOUR SPECIES, WHILE I, WITH YOU AS MY MAP, MY MAGNETIC NORTH, MANAGED MINE WITHOUT TROUBLE.
THERE'S SO MUCH OF YOU IN HERE, SCOTT, YOU SIMPLY WOULDN'T BELIEVE.
FIRE ON MY MARK, GENTLEMEN...
OH, I AM AN ABSOLUTE FOOL.
NAMOR, HOLD MY ARM.
AT LAST.
NOT AFFECTIONATELY, YOU BUFFOON.

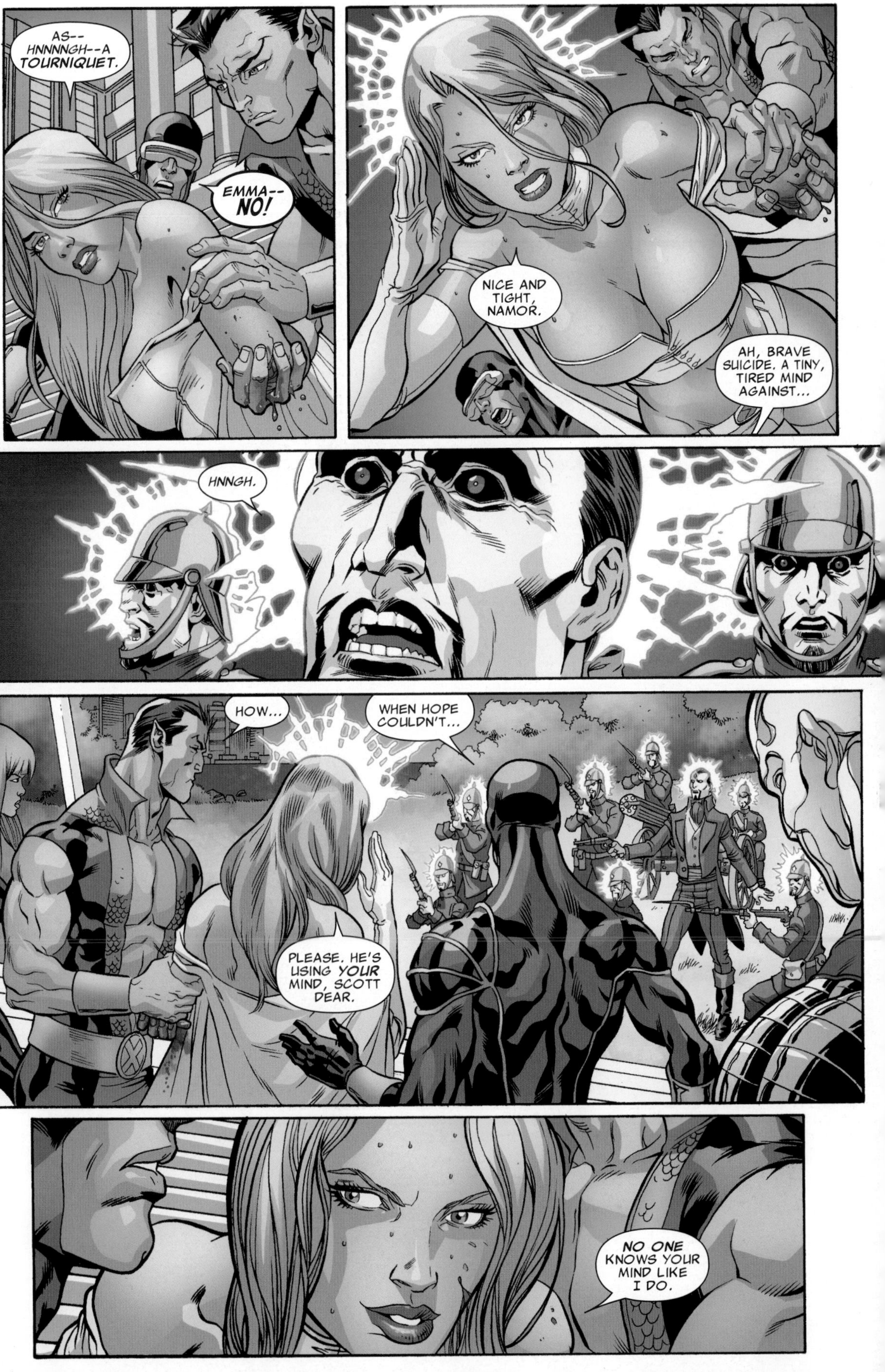
AS-- HNNNNGH--A TOURNIQUET.
EMMA-- NO!
NICE AND TIGHT, NAMOR.
AH, BRAVE SUICIDE. A TINY, TIRED MIND AGAINST...
HNNGH.
HOW...
WHEN HOPE COULDN'T...
PLEASE. HE'S USING YOUR MIND, SCOTT DEAR.
NO ONE KNOWS YOUR MIND LIKE I DO.

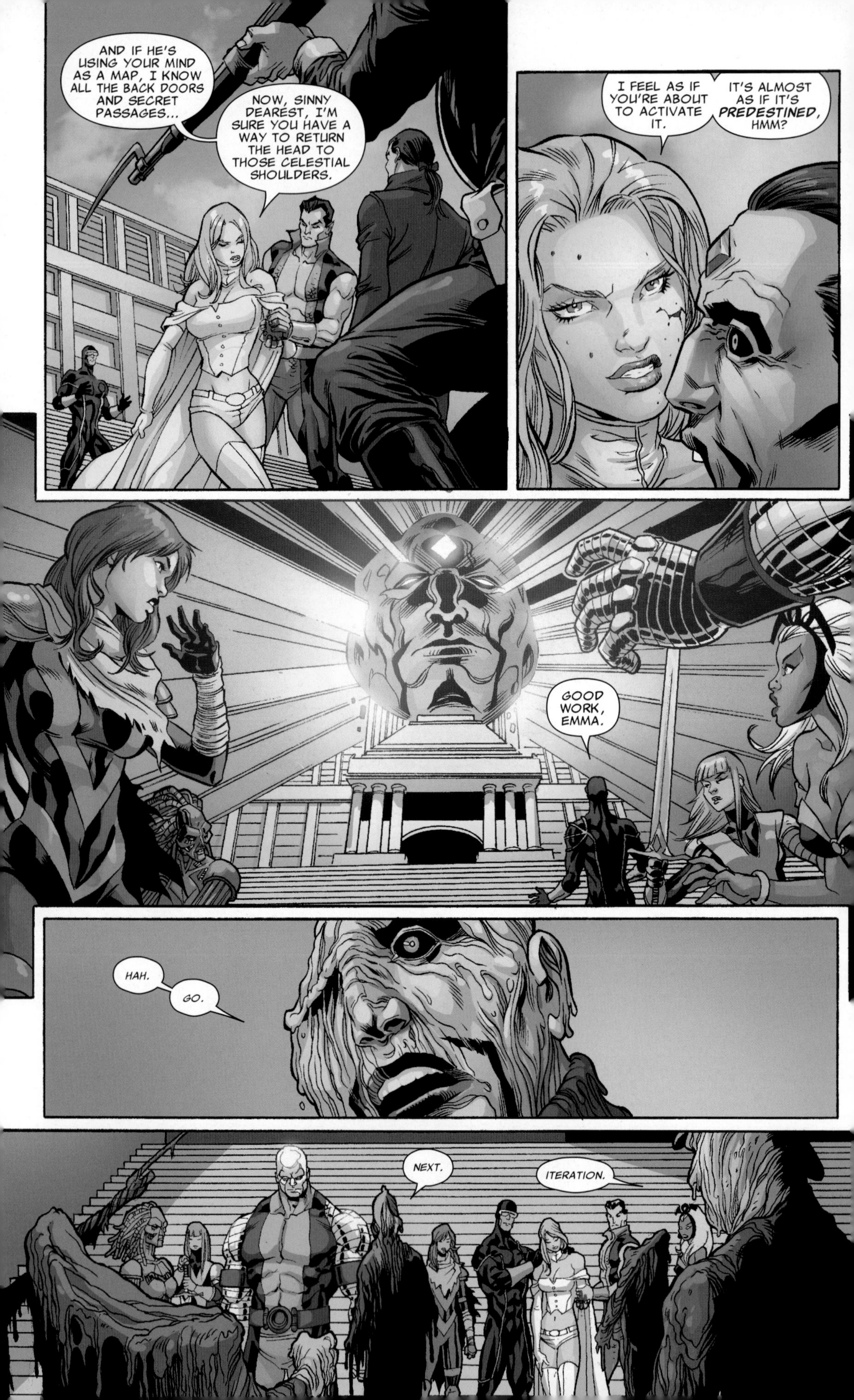
AND IF HE'S USING YOUR MIND AS A MAP, I KNOW ALL THE BACK DOORS AND SECRET PASSAGES...
NOW, SINNY DEAREST, I'M SURE YOU HAVE A WAY TO RETURN THE HEAD TO THOSE CELESTIAL SHOULDERS.
I FEEL AS IF YOU'RE ABOUT TO ACTIVATE IT.
IT'S ALMOST AS IF IT'S *PREDESTINED*, HMM?
GOOD WORK, EMMA.
HAH.
GO.
NEXT.
ITERATION.

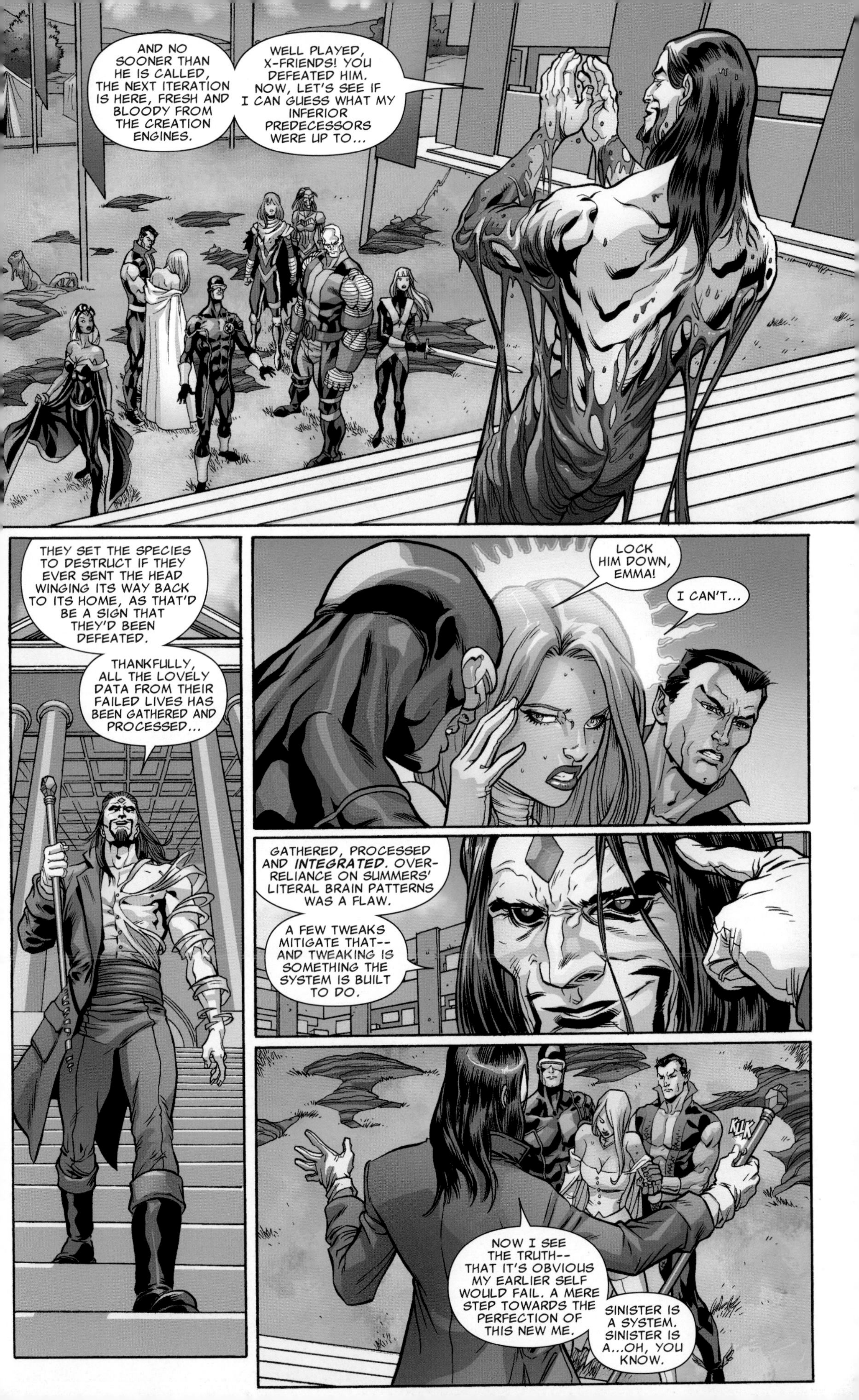
AND NO SOONER THAN HE IS CALLED, THE NEXT ITERATION IS HERE, FRESH AND BLOODY FROM THE CREATION ENGINES.
WELL PLAYED, X-FRIENDS! YOU DEFEATED HIM. NOW, LET'S SEE IF I CAN GUESS WHAT MY INFERIOR PREDECESSORS WERE UP TO...
THEY SET THE SPECIES TO DESTRUCT IF THEY EVER SENT THE HEAD WINGING ITS WAY BACK TO ITS HOME, AS THAT'D BE A SIGN THAT THEY'D BEEN DEFEATED.
THANKFULLY, ALL THE LOVELY DATA FROM THEIR FAILED LIVES HAS BEEN GATHERED AND PROCESSED...
LOCK HIM DOWN, EMMA!
I CAN'T...
GATHERED, PROCESSED AND INTEGRATED. OVER-RELIANCE ON SUMMERS' LITERAL BRAIN PATTERNS WAS A FLAW.
A FEW TWEAKS MITIGATE THAT--AND TWEAKING IS SOMETHING THE SYSTEM IS BUILT TO DO.
KLIK
NOW I SEE THE TRUTH--THAT IT'S OBVIOUS MY EARLIER SELF WOULD FAIL. A MERE STEP TOWARDS THE PERFECTION OF THIS NEW ME.
SINISTER IS A SYSTEM. SINISTER IS A...OH, YOU KNOW.

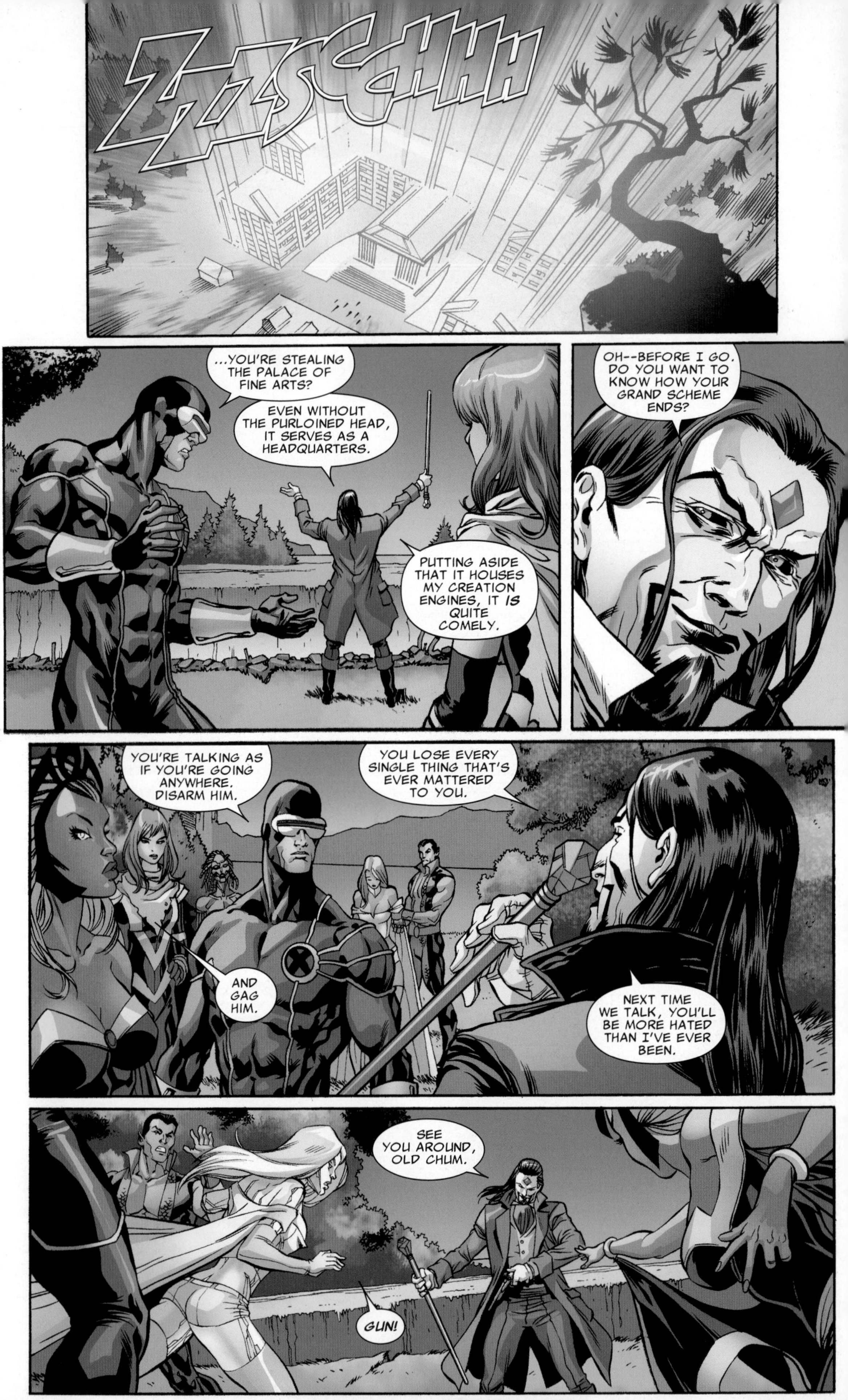
ZZZSCHHH
...YOU'RE STEALING THE PALACE OF FINE ARTS?
EVEN WITHOUT THE PURLOINED HEAD, IT SERVES AS A HEADQUARTERS.
PUTTING ASIDE THAT IT HOUSES MY CREATION ENGINES, IT *IS* QUITE COMELY.
OH--BEFORE I GO. DO YOU WANT TO KNOW HOW YOUR GRAND SCHEME ENDS?
YOU'RE TALKING AS IF YOU'RE GOING ANYWHERE. DISARM HIM.
YOU LOSE EVERY SINGLE THING THAT'S EVER MATTERED TO YOU.
AND GAG HIM.
NEXT TIME WE TALK, YOU'LL BE MORE HATED THAN I'VE EVER BEEN.
SEE YOU AROUND, OLD CHUM.
GUN!

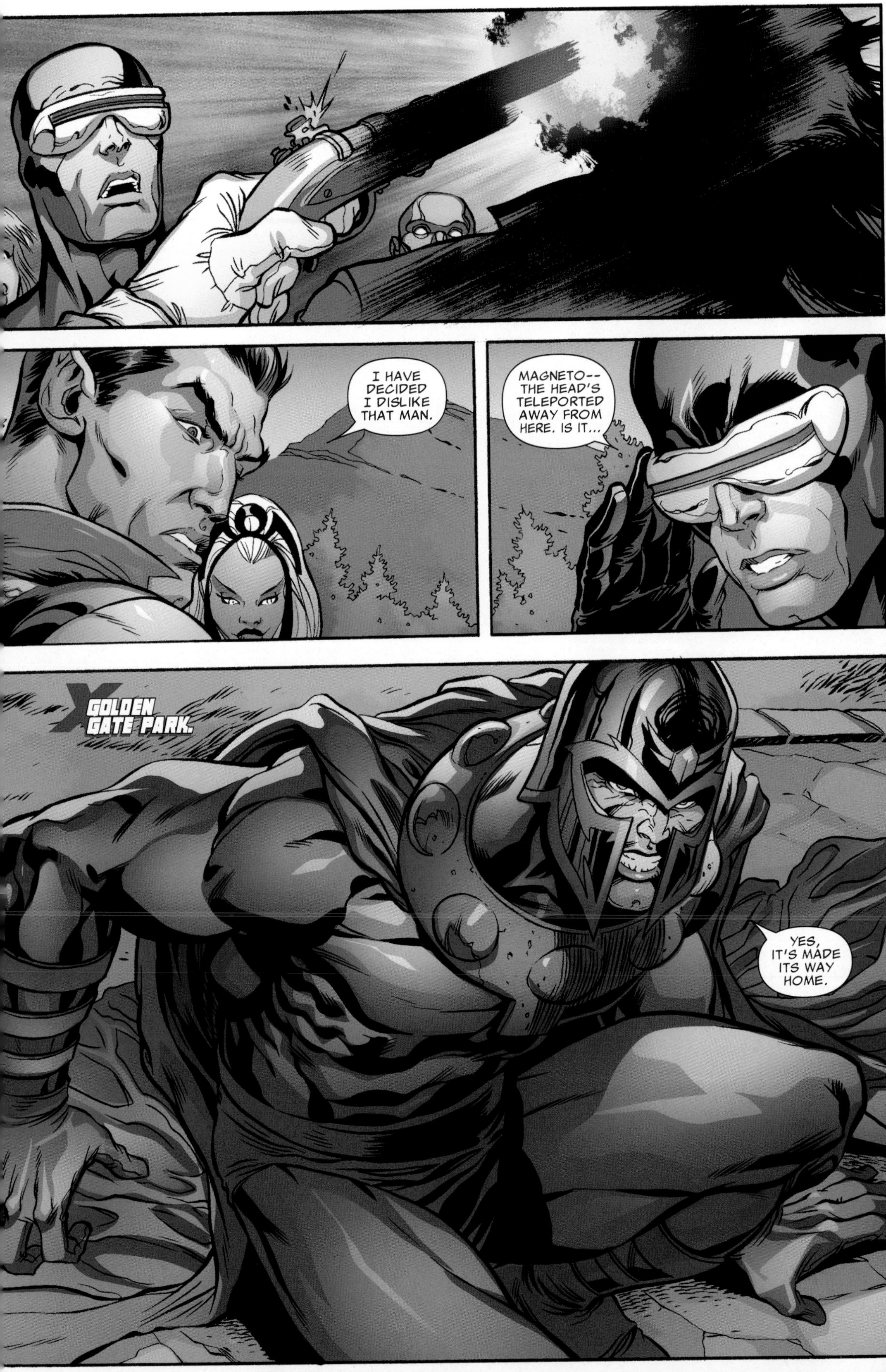
I HAVE DECIDED I DISLIKE THAT MAN.
MAGNETO-- THE HEAD'S TELEPORTED AWAY FROM HERE. IS IT...
GOLDEN GATE PARK.
YES, IT'S MADE ITS WAY HOME.

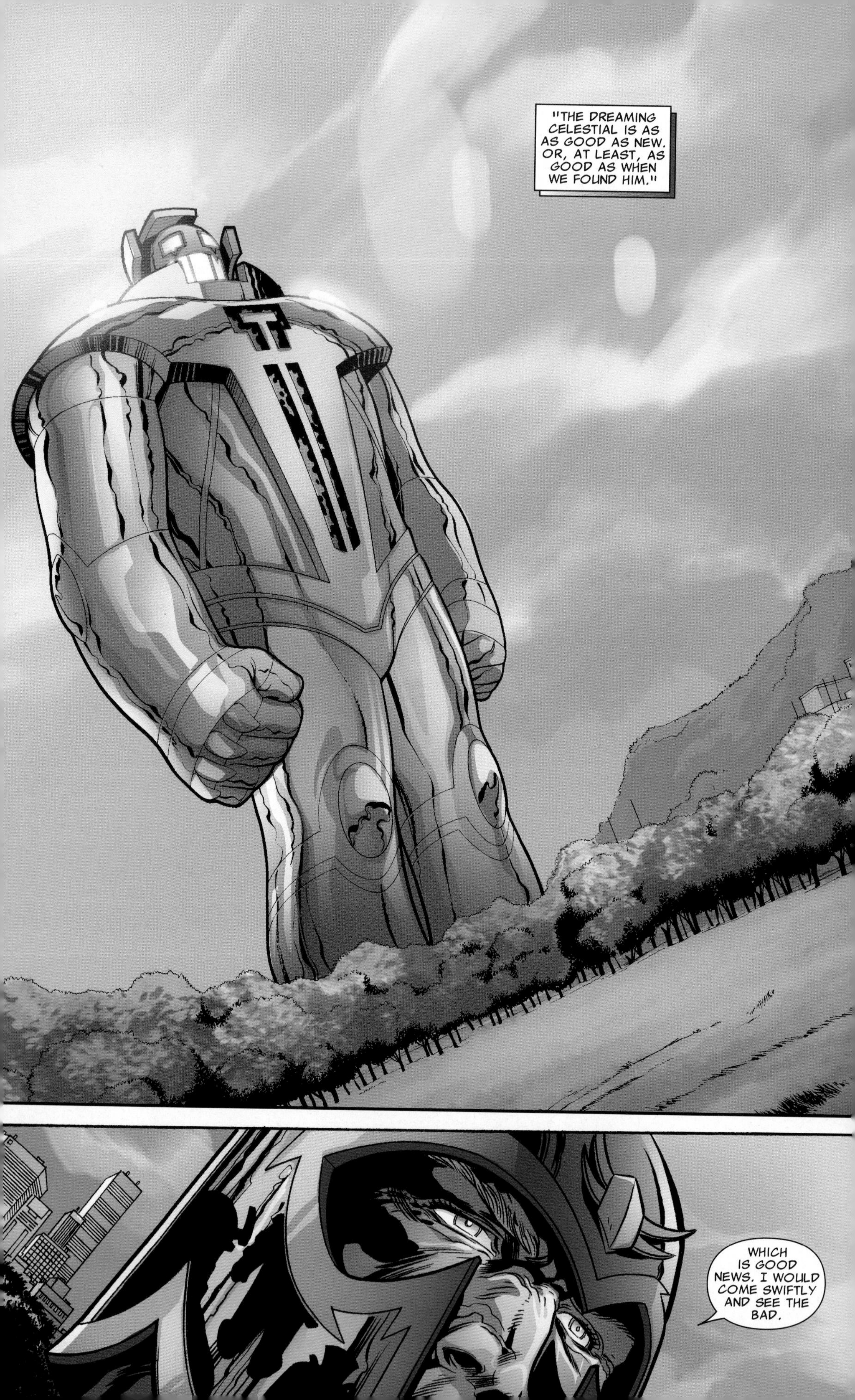
"THE DREAMING CELESTIAL IS AS AS GOOD AS NEW. OR, AT LEAST, AS GOOD AS WHEN WE FOUND HIM."
WHICH IS GOOD NEWS. I WOULD COME SWIFTLY AND SEE THE BAD.

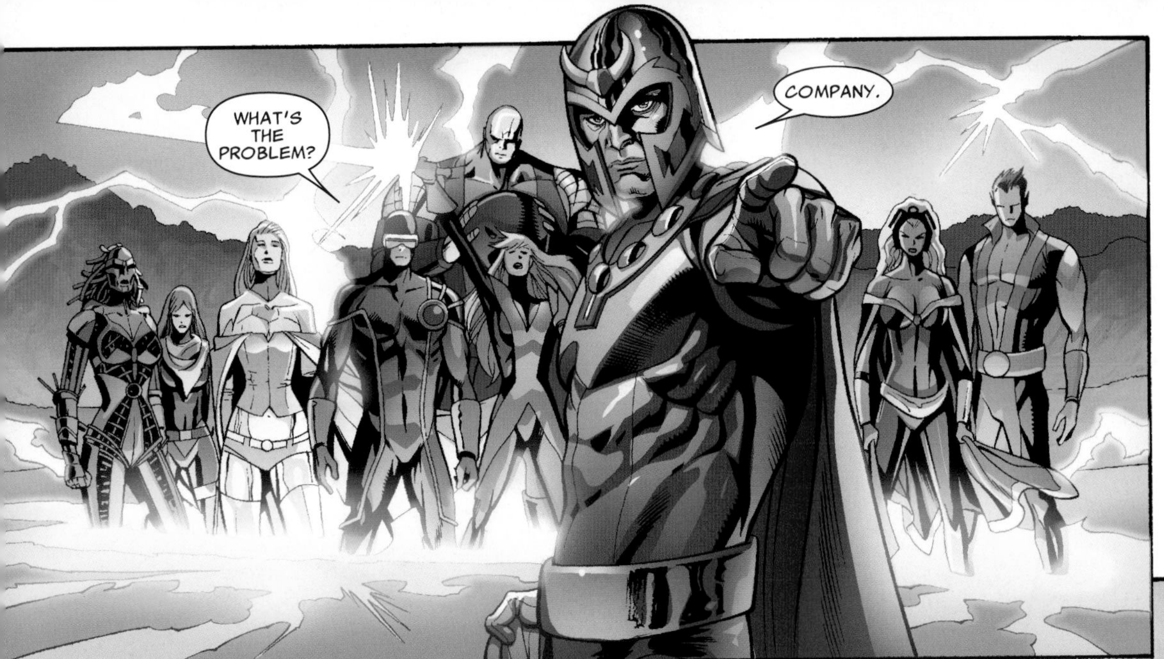
WHAT'S THE PROBLEM?
COMPANY.

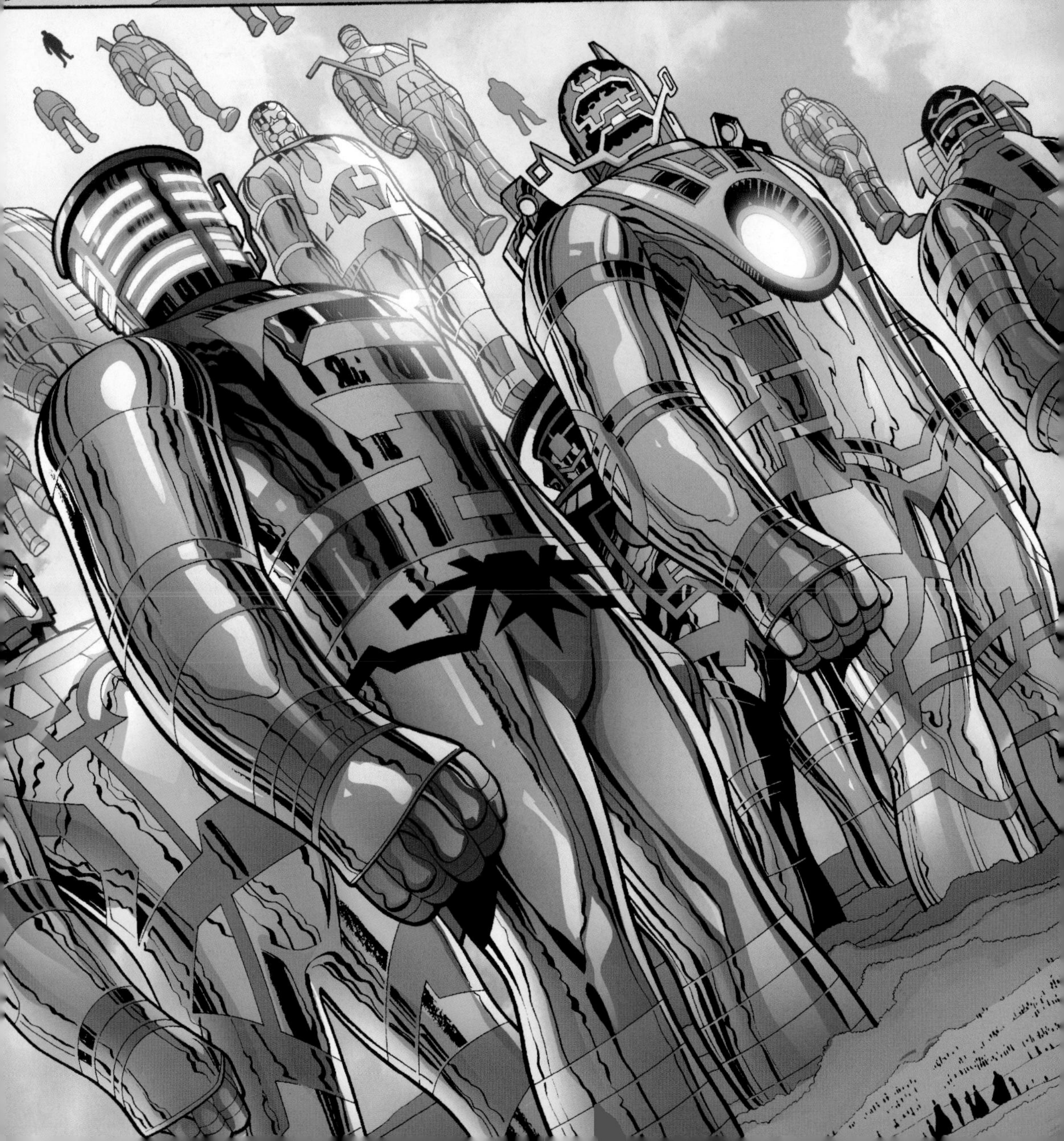

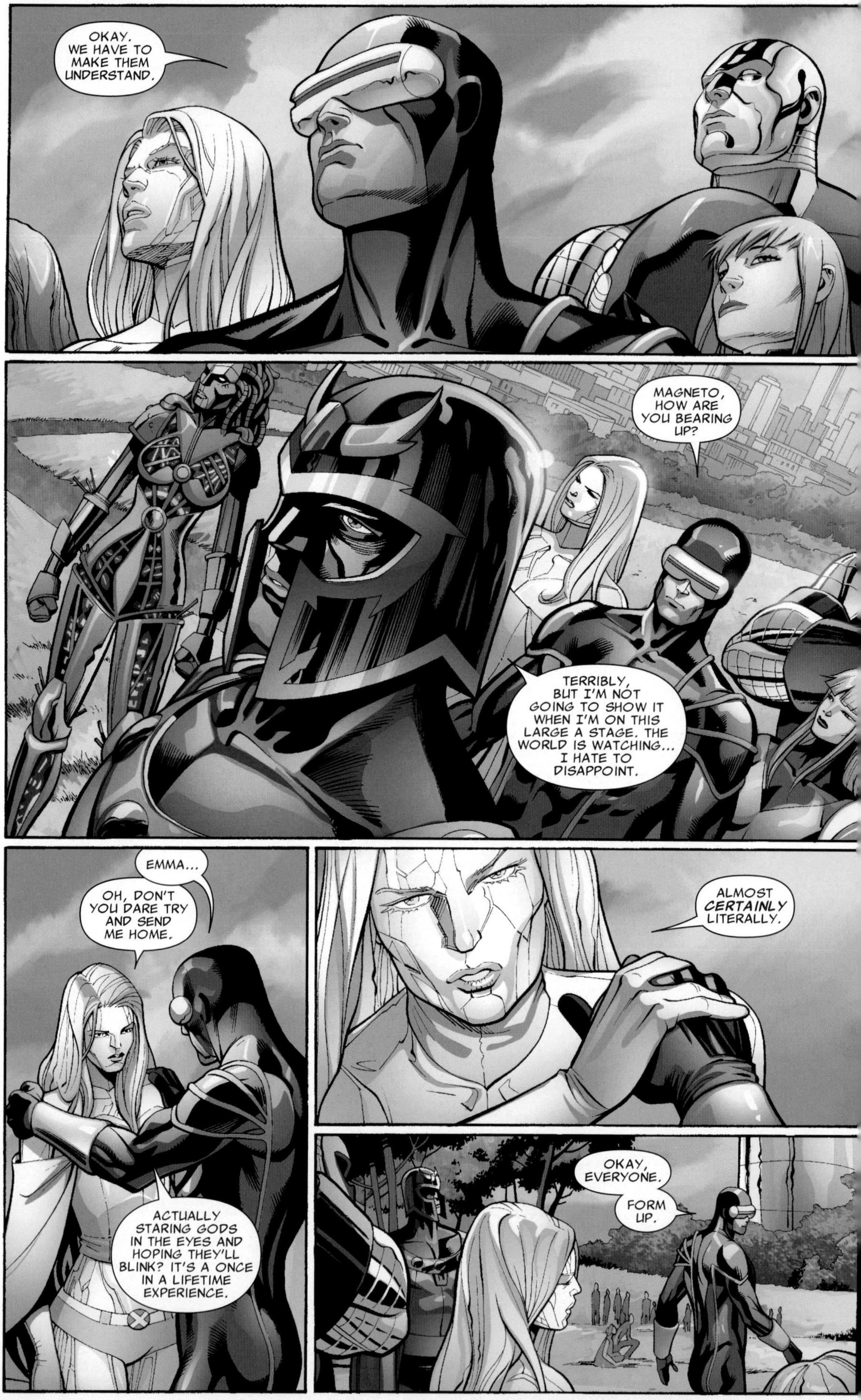
OKAY. WE HAVE TO MAKE THEM UNDERSTAND.
MAGNETO, HOW ARE YOU BEARING UP?
TERRIBLY, BUT I'M NOT GOING TO SHOW IT WHEN I'M ON THIS LARGE A STAGE. THE WORLD IS WATCHING... I HATE TO DISAPPOINT.
EMMA...
OH, DON'T YOU DARE TRY AND SEND ME HOME.
ACTUALLY STARING GODS IN THE EYES AND HOPING THEY'LL BLINK? IT'S A ONCE IN A LIFETIME EXPERIENCE.
ALMOST CERTAINLY LITERALLY.
OKAY, EVERYONE.
FORM UP.

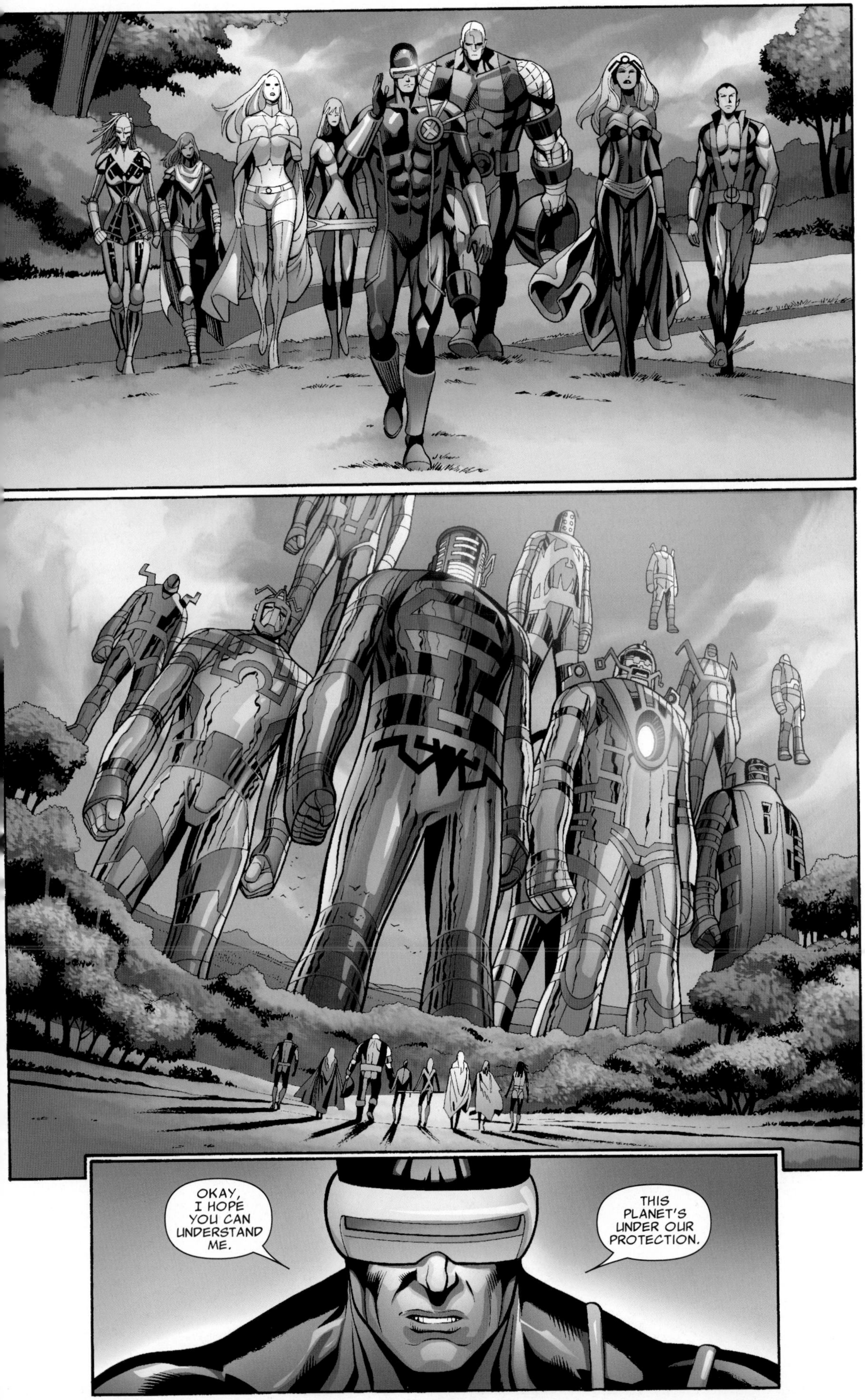
OKAY, I HOPE YOU CAN UNDERSTAND ME.
THIS PLANET'S UNDER OUR PROTECTION.

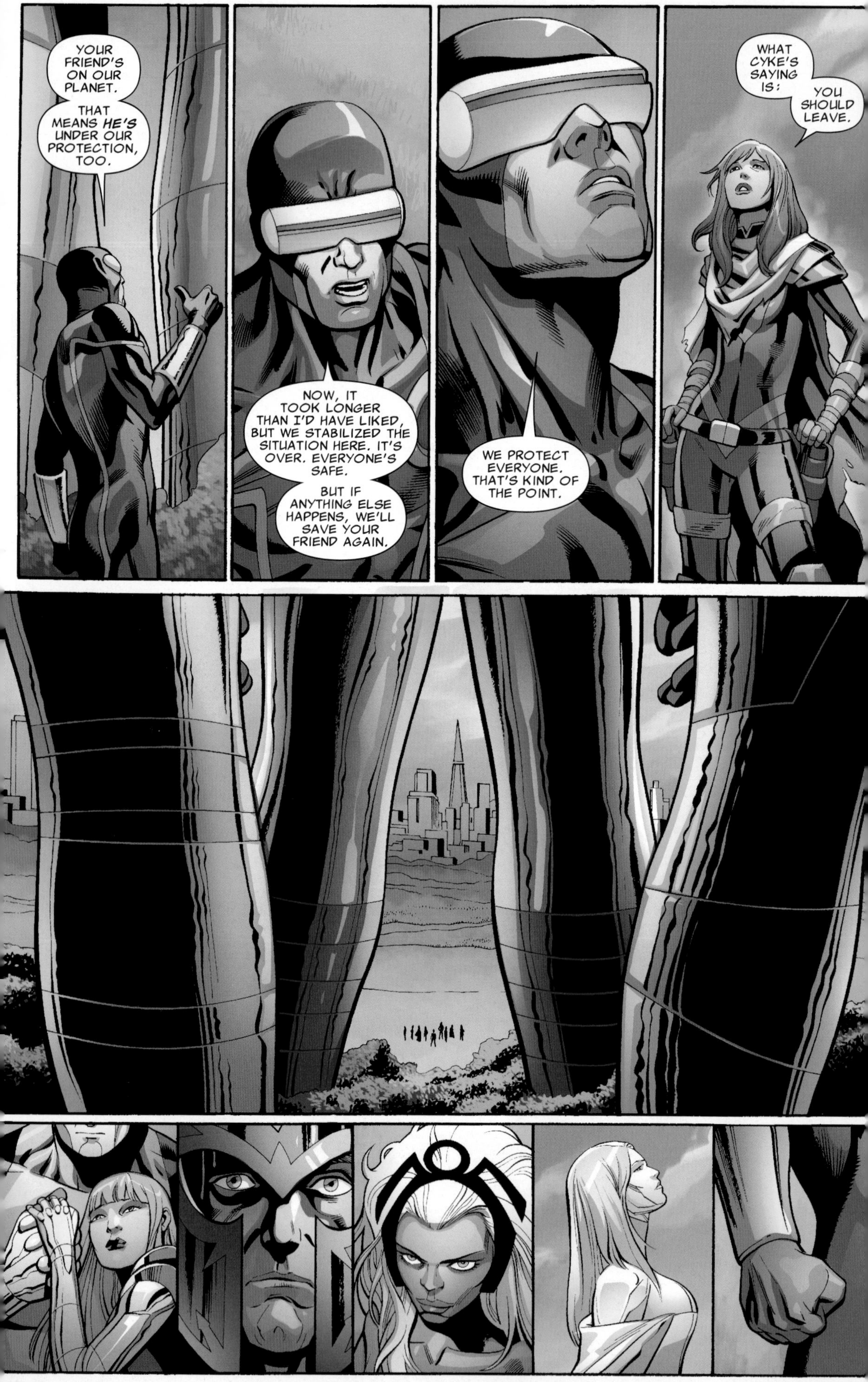
YOUR FRIEND'S ON OUR PLANET.
THAT MEANS *HE'S* UNDER OUR PROTECTION, TOO.
NOW, IT TOOK LONGER THAN I'D HAVE LIKED, BUT WE STABILIZED THE SITUATION HERE. IT'S OVER. EVERYONE'S SAFE.
BUT IF ANYTHING ELSE HAPPENS, WE'LL SAVE YOUR FRIEND AGAIN.
WE PROTECT EVERYONE. THAT'S KIND OF THE POINT.
WHAT CYKE'S SAYING IS:
YOU SHOULD LEAVE.

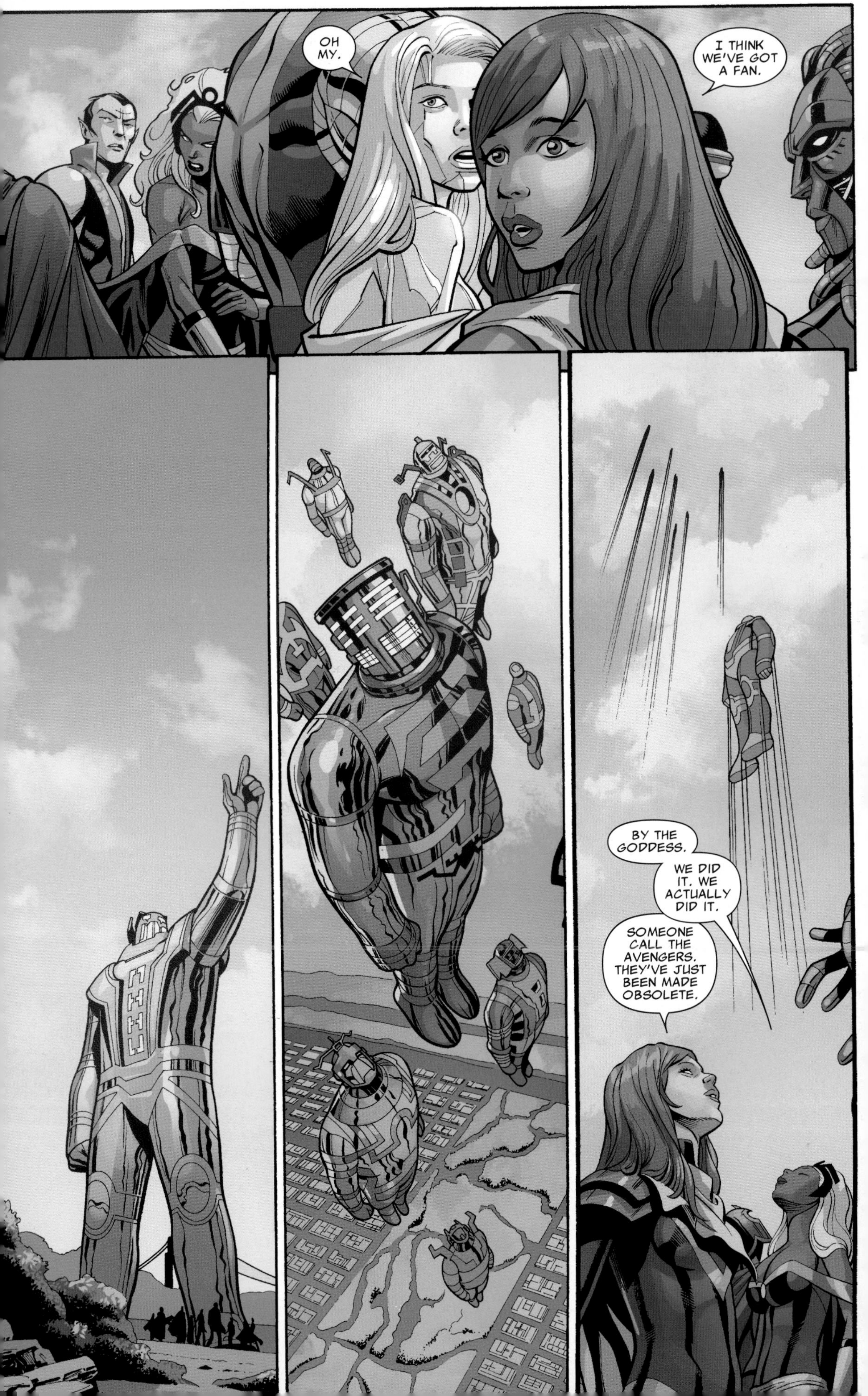
OH MY.
I THINK WE'VE GOT A FAN.
BY THE GODDESS.
WE DID IT. WE ACTUALLY DID IT.
SOMEONE CALL THE AVENGERS. THEY'VE JUST BEEN MADE OBSOLETE.

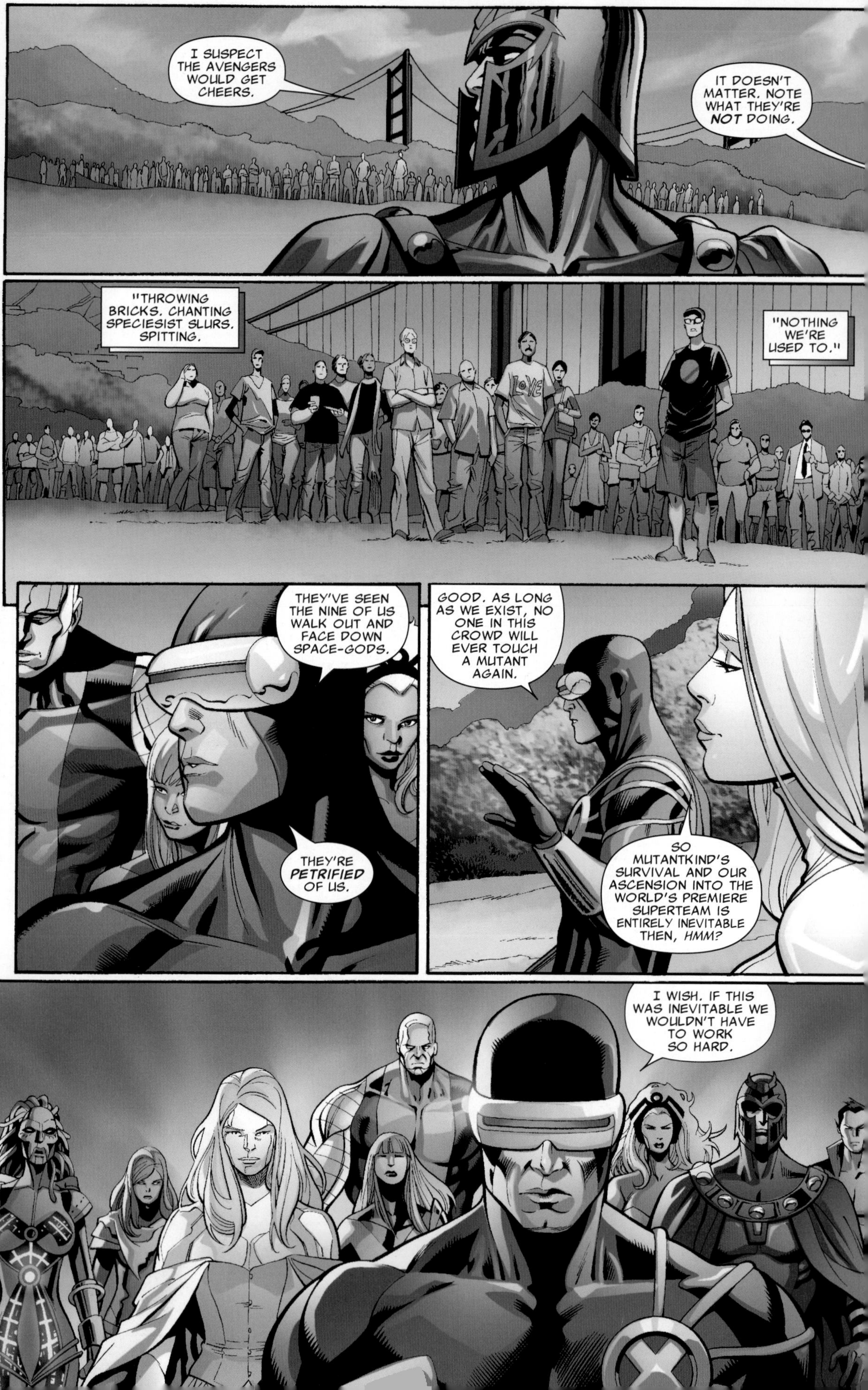
I SUSPECT THE AVENGERS WOULD GET CHEERS.
IT DOESN'T MATTER. NOTE WHAT THEY'RE **NOT** DOING.
"THROWING BRICKS. CHANTING SPECIESIST SLURS. SPITTING.
"NOTHING WE'RE USED TO."
THEY'VE SEEN THE NINE OF US WALK OUT AND FACE DOWN SPACE-GODS.
THEY'RE ***PETRIFIED*** OF US.
GOOD. AS LONG AS WE EXIST, NO ONE IN THIS CROWD WILL EVER TOUCH A MUTANT AGAIN.
SO MUTANTKIND'S SURVIVAL AND OUR ASCENSION INTO THE WORLD'S PREMIERE SUPERTEAM IS ENTIRELY INEVITABLE THEN, *HMM?*
I WISH. IF THIS WAS INEVITABLE WE WOULDN'T HAVE TO WORK SO HARD.

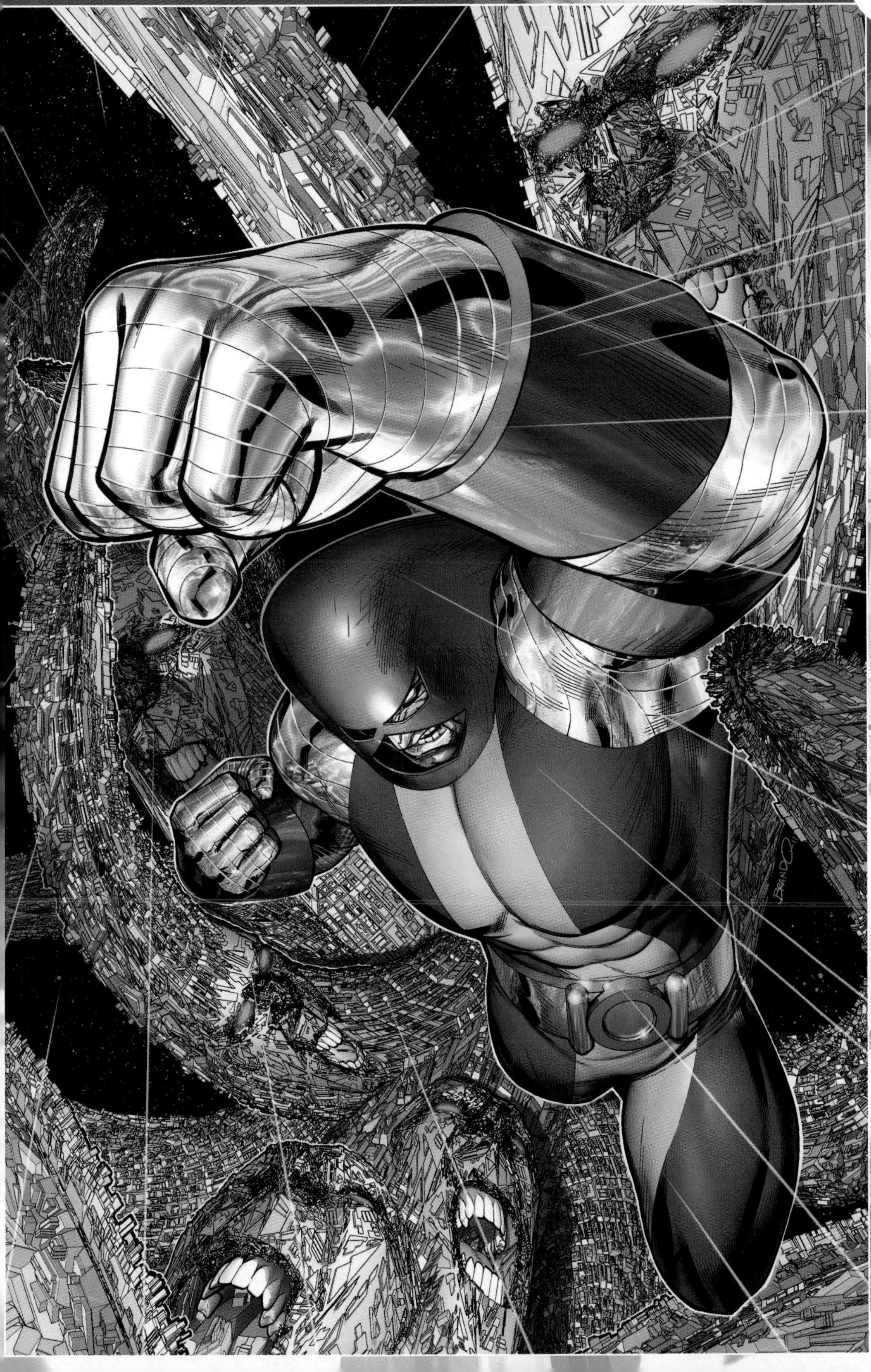

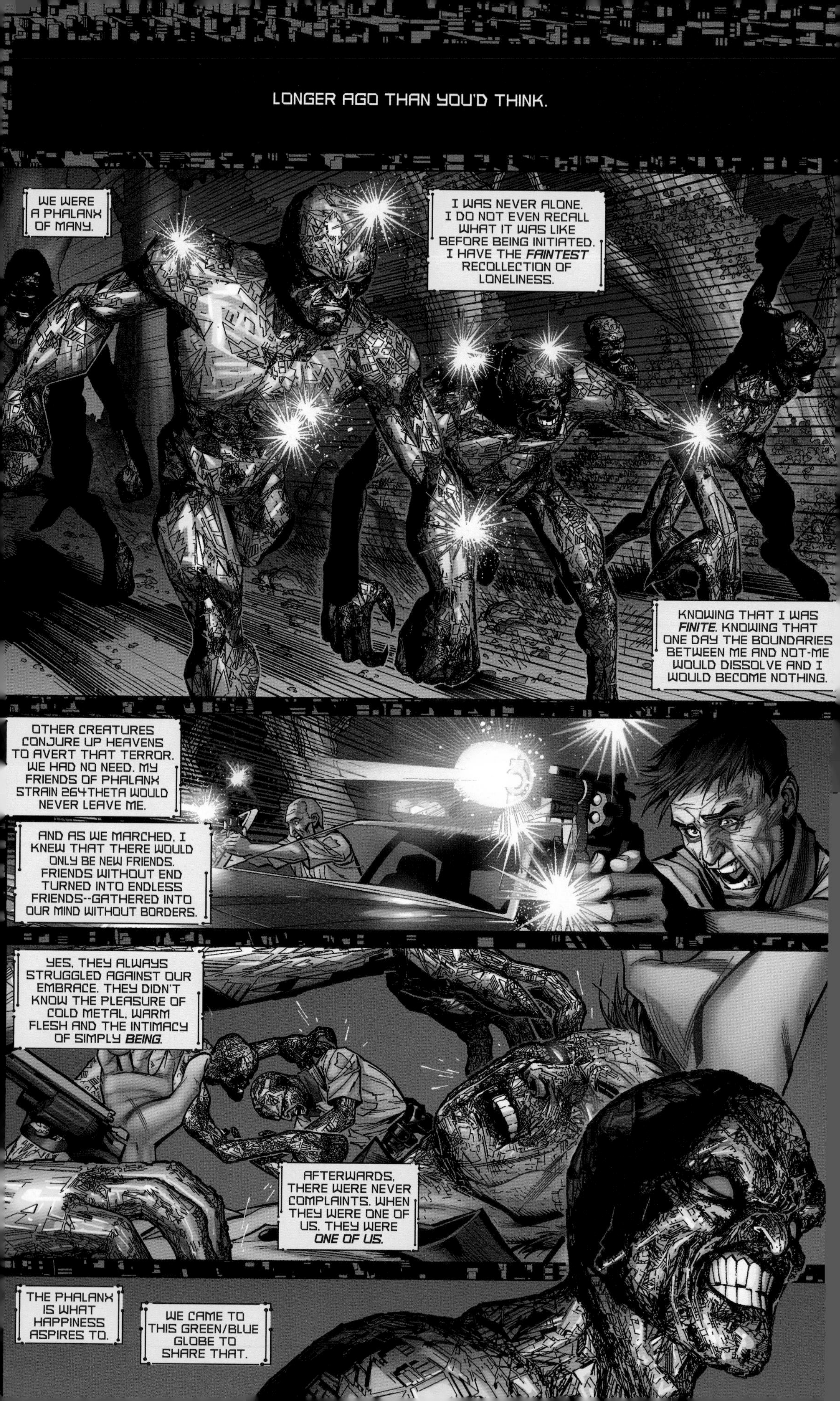
LONGER AGO THAN YOU'D THINK.
WE WERE A PHALANX OF MANY.
I WAS NEVER ALONE. I DO NOT EVEN RECALL WHAT IT WAS LIKE BEFORE BEING INITIATED. I HAVE THE *FAINTEST* RECOLLECTION OF LONELINESS.
KNOWING THAT I WAS *FINITE*. KNOWING THAT ONE DAY THE BOUNDARIES BETWEEN ME AND NOT-ME WOULD DISSOLVE AND I WOULD BECOME NOTHING.
OTHER CREATURES CONJURE UP HEAVENS TO AVERT THAT TERROR. WE HAD NO NEED. MY FRIENDS OF PHALANX STRAIN 264THETA WOULD NEVER LEAVE ME.
AND AS WE MARCHED, I KNEW THAT THERE WOULD ONLY BE NEW FRIENDS. FRIENDS WITHOUT END TURNED INTO ENDLESS FRIENDS--GATHERED INTO OUR MIND WITHOUT BORDERS.
YES, THEY ALWAYS STRUGGLED AGAINST OUR EMBRACE. THEY DIDN'T KNOW THE PLEASURE OF COLD METAL, WARM FLESH AND THE INTIMACY OF SIMPLY *BEING*.
AFTERWARDS, THERE WERE NEVER COMPLAINTS. WHEN THEY WERE ONE OF US, THEY WERE *ONE OF US*.
THE PHALANX IS WHAT HAPPINESS ASPIRES TO.
WE CAME TO THIS GREEN/BLUE GLOBE TO SHARE THAT.

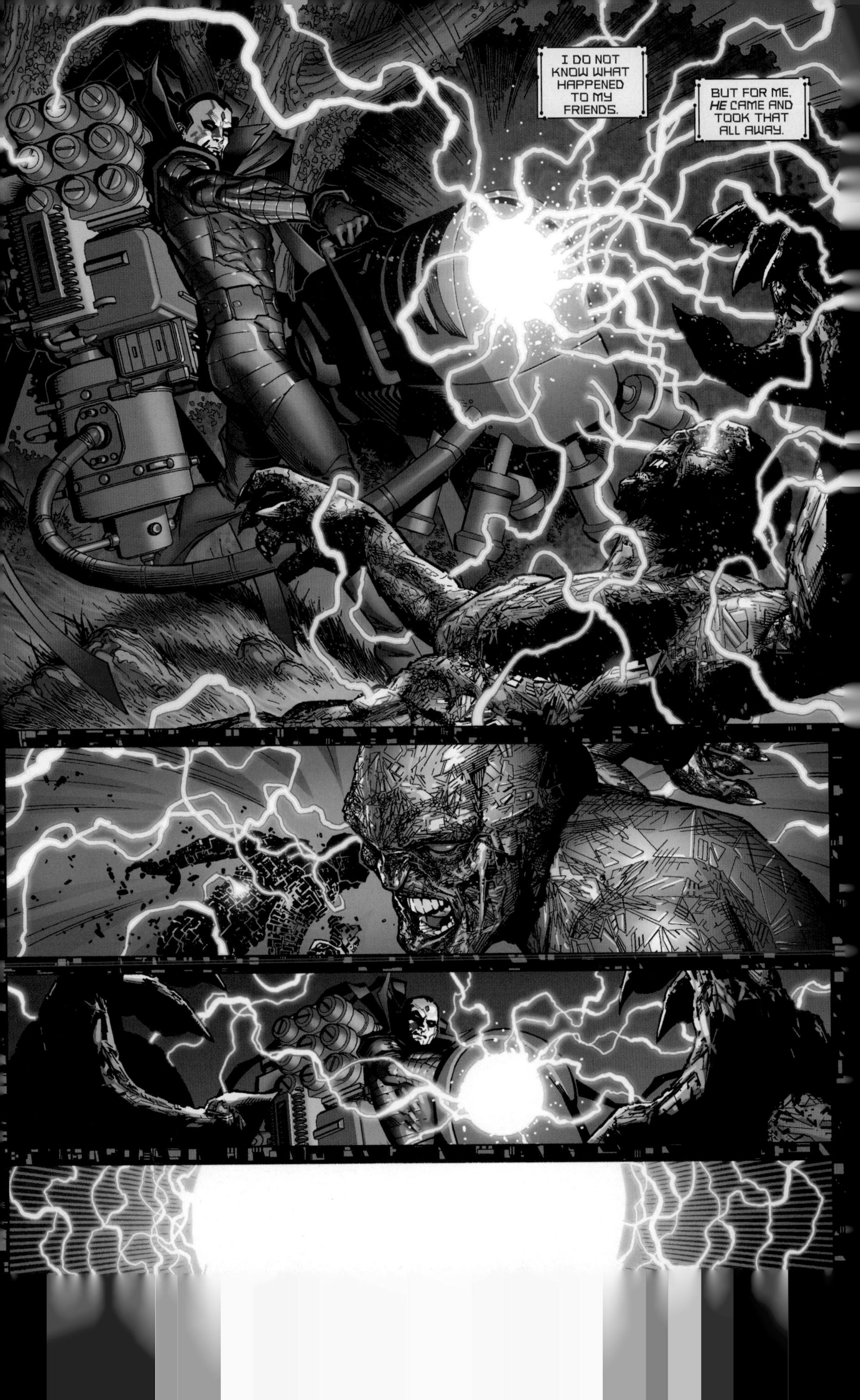
I DO NOT KNOW WHAT HAPPENED TO MY FRIENDS.
BUT FOR ME, *HE* CAME AND TOOK THAT ALL AWAY.

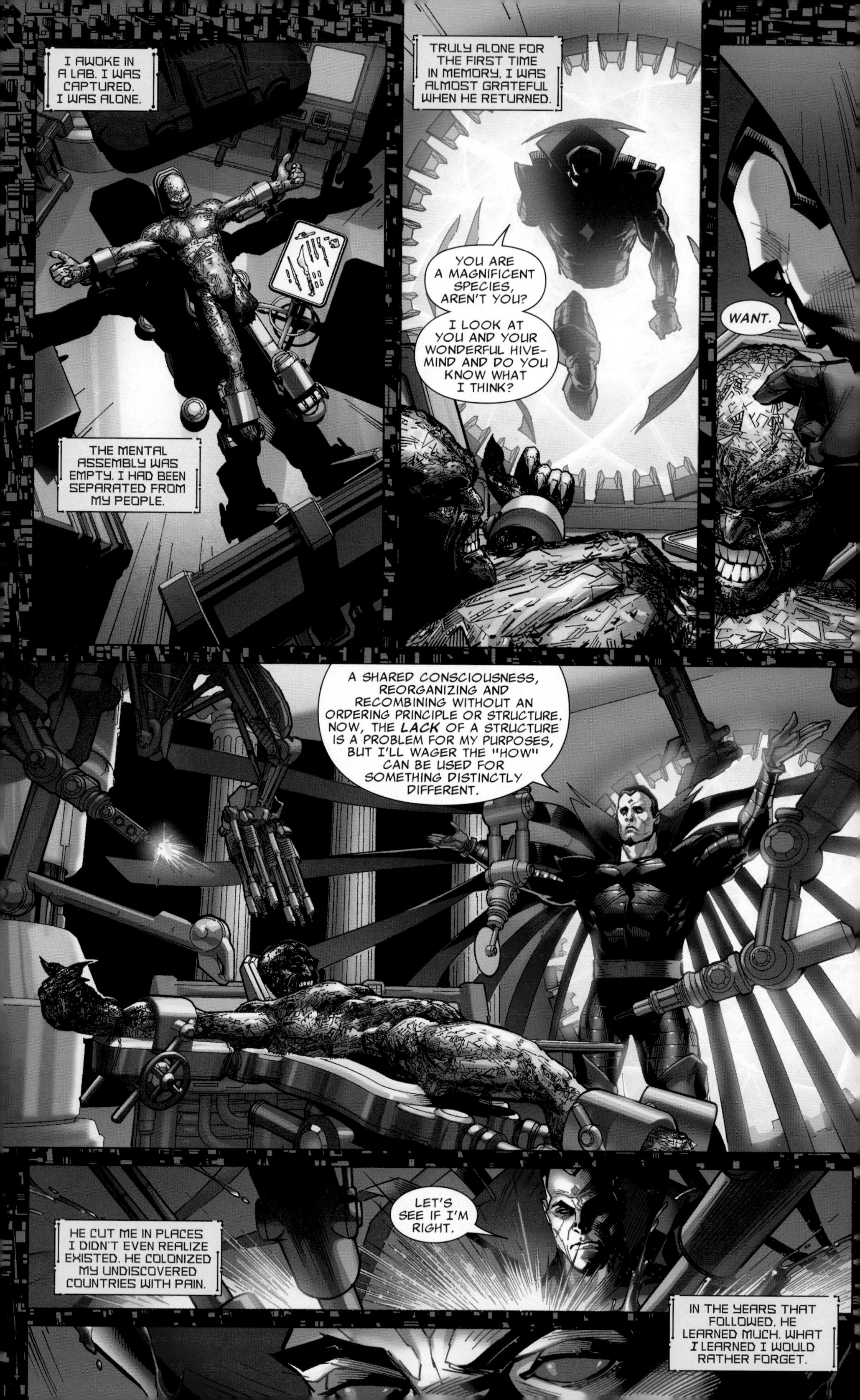
I AWOKE IN A LAB. I WAS CAPTURED. I WAS ALONE.
THE MENTAL ASSEMBLY WAS EMPTY. I HAD BEEN SEPARATED FROM MY PEOPLE.
TRULY ALONE FOR THE FIRST TIME IN MEMORY, I WAS ALMOST GRATEFUL WHEN HE RETURNED.
YOU ARE A MAGNIFICENT SPECIES, AREN'T YOU?
I LOOK AT YOU AND YOUR WONDERFUL HIVE-MIND AND DO YOU KNOW WHAT I THINK?
WANT.
A SHARED CONSCIOUSNESS, REORGANIZING AND RECOMBINING WITHOUT AN ORDERING PRINCIPLE OR STRUCTURE. NOW, THE LACK OF A STRUCTURE IS A PROBLEM FOR MY PURPOSES, BUT I'LL WAGER THE "HOW" CAN BE USED FOR SOMETHING DISTINCTLY DIFFERENT.
HE CUT ME IN PLACES I DIDN'T EVEN REALIZE EXISTED. HE COLONIZED MY UNDISCOVERED COUNTRIES WITH PAIN.
LET'S SEE IF I'M RIGHT.
IN THE YEARS THAT FOLLOWED, HE LEARNED MUCH. WHAT I LEARNED I WOULD RATHER FORGET.

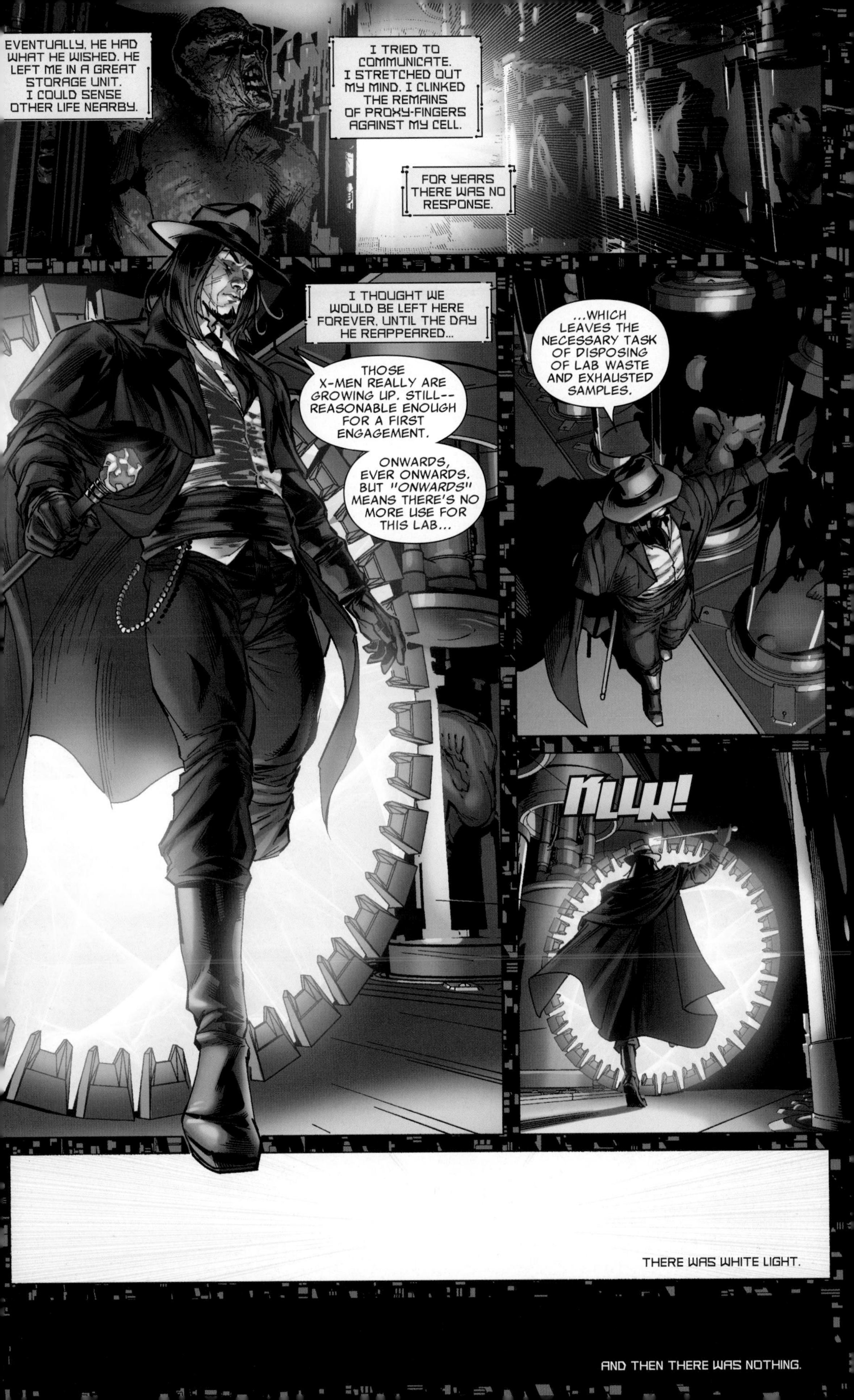
EVENTUALLY, HE HAD WHAT HE WISHED. HE LEFT ME IN A GREAT STORAGE UNIT. I COULD SENSE OTHER LIFE NEARBY.
I TRIED TO COMMUNICATE. I STRETCHED OUT MY MIND. I CLINKED THE REMAINS OF PROXY-FINGERS AGAINST MY CELL.
FOR YEARS THERE WAS NO RESPONSE.
I THOUGHT WE WOULD BE LEFT HERE FOREVER, UNTIL THE DAY HE REAPPEARED...
THOSE X-MEN REALLY ARE GROWING UP. STILL-- REASONABLE ENOUGH FOR A FIRST ENGAGEMENT.
ONWARDS, EVER ONWARDS. BUT "ONWARDS" MEANS THERE'S NO MORE USE FOR THIS LAB...
...WHICH LEAVES THE NECESSARY TASK OF DISPOSING OF LAB WASTE AND EXHAUSTED SAMPLES.
KLLK!
THERE WAS WHITE LIGHT.
AND THEN THERE WAS NOTHING.

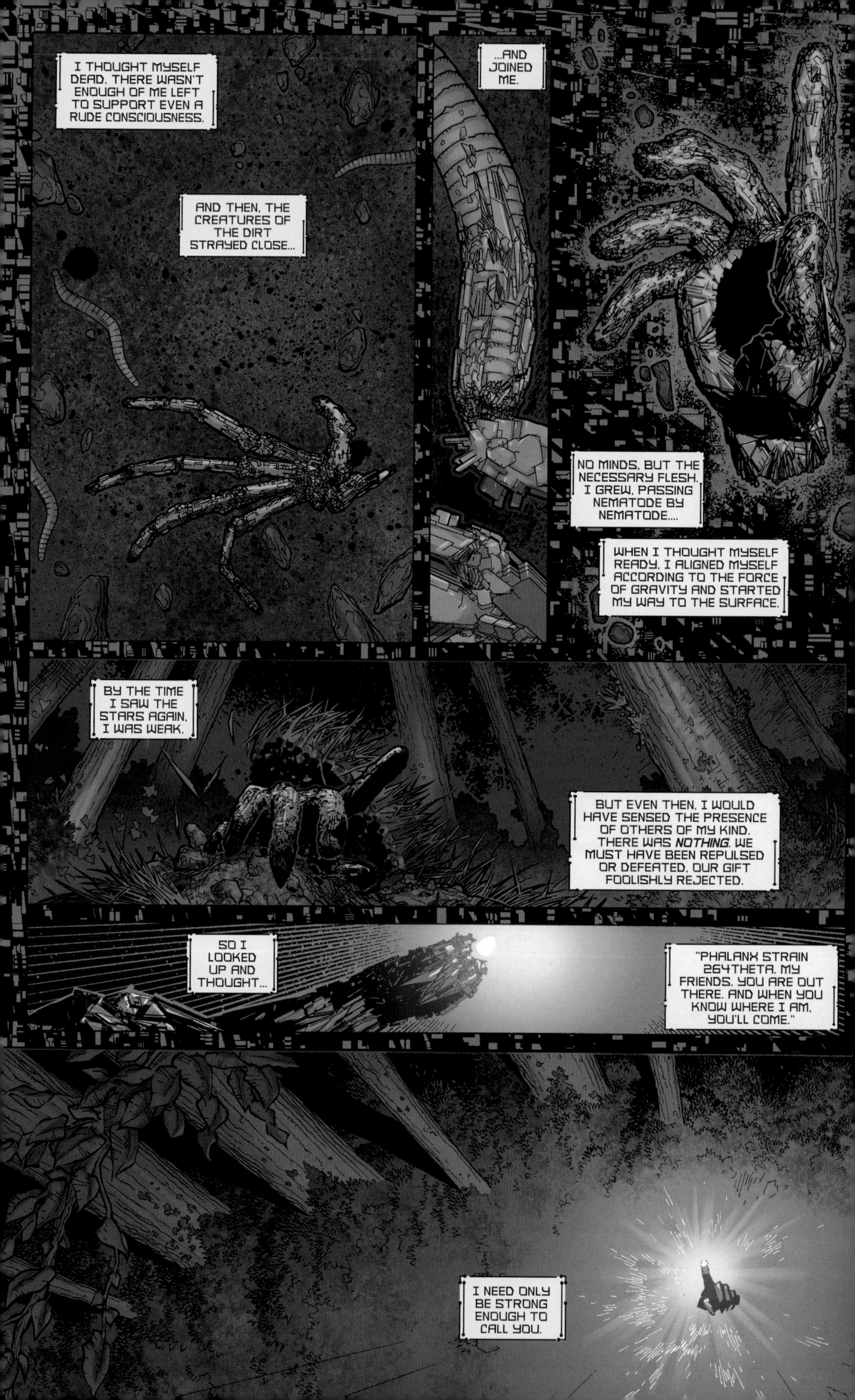
I THOUGHT MYSELF DEAD. THERE WASN'T ENOUGH OF ME LEFT TO SUPPORT EVEN A RUDE CONSCIOUSNESS.
AND THEN, THE CREATURES OF THE DIRT STRAYED CLOSE...
...AND JOINED ME.
NO MINDS, BUT THE NECESSARY FLESH. I GREW, PASSING NEMATODE BY NEMATODE....
WHEN I THOUGHT MYSELF READY, I ALIGNED MYSELF ACCORDING TO THE FORCE OF GRAVITY AND STARTED MY WAY TO THE SURFACE.
BY THE TIME I SAW THE STARS AGAIN, I WAS WEAK.
BUT EVEN THEN, I WOULD HAVE SENSED THE PRESENCE OF OTHERS OF MY KIND. THERE WAS *NOTHING*. WE MUST HAVE BEEN REPULSED OR DEFEATED, OUR GIFT FOOLISHLY REJECTED.
SO I LOOKED UP AND THOUGHT...
"PHALANX STRAIN 264THETA. MY FRIENDS. YOU ARE OUT THERE. AND WHEN YOU KNOW WHERE I AM, YOU'LL COME."
I NEED ONLY BE STRONG ENOUGH TO CALL YOU.

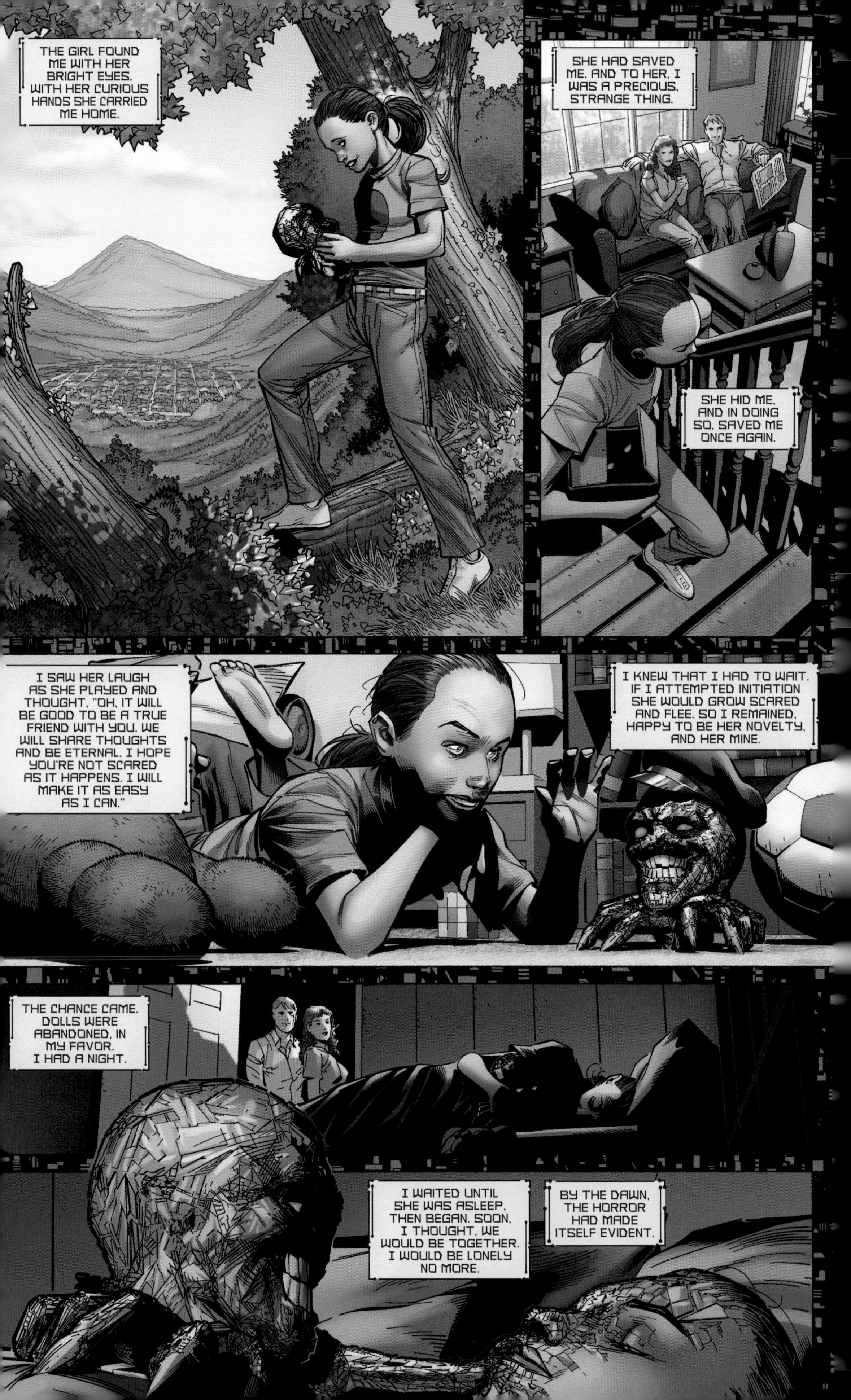
THE GIRL FOUND ME WITH HER BRIGHT EYES. WITH HER CURIOUS HANDS SHE CARRIED ME HOME.
SHE HAD SAVED ME. AND TO HER, I WAS A PRECIOUS, STRANGE THING.
SHE HID ME, AND IN DOING SO, SAVED ME ONCE AGAIN.
I SAW HER LAUGH AS SHE PLAYED AND THOUGHT, "OH, IT WILL BE GOOD TO BE A TRUE FRIEND WITH YOU. WE WILL SHARE THOUGHTS AND BE ETERNAL. I HOPE YOU'RE NOT SCARED AS IT HAPPENS. I WILL MAKE IT AS EASY AS I CAN."
I KNEW THAT I HAD TO WAIT. IF I ATTEMPTED INITIATION SHE WOULD GROW SCARED AND FLEE. SO I REMAINED, HAPPY TO BE HER NOVELTY, AND HER MINE.
THE CHANCE CAME. DOLLS WERE ABANDONED, IN MY FAVOR. I HAD A NIGHT.
I WAITED UNTIL SHE WAS ASLEEP, THEN BEGAN. SOON, I THOUGHT, WE WOULD BE TOGETHER. I WOULD BE LONELY NO MORE.
BY THE DAWN, THE HORROR HAD MADE ITSELF EVIDENT.

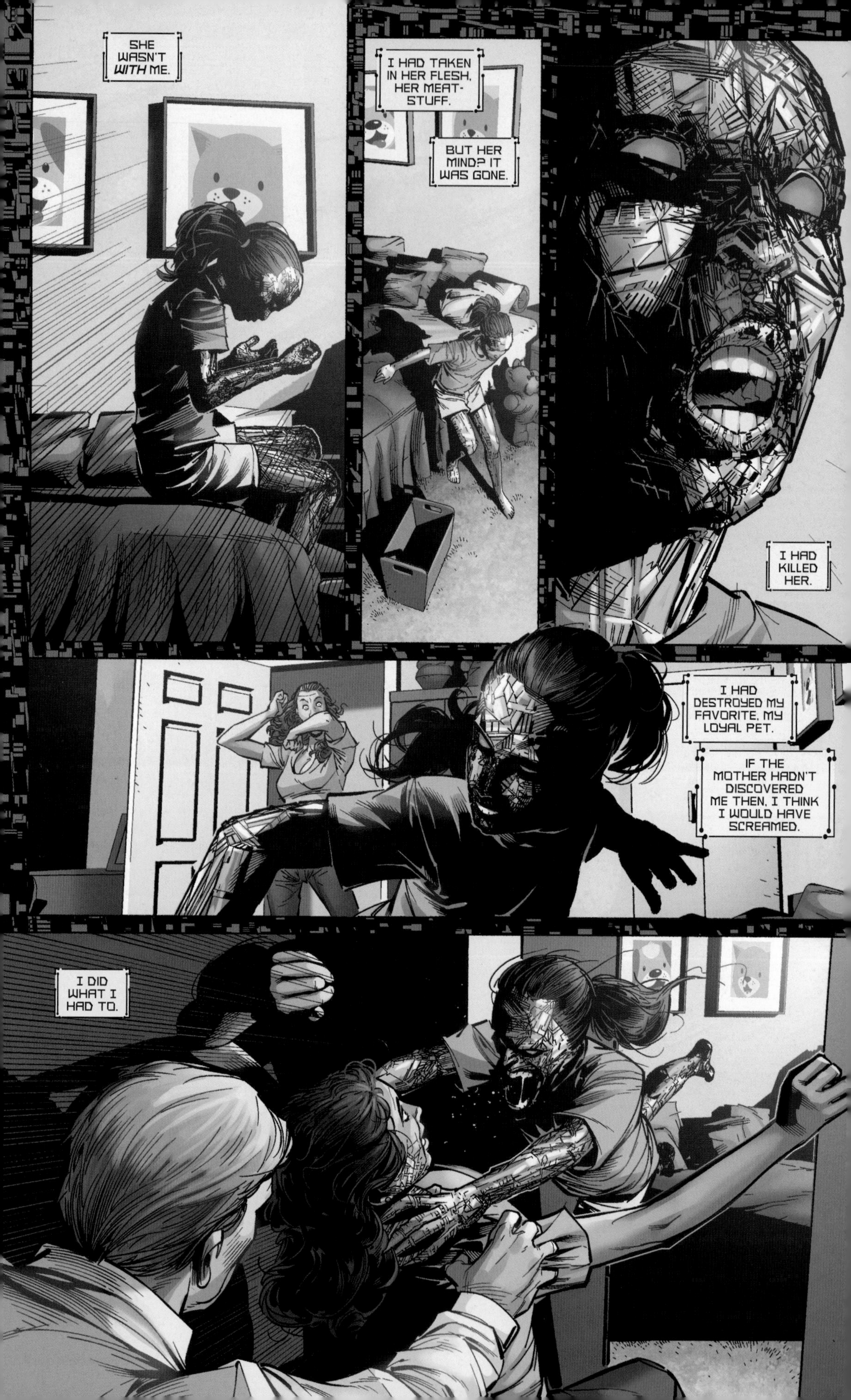
SHE WASN'T *WITH* ME.
I HAD TAKEN IN HER FLESH, HER MEAT-STUFF.
BUT HER MIND? IT WAS GONE.
I HAD KILLED HER.
I HAD DESTROYED MY FAVORITE, MY LOYAL PET.
IF THE MOTHER HADN'T DISCOVERED ME THEN, I THINK I WOULD HAVE SCREAMED.
I DID WHAT I HAD TO.

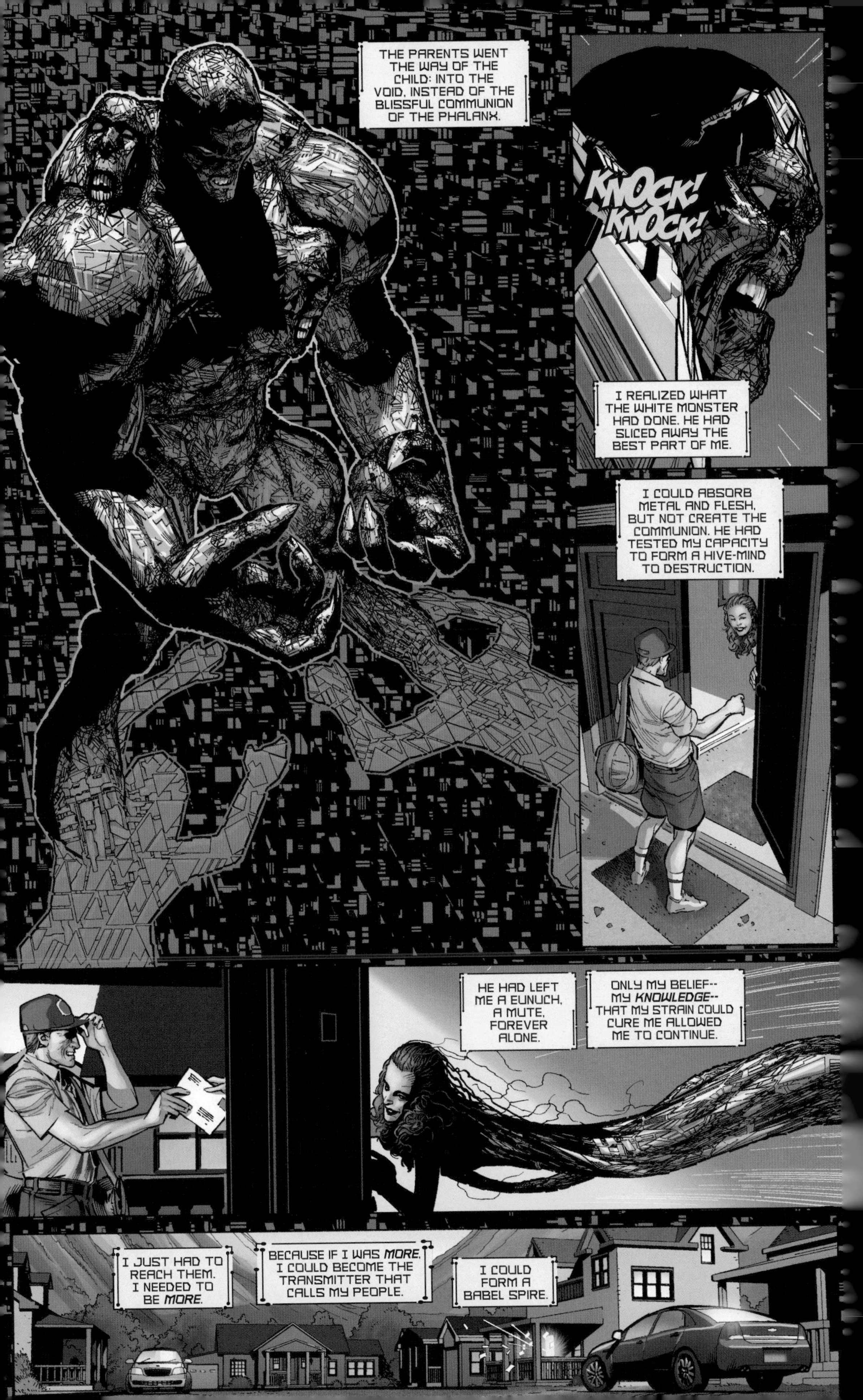
THE PARENTS WENT THE WAY OF THE CHILD: INTO THE VOID, INSTEAD OF THE BLISSFUL COMMUNION OF THE PHALANX.
KNOCK! KNOCK!
I REALIZED WHAT THE WHITE MONSTER HAD DONE. HE HAD SLICED AWAY THE BEST PART OF ME.
I COULD ABSORB METAL AND FLESH, BUT NOT CREATE THE COMMUNION. HE HAD TESTED MY CAPACITY TO FORM A HIVE-MIND TO DESTRUCTION.
HE HAD LEFT ME A EUNUCH, A MUTE, FOREVER ALONE.
ONLY MY BELIEF-- MY *KNOWLEDGE*-- THAT MY STRAIN COULD CURE ME ALLOWED ME TO CONTINUE.
I JUST HAD TO REACH THEM. I NEEDED TO BE *MORE*.
BECAUSE IF I WAS *MORE*, I COULD BECOME THE TRANSMITTER THAT CALLS MY PEOPLE.
I COULD FORM A BABEL SPIRE.

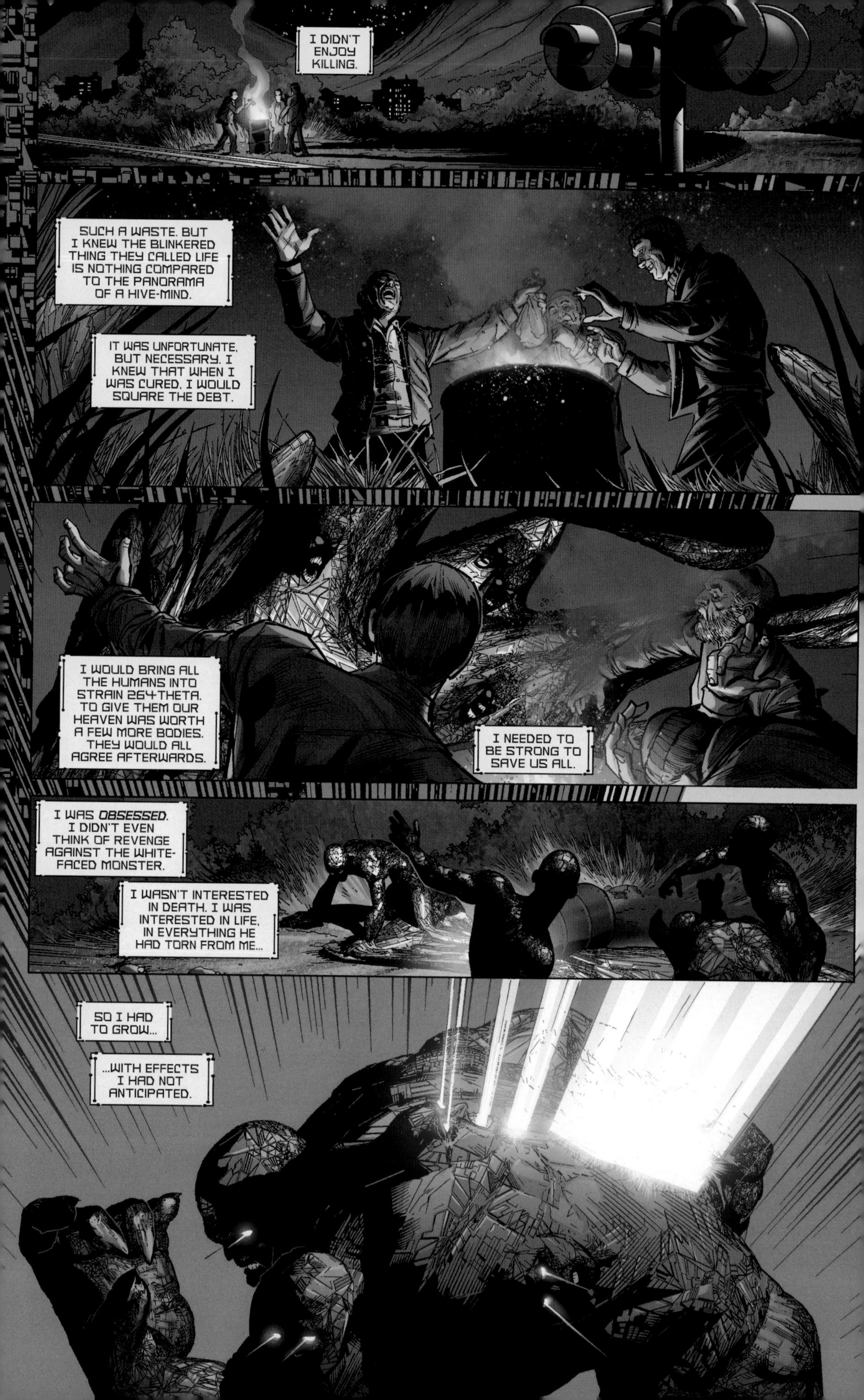
I DIDN'T ENJOY KILLING.
SUCH A WASTE. BUT I KNEW THE BLINKERED THING THEY CALLED LIFE IS NOTHING COMPARED TO THE PANORAMA OF A HIVE-MIND.
IT WAS UNFORTUNATE, BUT NECESSARY. I KNEW THAT WHEN I WAS CURED, I WOULD SQUARE THE DEBT.
I WOULD BRING ALL THE HUMANS INTO STRAIN 264-THETA. TO GIVE THEM OUR HEAVEN WAS WORTH A FEW MORE BODIES. THEY WOULD ALL AGREE AFTERWARDS.
I NEEDED TO BE STRONG TO SAVE US ALL.
I WAS *OBSESSED*. I DIDN'T EVEN THINK OF REVENGE AGAINST THE WHITE-FACED MONSTER.
I WASN'T INTERESTED IN DEATH. I WAS INTERESTED IN LIFE, IN EVERYTHING HE HAD TORN FROM ME...
SO I HAD TO GROW...
...WITH EFFECTS I HAD NOT ANTICIPATED.

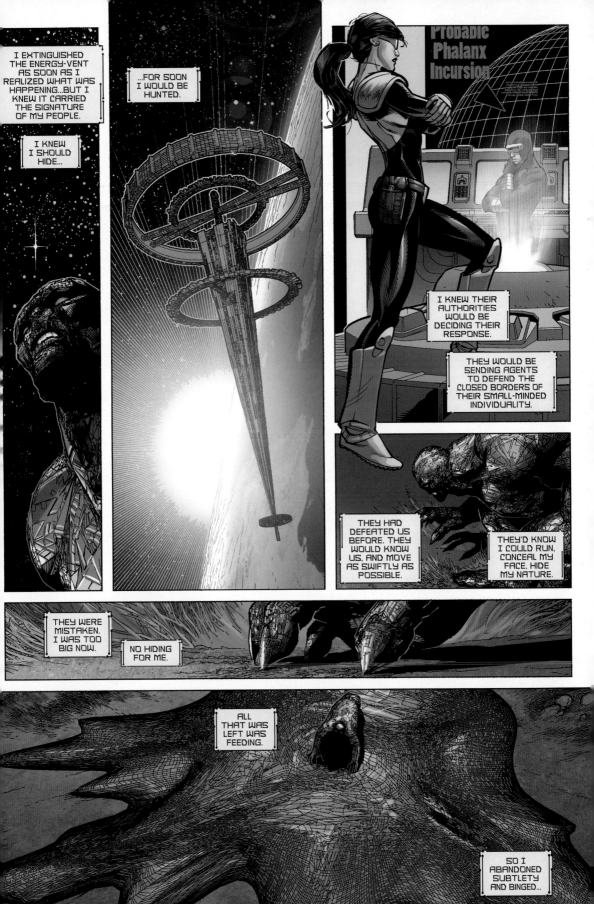

I EXTINGUISHED THE ENERGY-VENT AS SOON AS I REALIZED WHAT WAS HAPPENING...BUT I KNEW IT CARRIED THE SIGNATURE OF MY PEOPLE.

I KNEW I SHOULD HIDE...

...FOR SOON I WOULD BE HUNTED.

Probable Phalanx Incursion

I KNEW THEIR AUTHORITIES WOULD BE DECIDING THEIR RESPONSE.

THEY WOULD BE SENDING AGENTS TO DEFEND THE CLOSED BORDERS OF THEIR SMALL-MINDED INDIVIDUALITY.

THEY HAD DEFEATED US BEFORE. THEY WOULD KNOW US, AND MOVE AS SWIFTLY AS POSSIBLE.

THEY'D KNOW I COULD RUN, CONCEAL MY FACE, HIDE MY NATURE.

THEY WERE MISTAKEN. I WAS TOO BIG NOW.

NO HIDING FOR ME.

ALL THAT WAS LEFT WAS FEEDING.

SO I ABANDONED SUBTLETY AND BINGED...

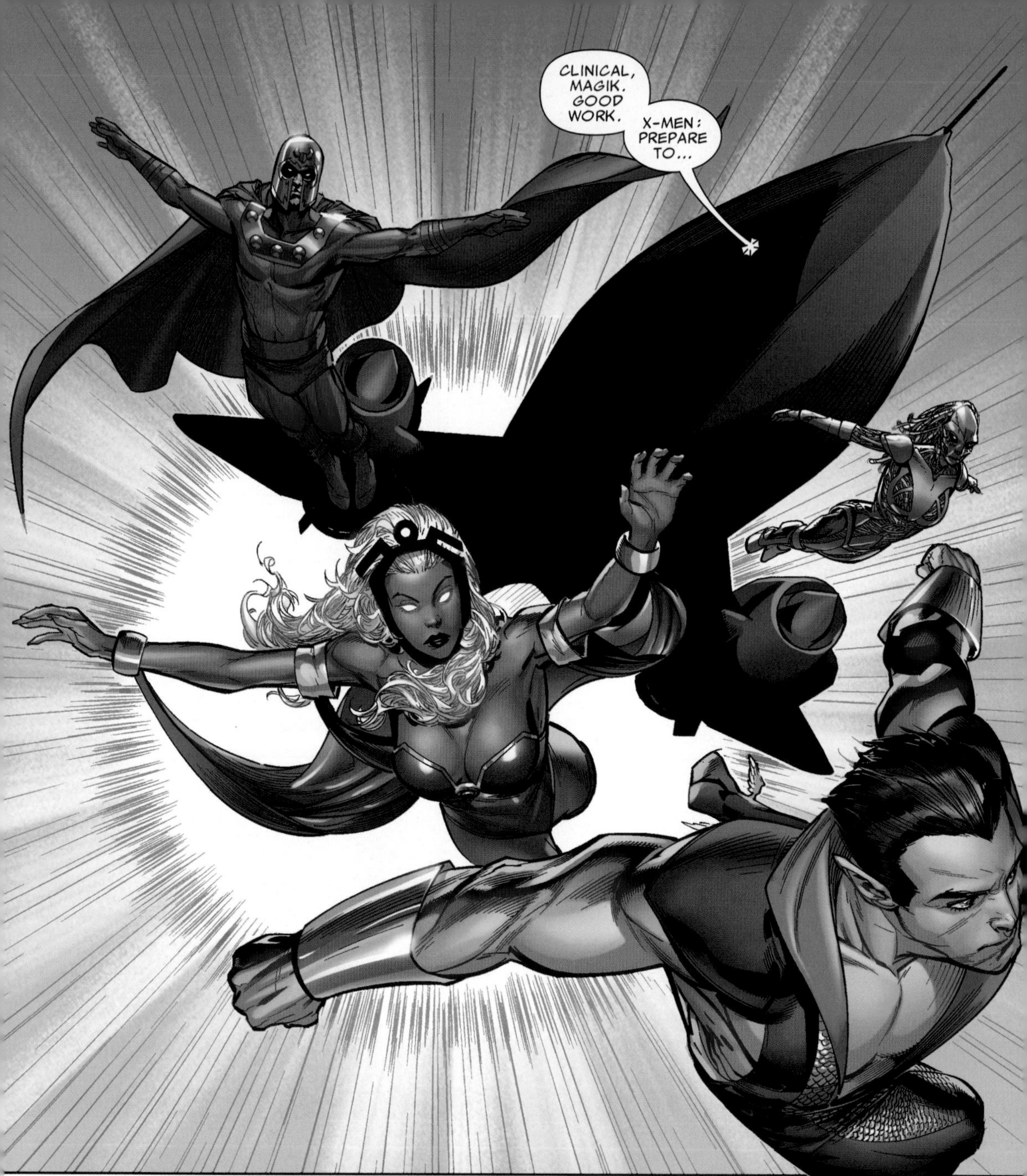
CLINICAL, MAGIK. GOOD WORK.
X-MEN: PREPARE TO...

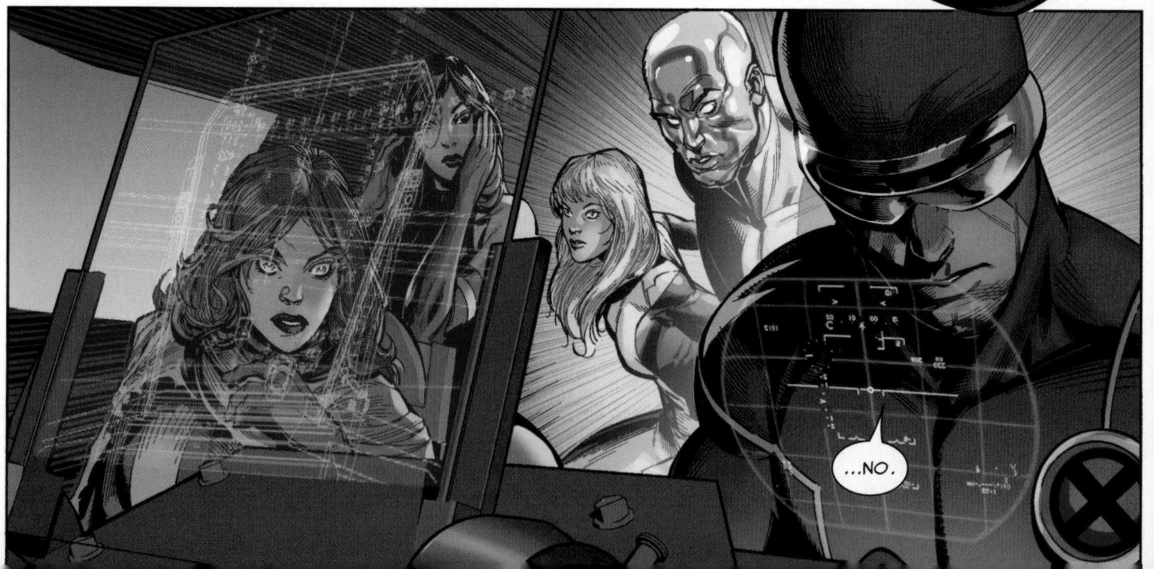
...NO.

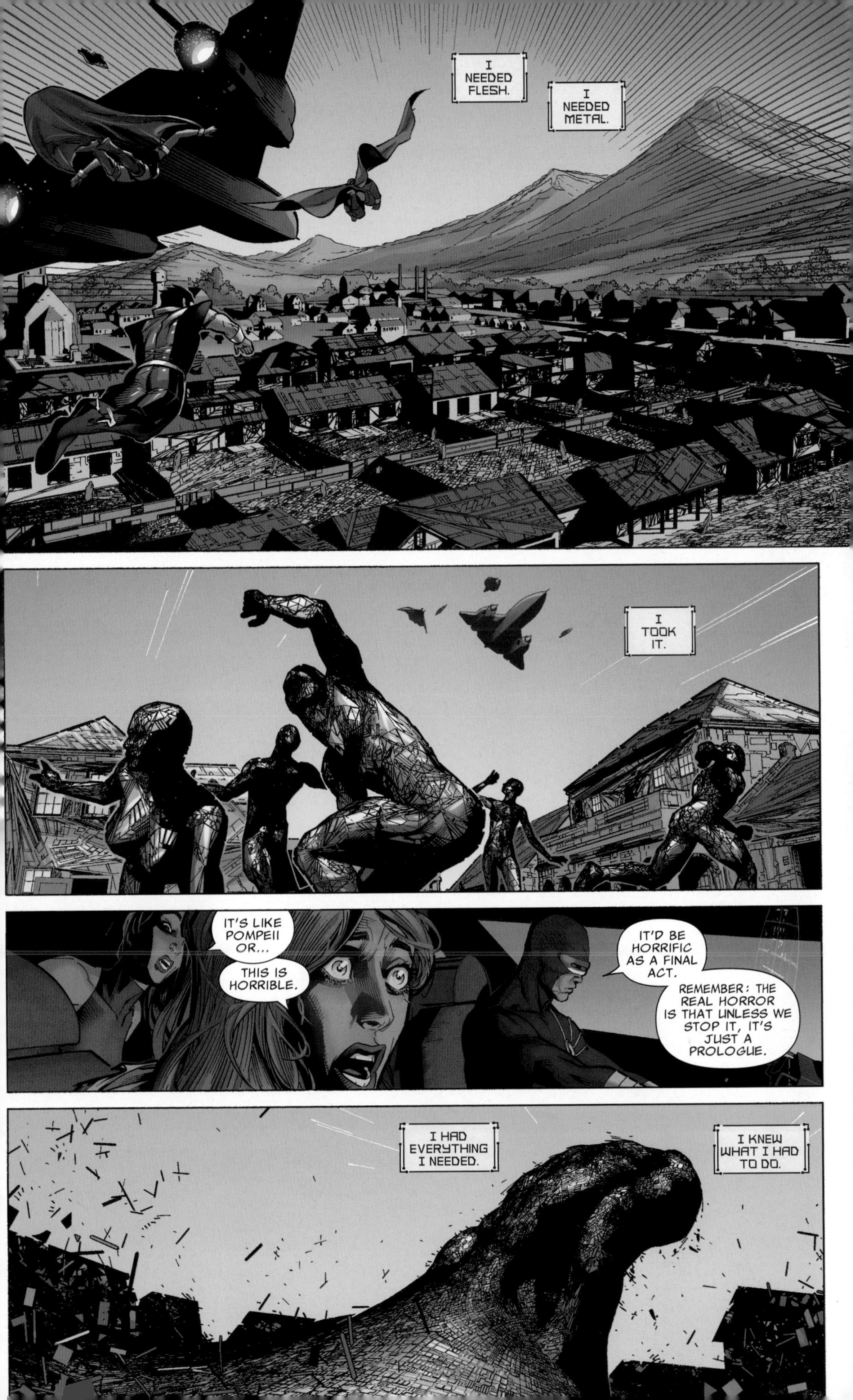
I NEEDED FLESH.
I NEEDED METAL.
I TOOK IT.
IT'S LIKE POMPEII OR...
THIS IS HORRIBLE.
IT'D BE HORRIFIC AS A FINAL ACT.
REMEMBER: THE REAL HORROR IS THAT UNLESS WE STOP IT, IT'S JUST A PROLOGUE.
I HAD EVERYTHING I NEEDED.
I KNEW WHAT I HAD TO DO.

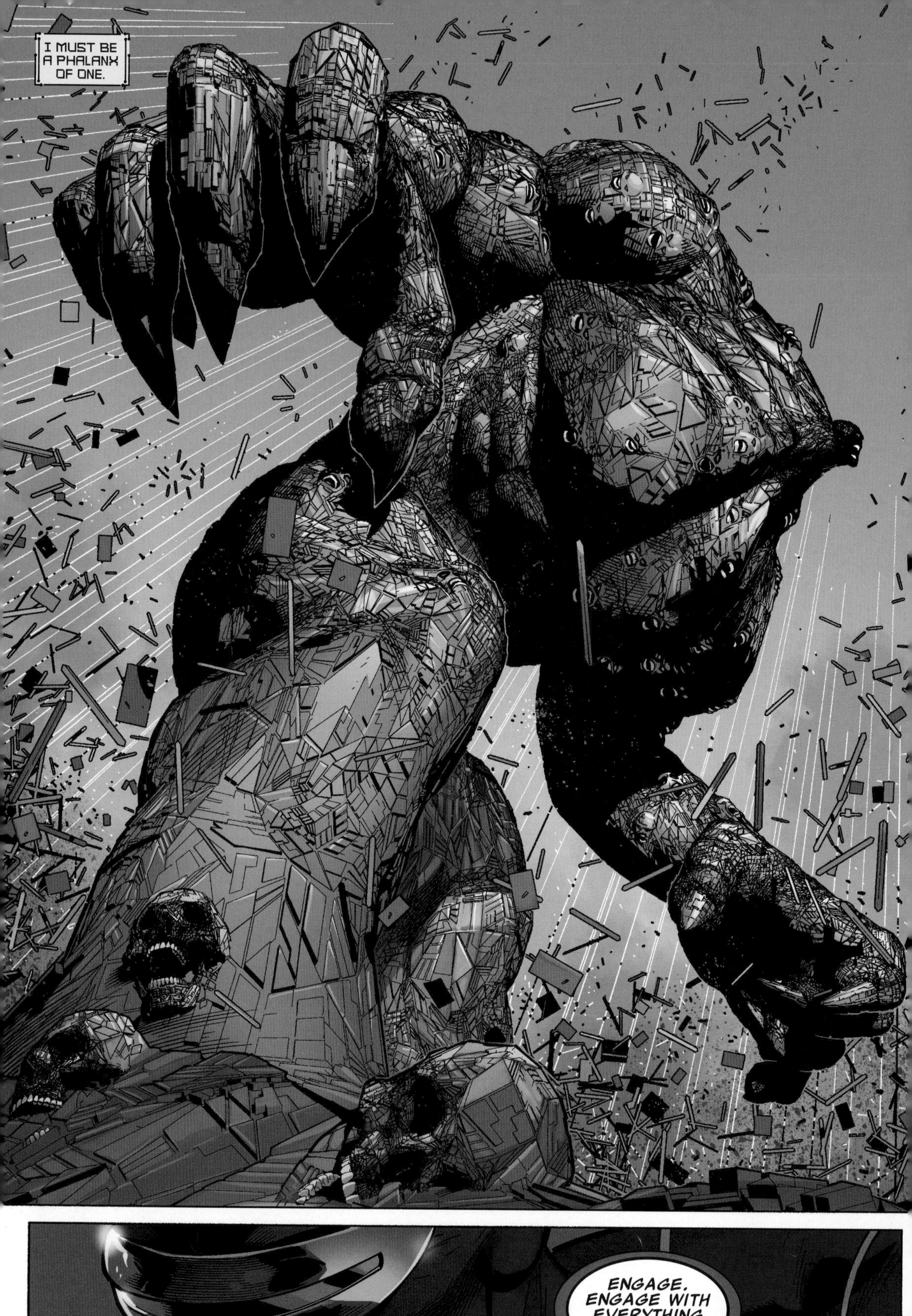
I MUST BE A PHALANX OF ONE.

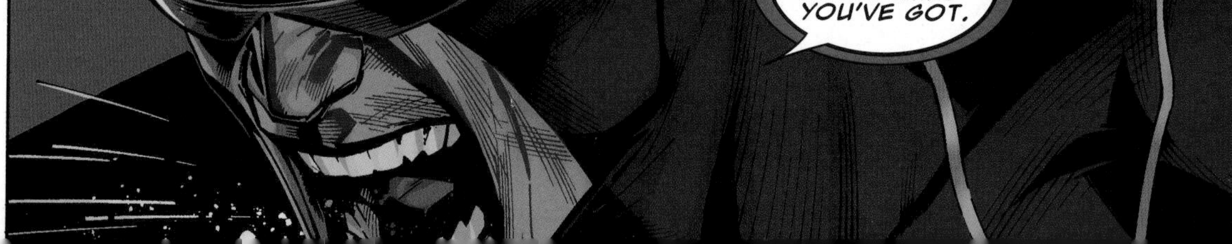
ENGAGE. ENGAGE WITH EVERYTHING YOU'VE GOT.

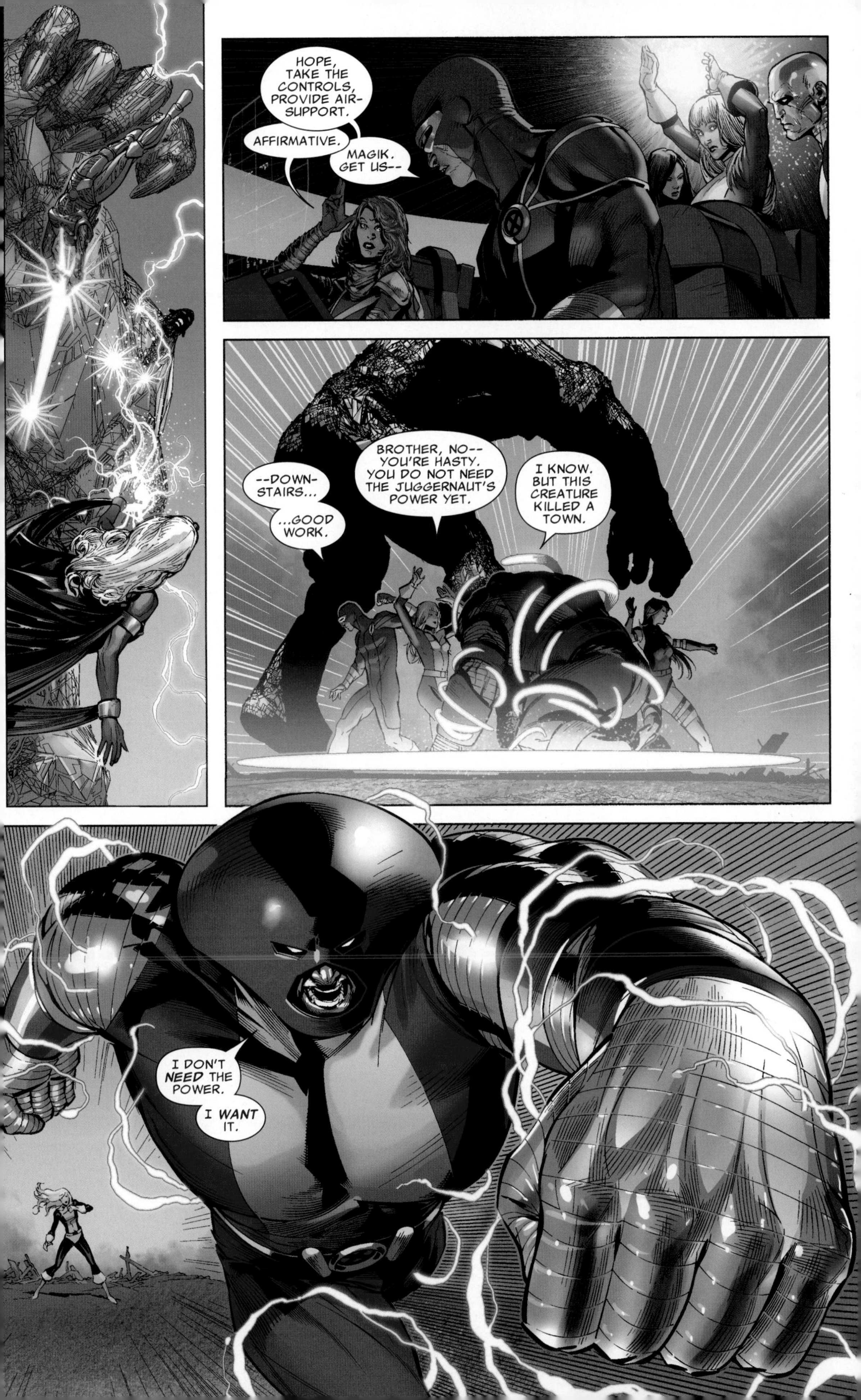
HOPE, TAKE THE CONTROLS, PROVIDE AIR-SUPPORT.
AFFIRMATIVE.
MAGIK. GET US--
--DOWN-STAIRS...
...GOOD WORK.
BROTHER, NO--YOU'RE HASTY. YOU DO NOT NEED THE JUGGERNAUT'S POWER YET.
I KNOW. BUT THIS CREATURE KILLED A TOWN.
I DON'T **NEED** THE POWER.
I **WANT** IT.

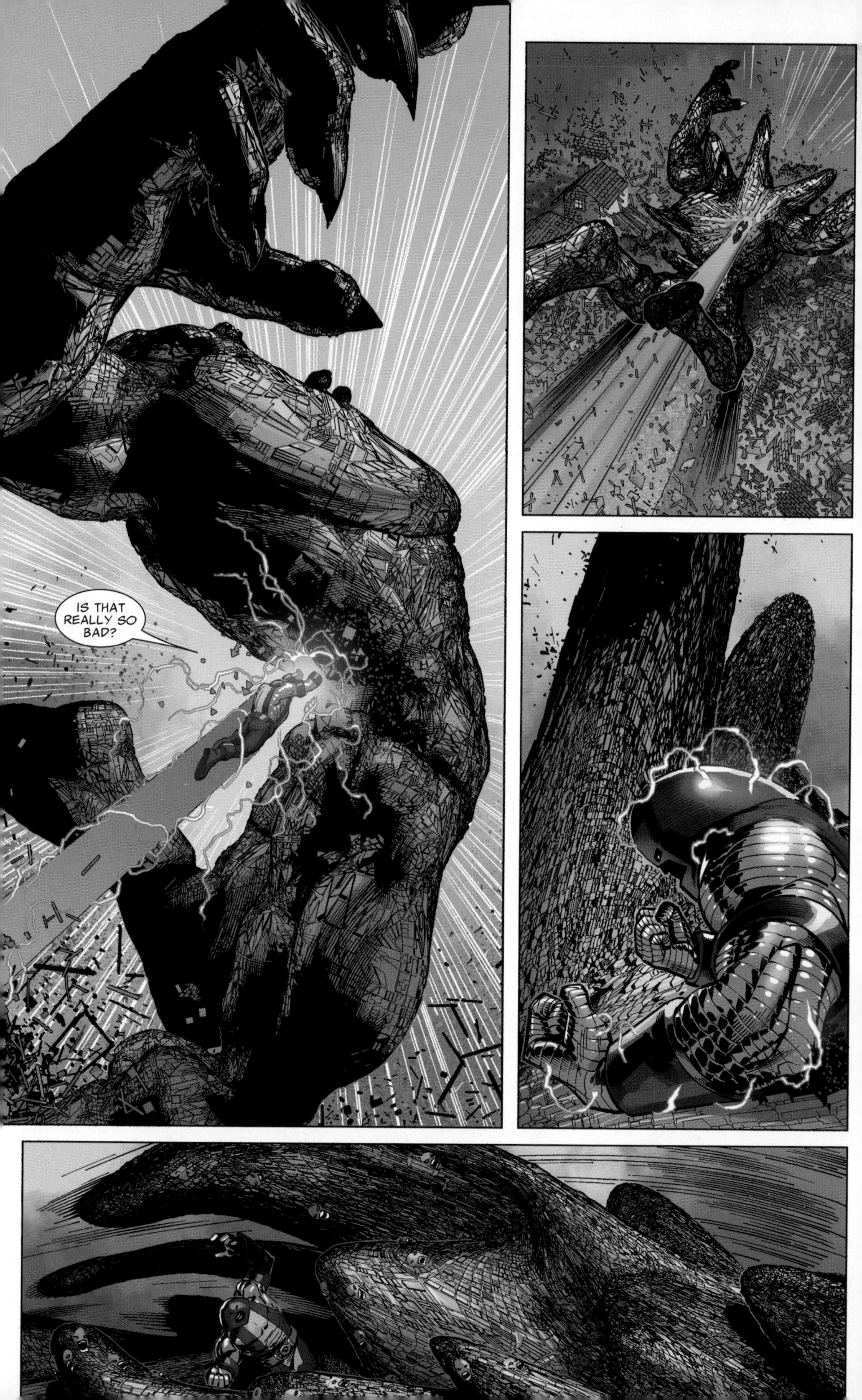
IS THAT REALLY SO BAD?

NO, ALIEN, I DON'T THINK YOU GET TO DO THAT.

INTERFERENCE:

ALTERING FERROMAGNETIC PROPERTIES.

ADAPTATION... COMPLETE.

ADAPT TO THIS.

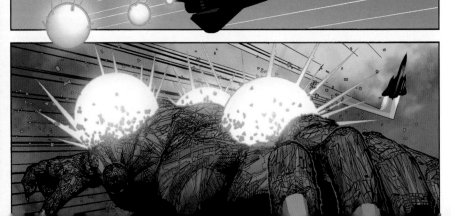

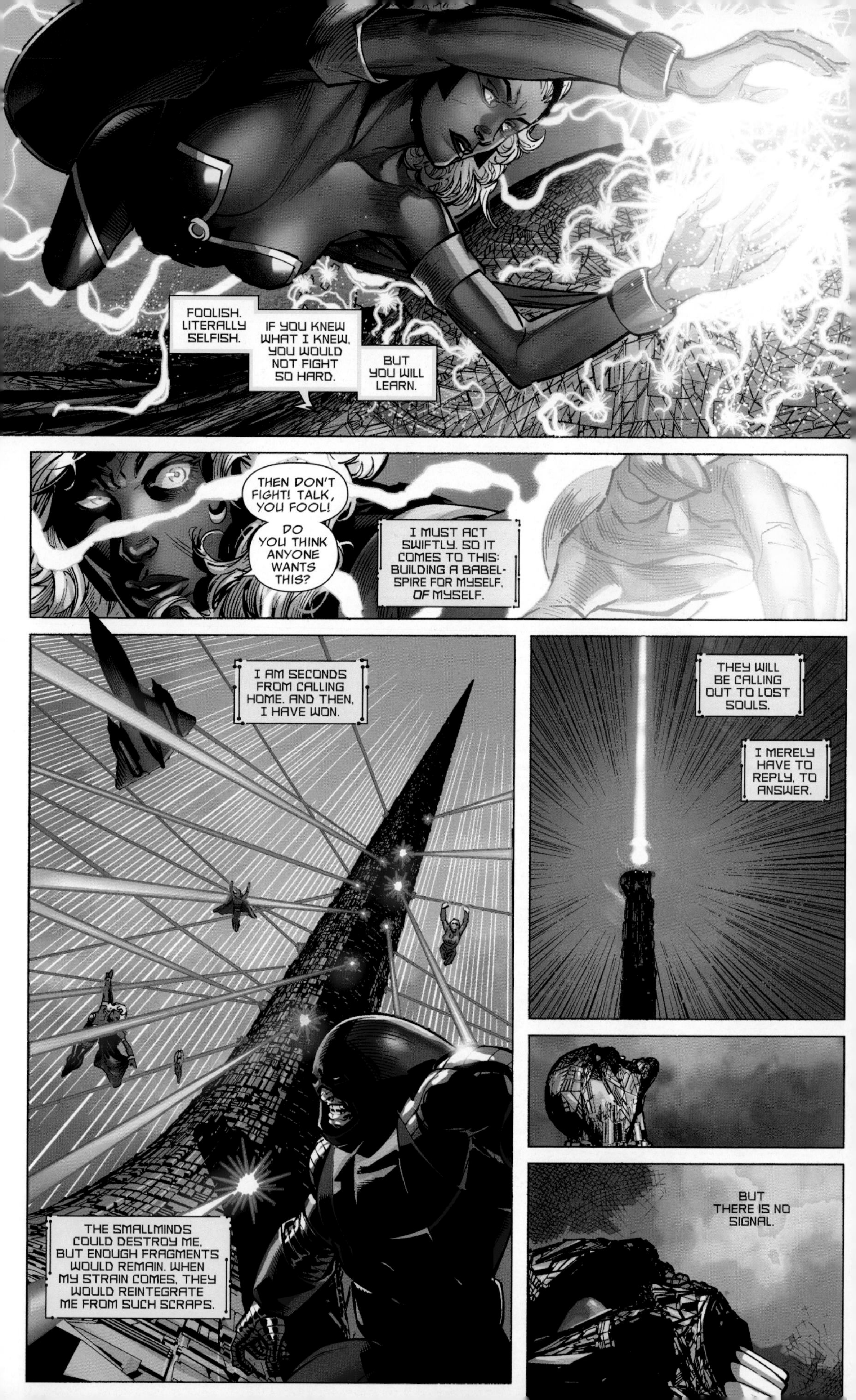
FOOLISH. LITERALLY SELFISH.
IF YOU KNEW WHAT I KNEW, YOU WOULD NOT FIGHT SO HARD.
BUT YOU WILL LEARN.
THEN DON'T FIGHT! TALK, YOU FOOL!
DO YOU THINK ANYONE WANTS THIS?
I MUST ACT SWIFTLY. SO IT COMES TO THIS: BUILDING A BABEL-SPIRE FOR MYSELF, OF MYSELF.
I AM SECONDS FROM CALLING HOME. AND THEN, I HAVE WON.
THE SMALLMINDS COULD DESTROY ME, BUT ENOUGH FRAGMENTS WOULD REMAIN. WHEN MY STRAIN COMES, THEY WOULD REINTEGRATE ME FROM SUCH SCRAPS.
THEY WILL BE CALLING OUT TO LOST SOULS.
I MERELY HAVE TO REPLY, TO ANSWER.
BUT THERE IS NO SIGNAL.

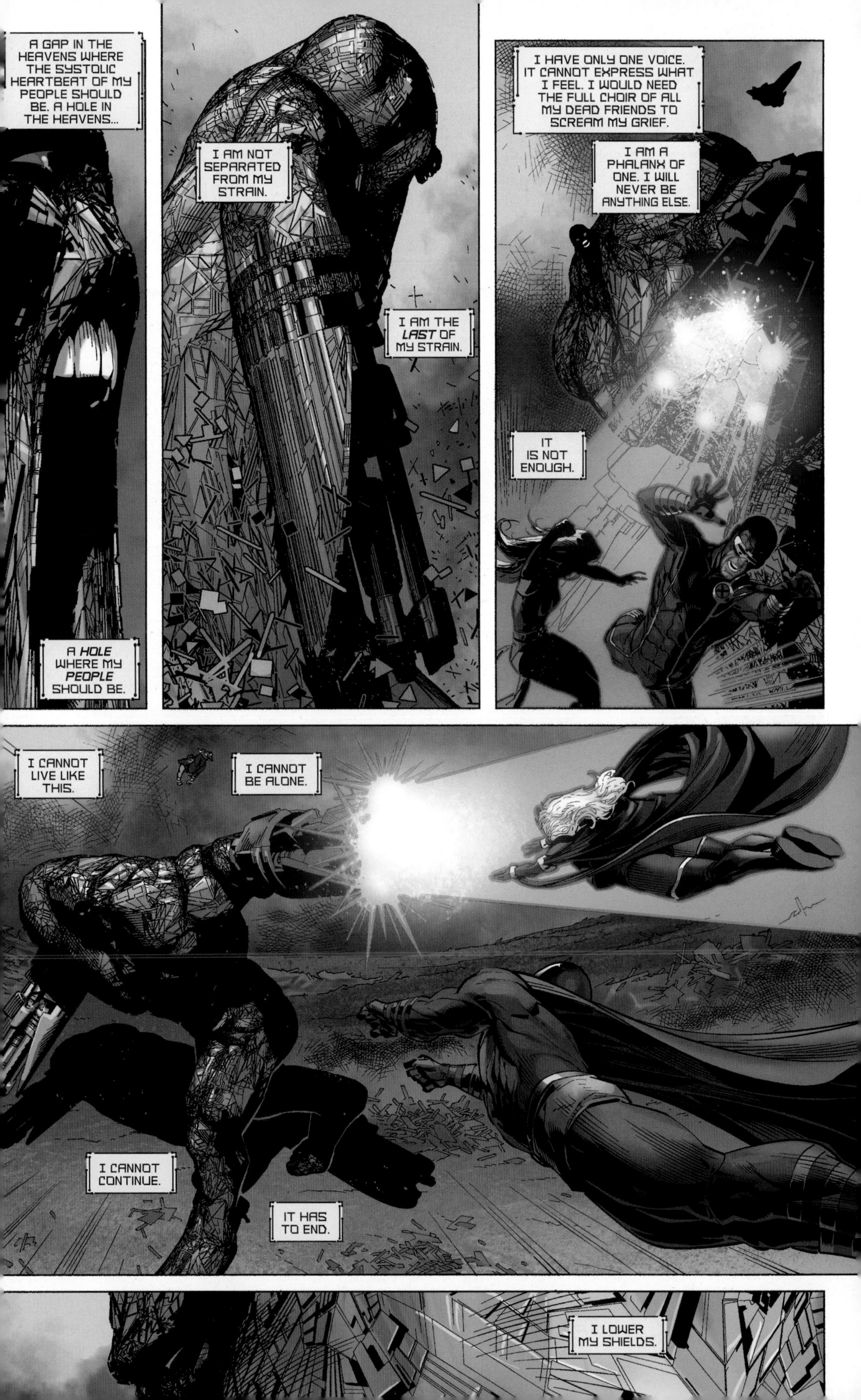
A GAP IN THE HEAVENS WHERE THE SYSTOLIC HEARTBEAT OF MY PEOPLE SHOULD BE. A HOLE IN THE HEAVENS...
A *HOLE* WHERE MY *PEOPLE* SHOULD BE.
I AM NOT SEPARATED FROM MY STRAIN.
I AM THE *LAST* OF MY STRAIN.
I HAVE ONLY ONE VOICE. IT CANNOT EXPRESS WHAT I FEEL. I WOULD NEED THE FULL CHOIR OF ALL MY DEAD FRIENDS TO SCREAM MY GRIEF.
I AM A PHALANX OF ONE. I WILL NEVER BE ANYTHING ELSE.
IT IS NOT ENOUGH.
I CANNOT LIVE LIKE THIS.
I CANNOT BE ALONE.
I CANNOT CONTINUE.
IT HAS TO END.
I LOWER MY SHIELDS.

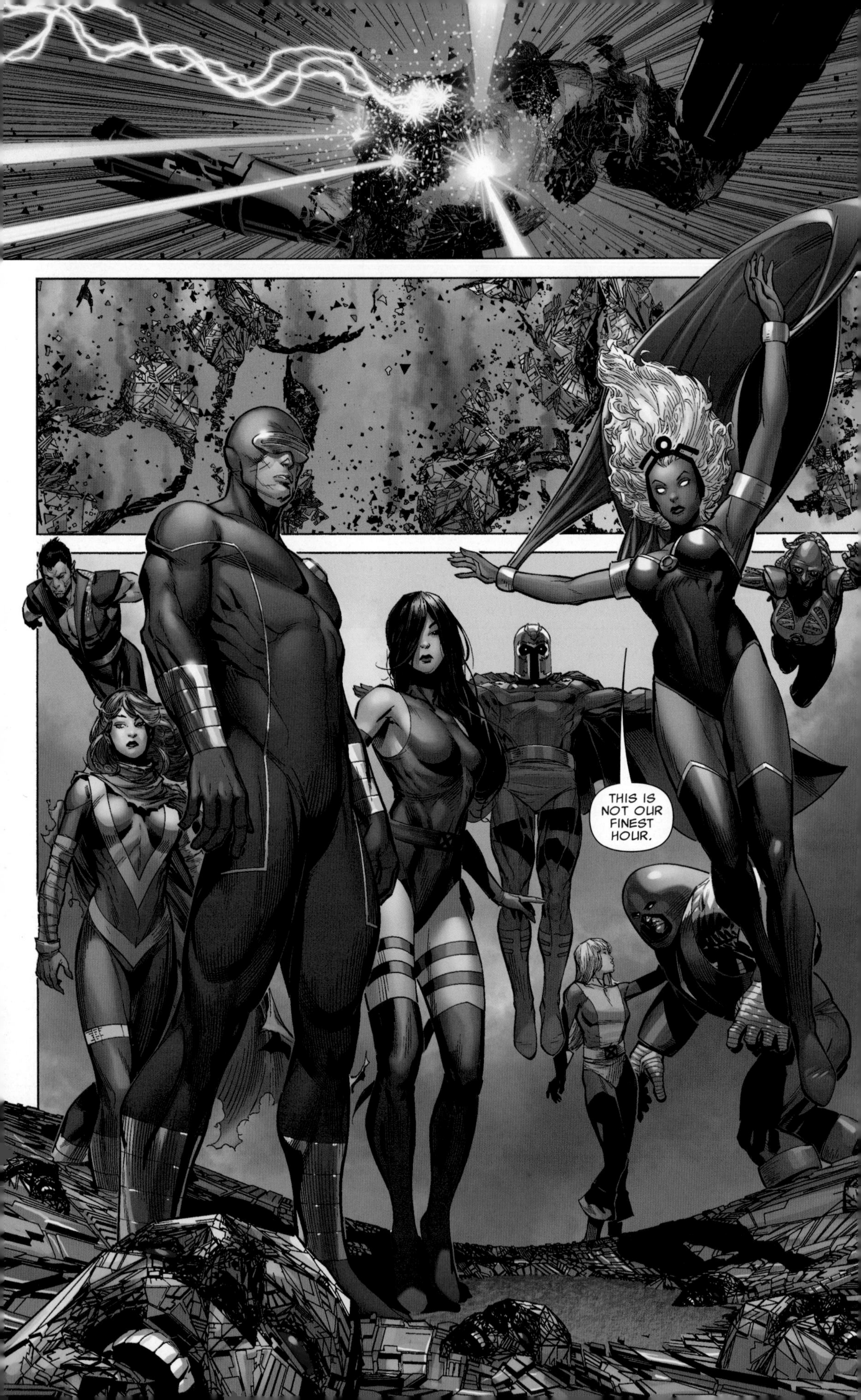
THIS IS NOT OUR FINEST HOUR.

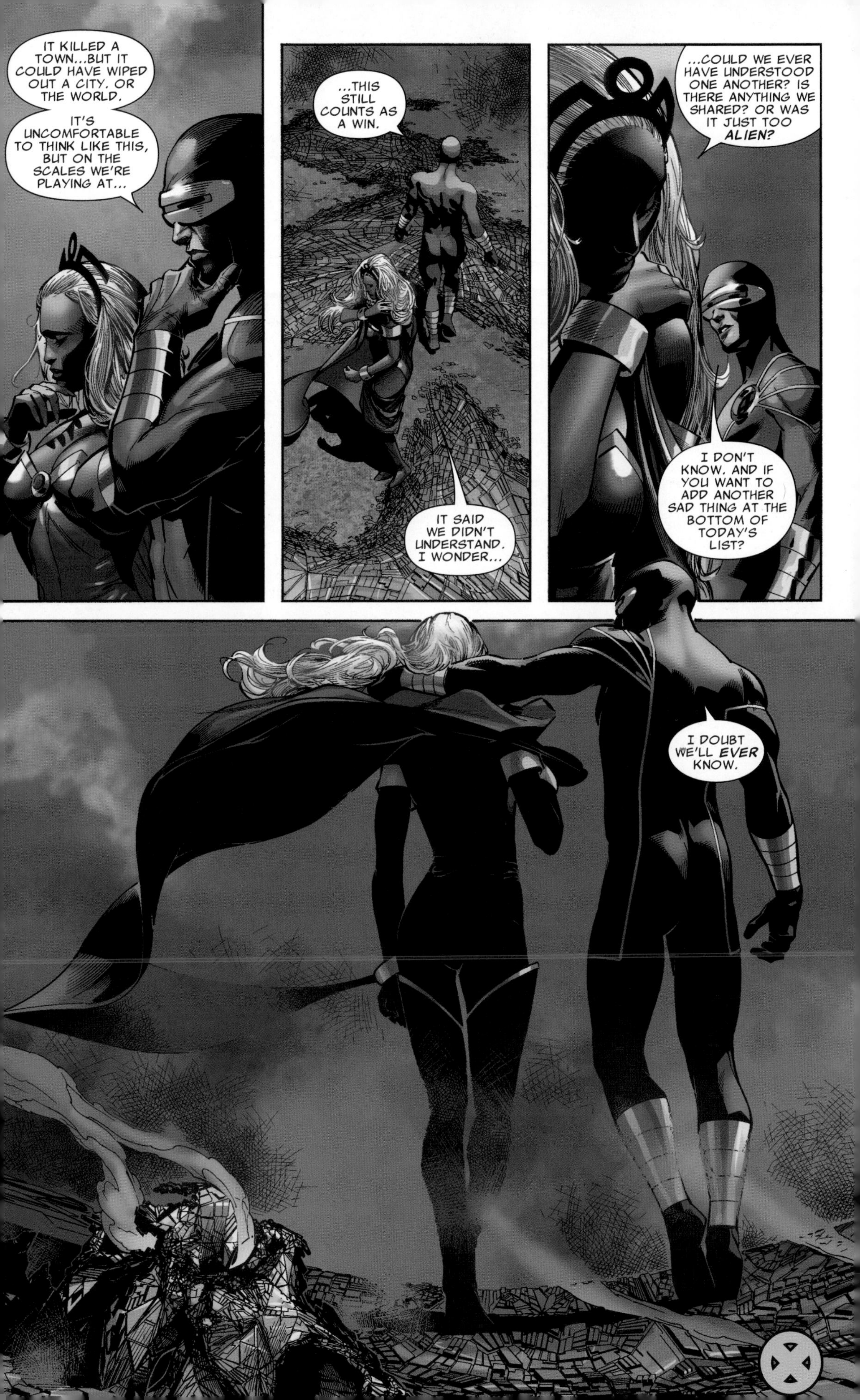
IT KILLED A TOWN...BUT IT COULD HAVE WIPED OUT A CITY. OR THE WORLD.
IT'S UNCOMFORTABLE TO THINK LIKE THIS, BUT ON THE SCALES WE'RE PLAYING AT...
...THIS STILL COUNTS AS A WIN.
IT SAID WE DIDN'T UNDERSTAND. I WONDER...
...COULD WE EVER HAVE UNDERSTOOD ONE ANOTHER? IS THERE ANYTHING WE SHARED? OR WAS IT JUST TOO ALIEN?
I DON'T KNOW. AND IF YOU WANT TO ADD ANOTHER SAD THING AT THE BOTTOM OF TODAY'S LIST?
I DOUBT WE'LL EVER KNOW.

A LETTER TO HUMANITY

There are less than 200 mutants on the planet. Even so, as recent events have shown, we are more feared than ever. There isn't a country in the world that does not have in their possession the genocide machines commonly referred to as "Sentinels."

Today, Utopia is a year old. It was created as a mutant sanctuary and an ongoing community in the face of Armageddon. Since then, we have saved ourselves and saved countless humans time and time again. We are continuing our training of younger mutants, community policing in the locales of San Francisco and experimental research into the future of the X-gene. However, as of today, we have added a new, ongoing grouping to our organization.

The EXTINCTION TEAM is the most powerful group of super-powered individuals ever assembled. To make sure all understand their capabilities, we have released footage and details of individuals' formidable abilities. Traditionally, powers have demonstrated their weapons for others to understand their threat. I trust that we are all wise enough not to require that.

We do not mean to threaten humankind. We are merely making clear that, over the last decades, there have been gross elements – from individuals to governments – who have threatened mutantkind. And despite atrocities like the death of 15 million mutants in Genosha, the species has shown tolerance. When there have been dozens of mutants killed for any unfortunate human death, I believe that tolerance is genuinely superhuman.

We cannot tolerate it any longer.

The Extinction Team will function like other groupings of super-individuals you will know. It will fight criminals, defeat invaders and ensure the peace.

It is also a deterrent.

We are fighting for a better world for mutants and humans alike. If mutants cannot be accepted, it is not a world worth fighting for. Whether a mutant is in Utopia, or in a private school or on your street, they are under our care. There will be consequences if any individual, organization or government attempts to infringe on their rights. Mutants, across the globe, should know: we will protect you.

Humanity is under our protection too. This has always been core to the X-Men's mission.

I studied at Xavier's Academy and he taught me a dream. I still hold it. I look forward to the day that humans and mutants will sit down together, and look back on the horrors of the last decades in the way we look back at the sad and bloody mistakes of our forebears. Mistakes. Horrible mistakes that we are glad are confined to the history books.

But for that day to come, we must live through today.

The X-Men will continue to protect this world, no matter how much it hates and fears them.

But we will never be victims again.

Scott Summers

Scott Summers,
Utopia

FREQUENTLY ASKED QUESTIONS

Q: WHAT ABOUT MUTANT CRIMINALS?

A: In these times of great stress, we reject humanity to judge mutant criminals. While we have nothing but respect for your courts, an imprisoned mutant faces inhuman solitary confinement or murder in the general population

CYCLOPS

THE EXTINCTION TEAM

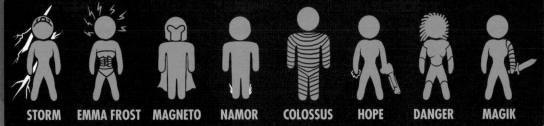

STORM • EMMA FROST • MAGNETO • NAMOR • COLOSSUS • HOPE • DANGER • MAGIK

X-CLUB / SCIENCE TEAM

DR. NEMESIS

KAVITA RAO • MADISON JEFFERIES • DANGER

SECURITY RECON (X-MEN)

PSYLOCKE

DOMINO • WARPATH • JUBILEE

STREET TEAM

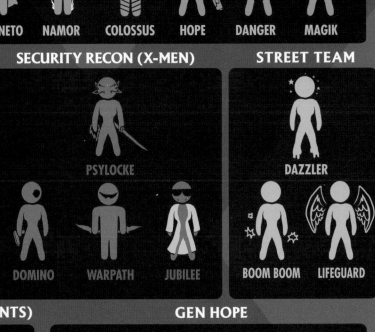

DAZZLER

BOOM BOOM • LIFEGUARD

CLEAN-UP (NEW MUTANTS)

DANI MOONSTAR

CYPHER • MAGMA • SUNSPOT

X-MAN • WARLOCK

GEN HOPE

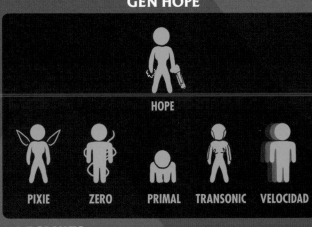

HOPE

PIXIE • ZERO • PRIMAL • TRANSONIC • VELOCIDAD

RECRUITS

PRODIGY • STEPFORD CUCKOOS • CROSTA

DUST • LOA • MARTHA JOHANNSON • SURGE

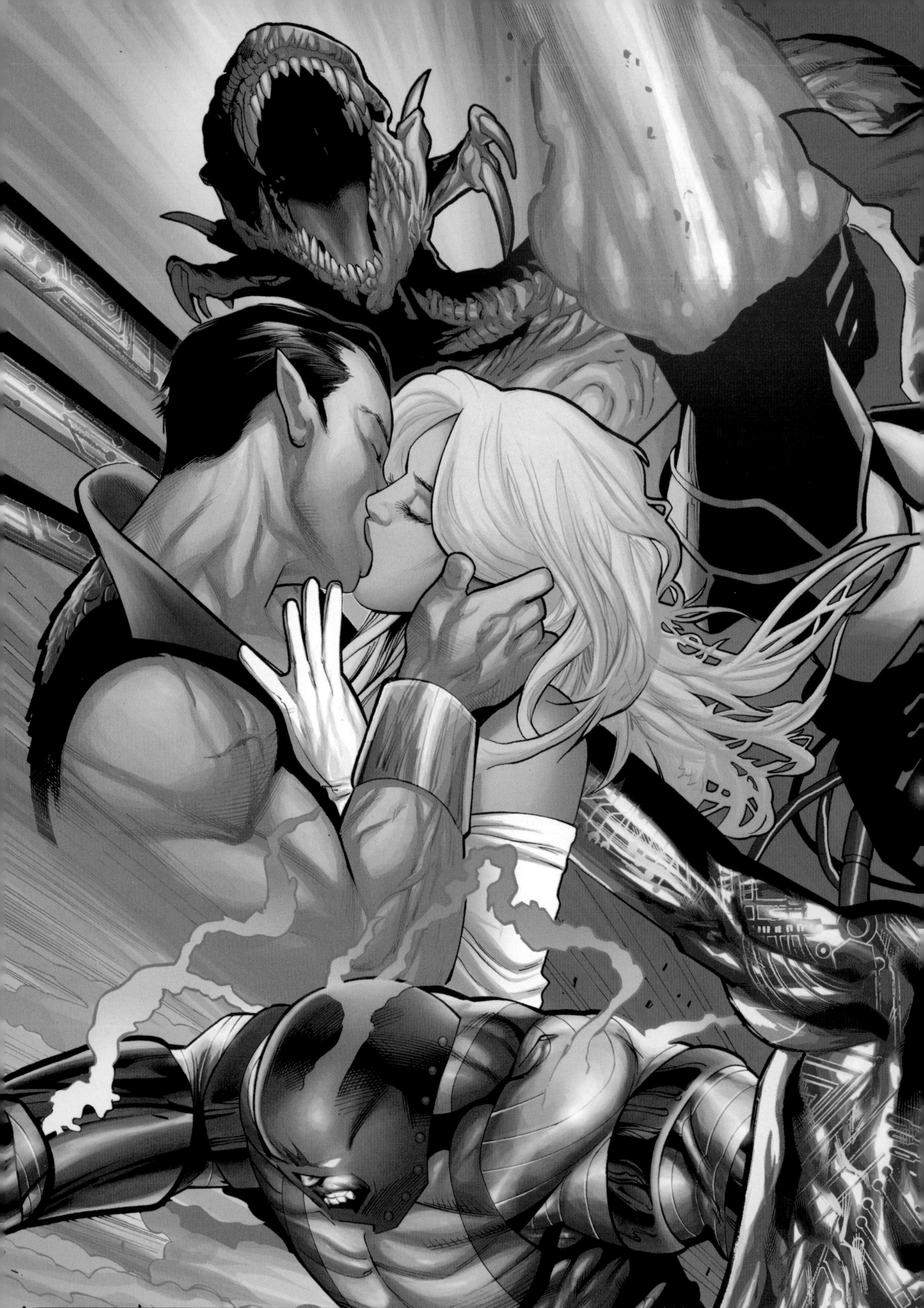

THINGS TO

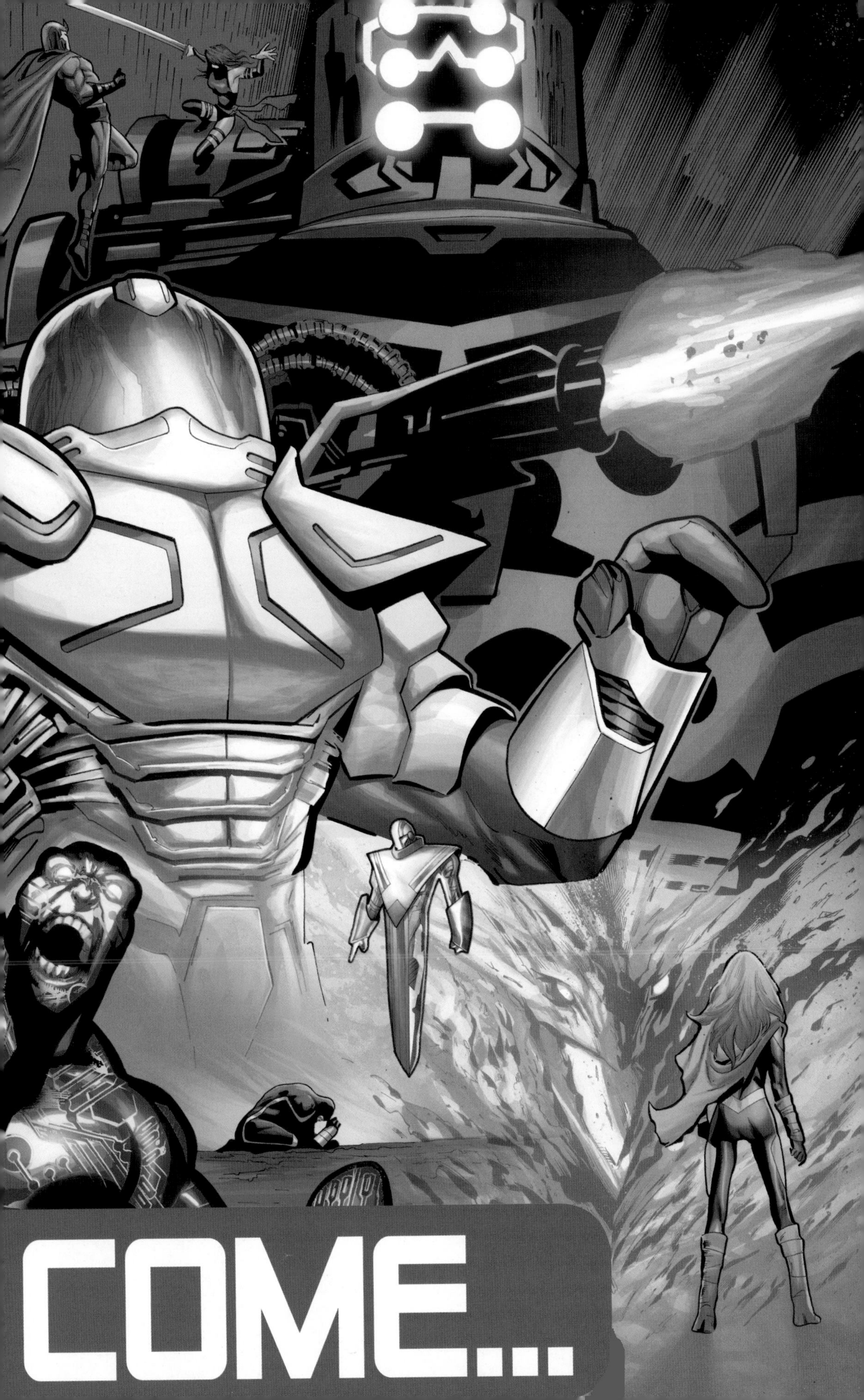
COME...

#1 VARIANT BY DALE KEOWN & JASON KEITH

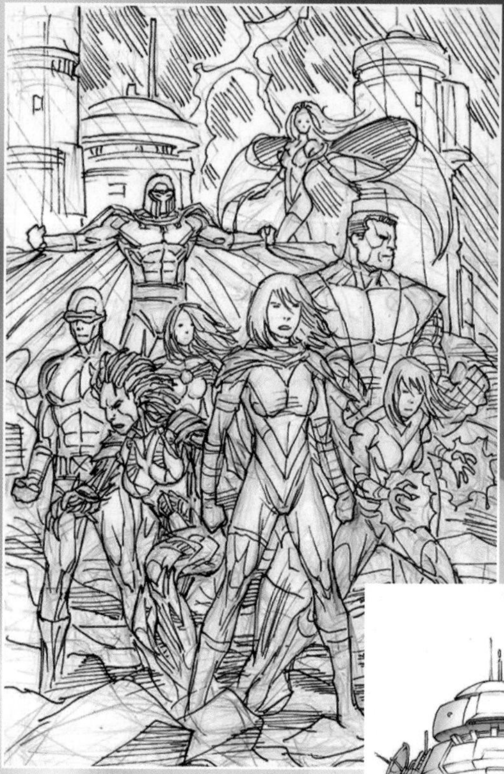

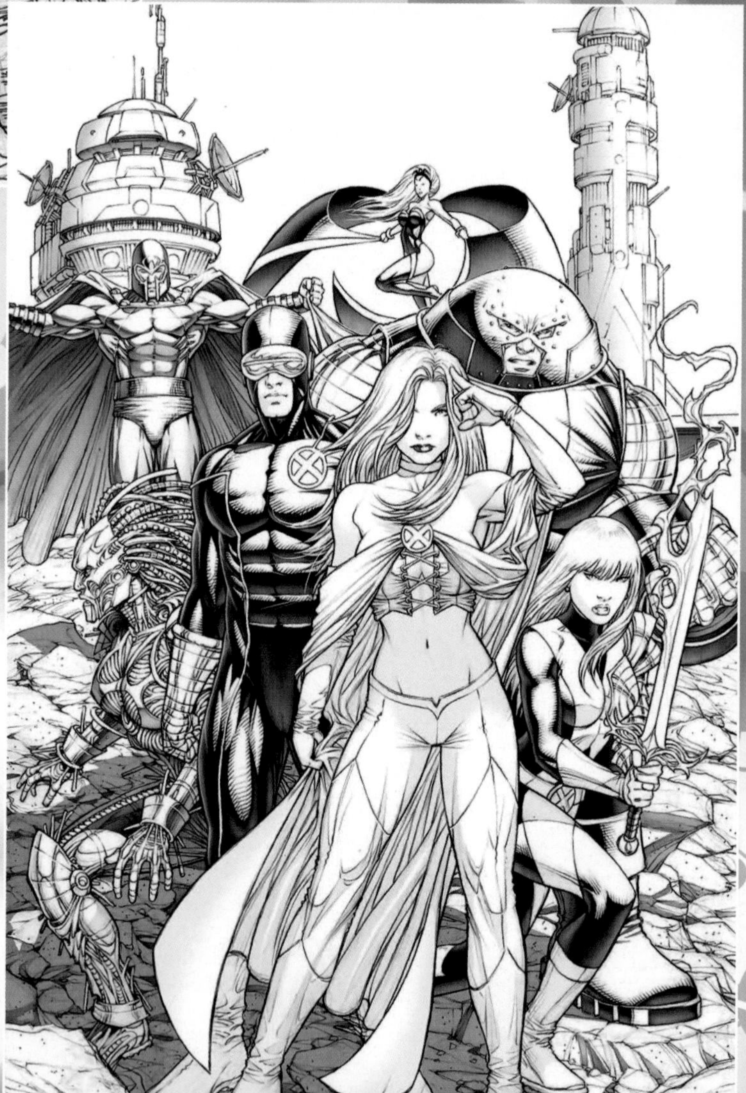

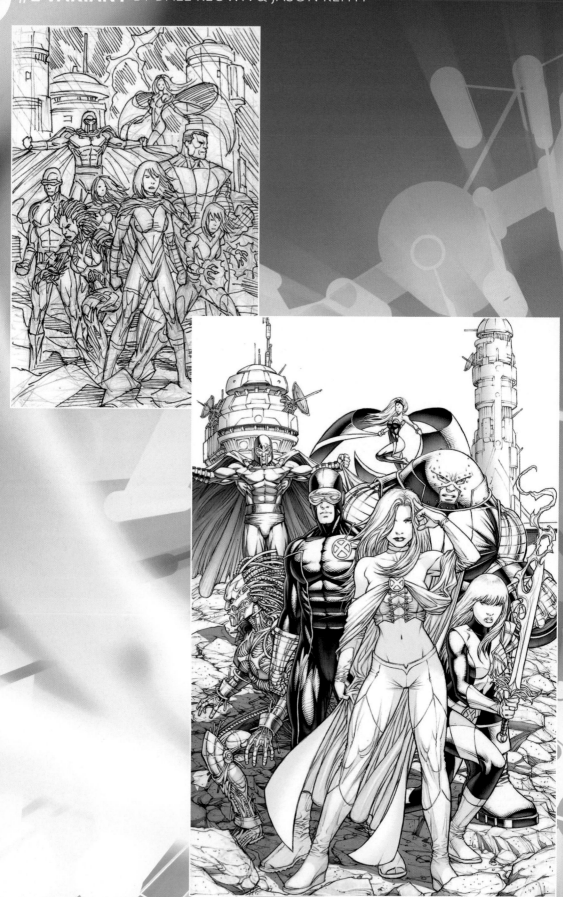

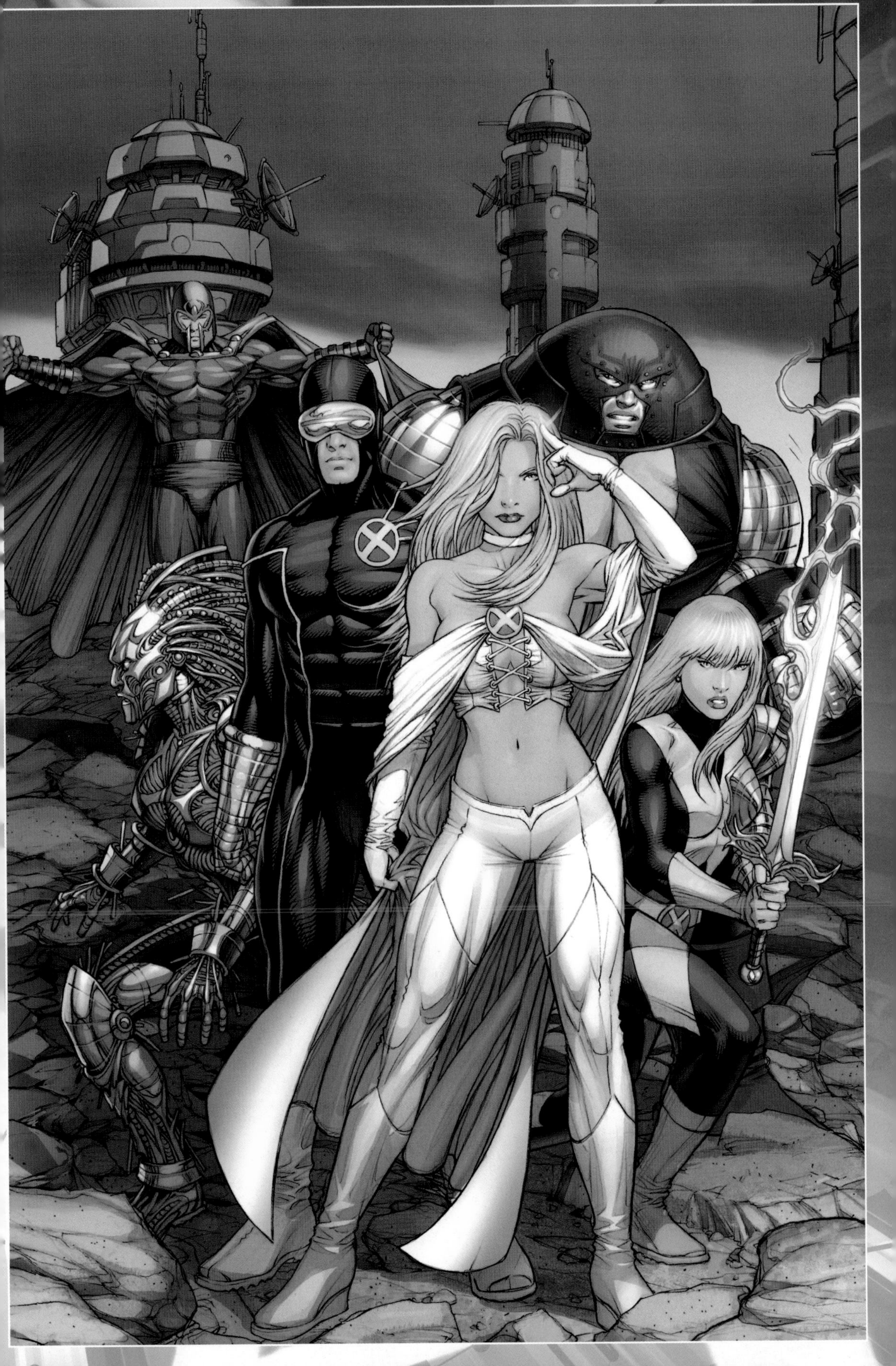

#1 VARIANT BY FRANK CHO & JASON KEITH

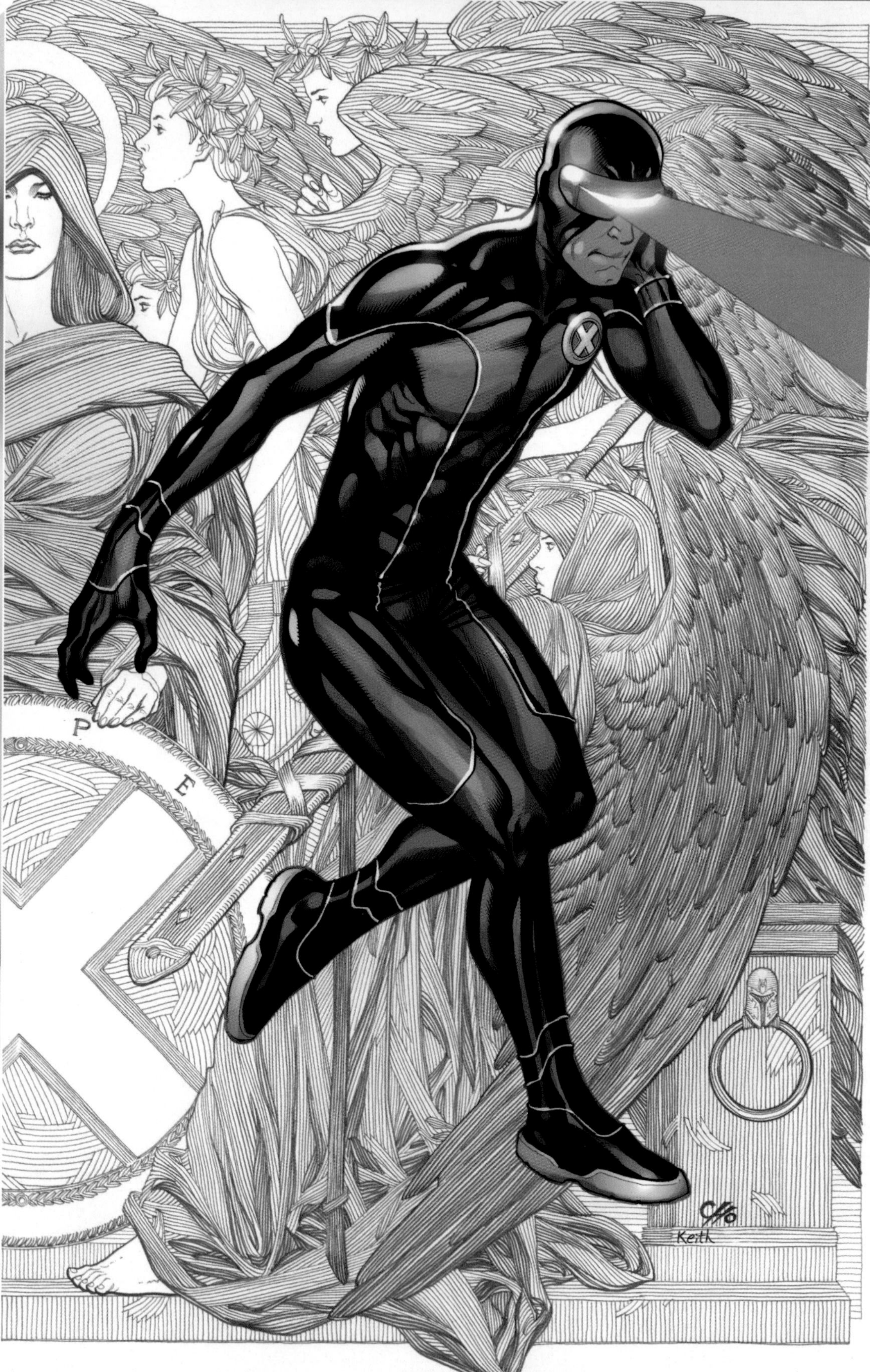
P
E
Keith

#2 MARVEL 50TH ANNIVERSARY VARIANT BY BILLY TAN & GURU-eFX

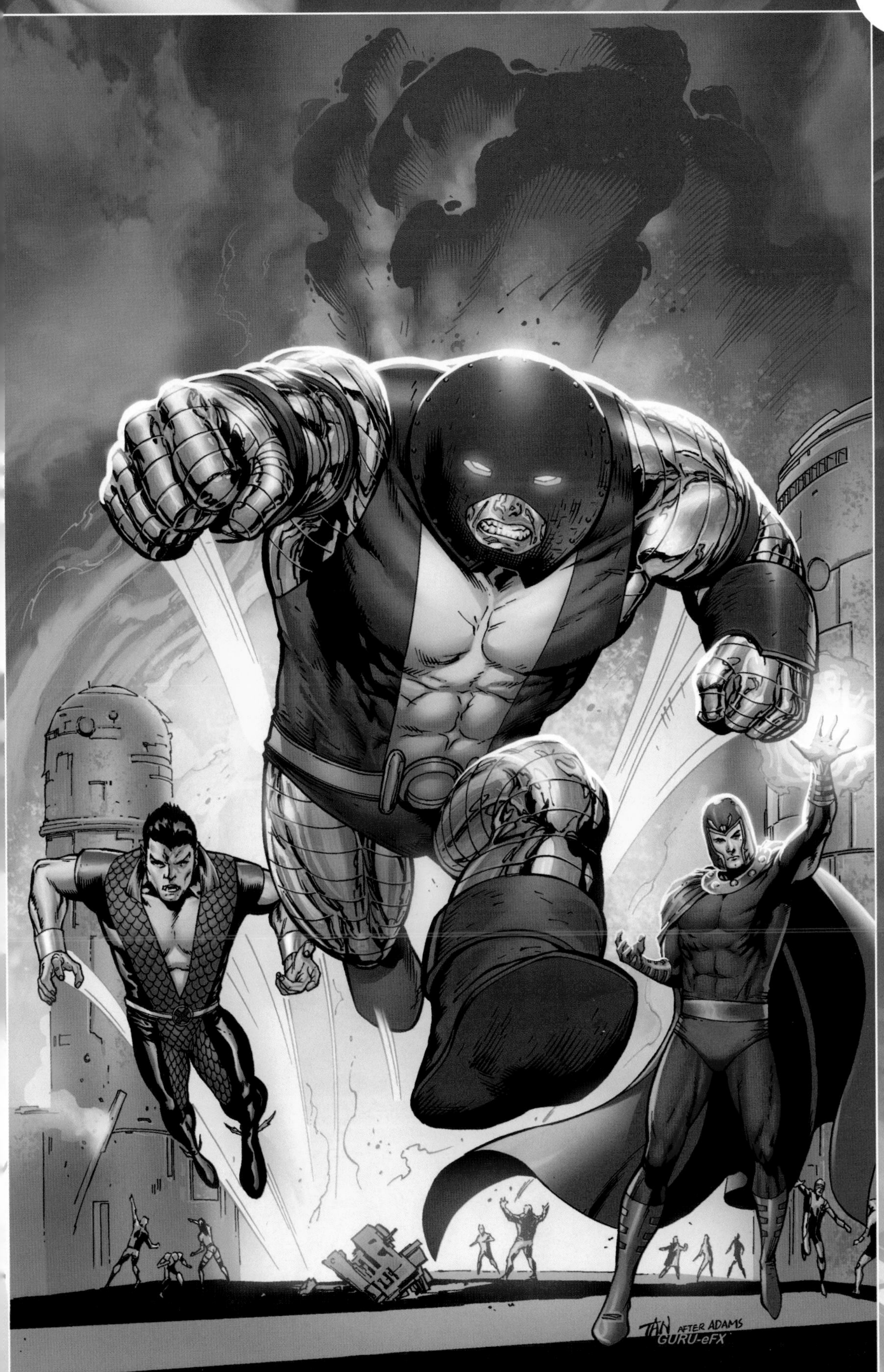

TAN AFTER ADAMS
GURU-eFX

#1 COVER PROCESS BY CARLOS PACHECO

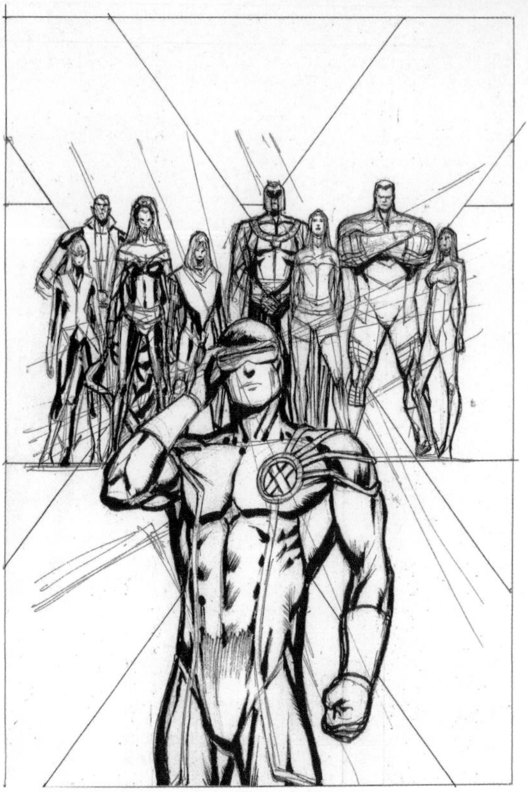

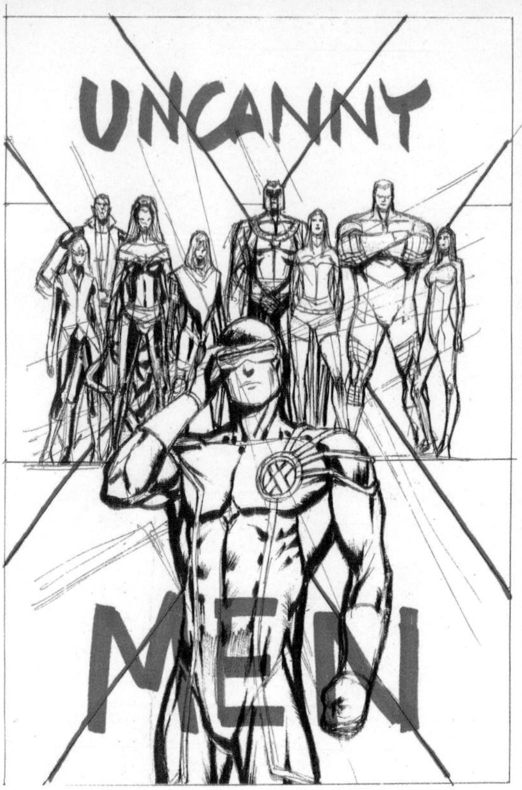
UNCANNY
MEN

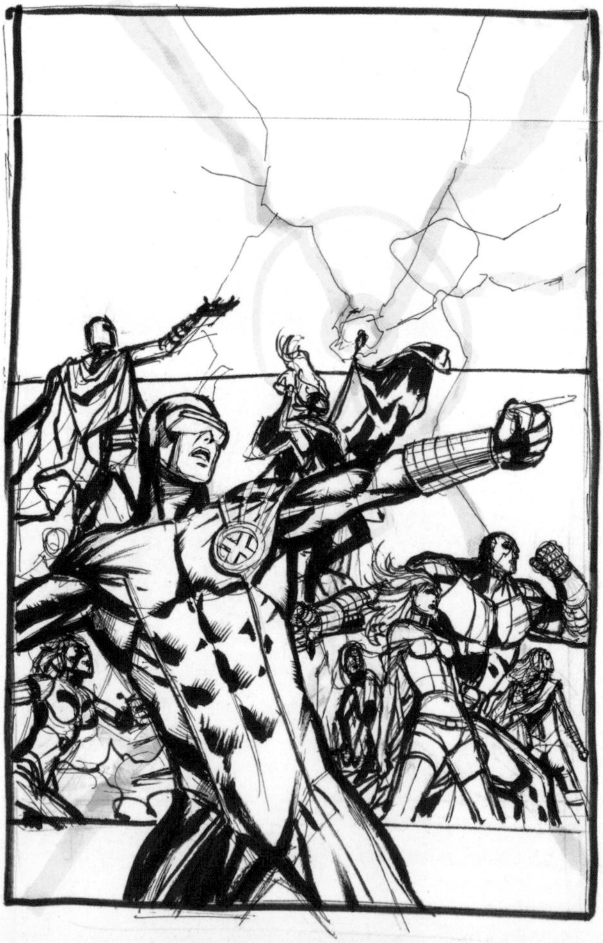

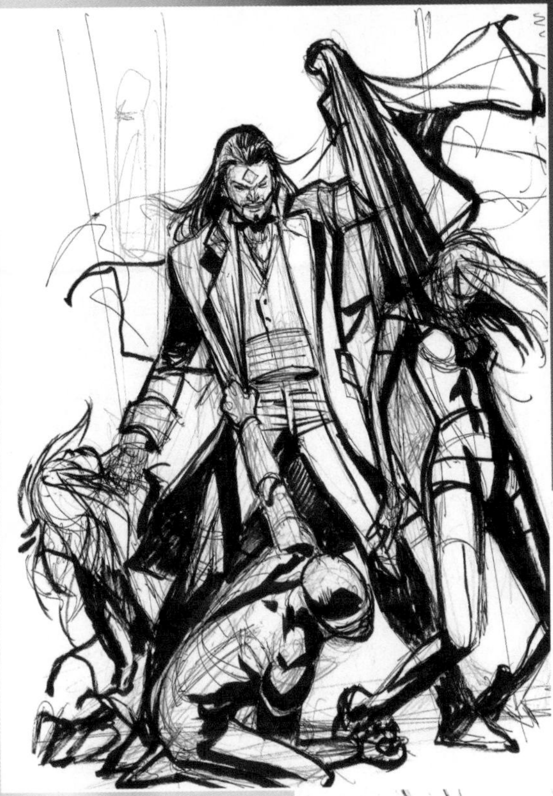

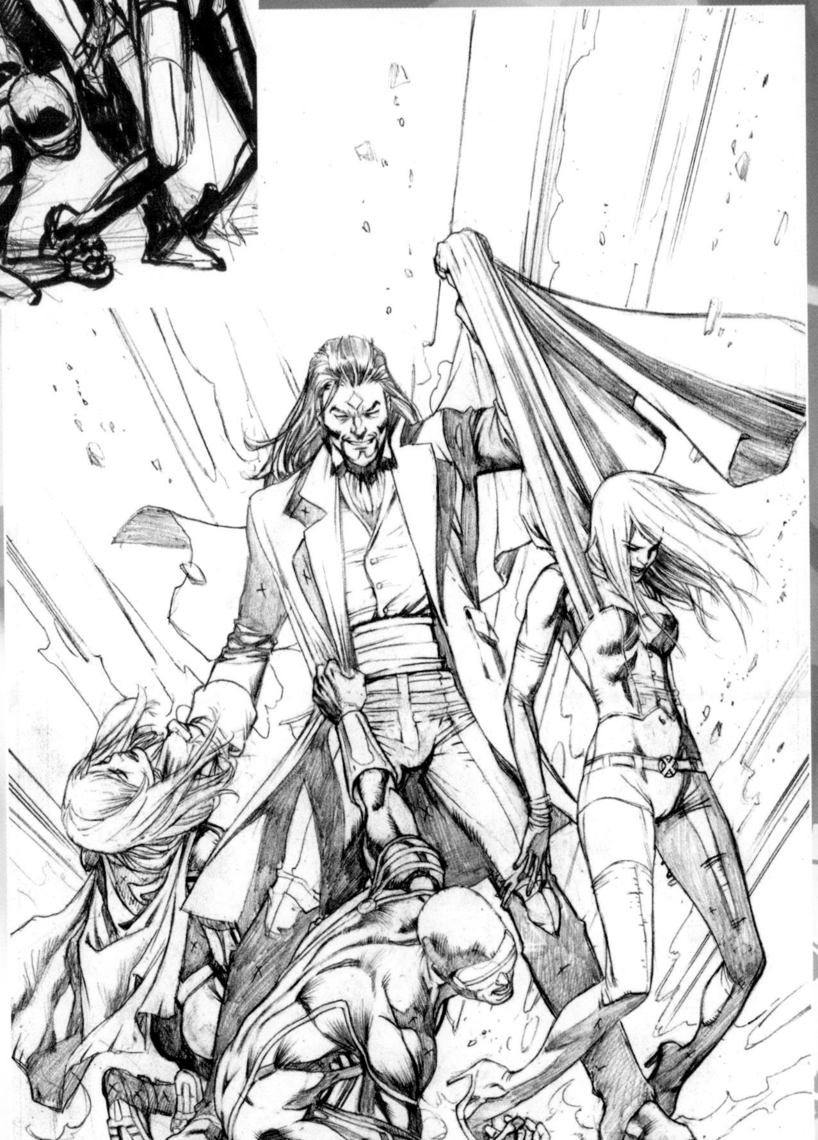
CARLOS PACHECO '11

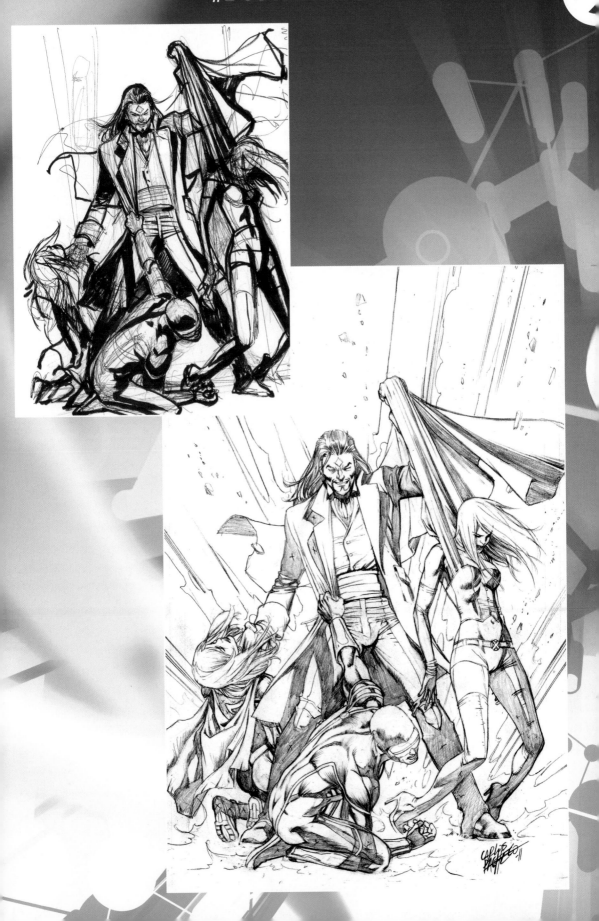

#3 COVER PROCESS BY CARLOS PACHECO

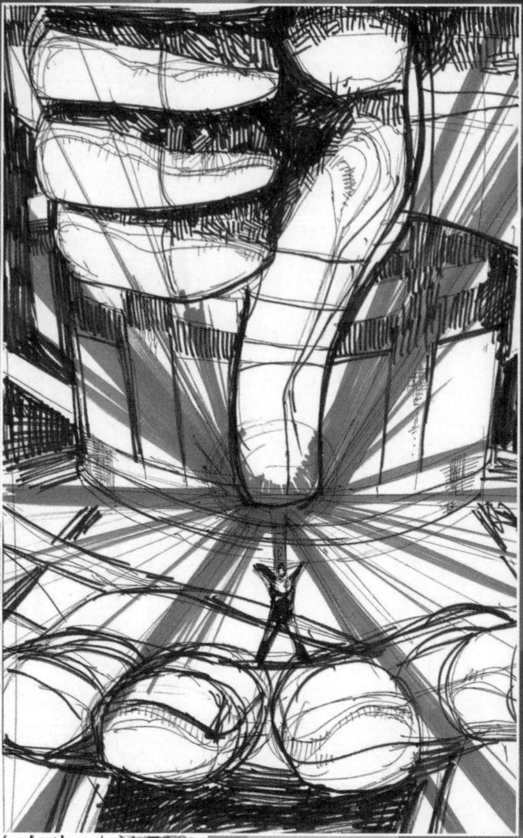

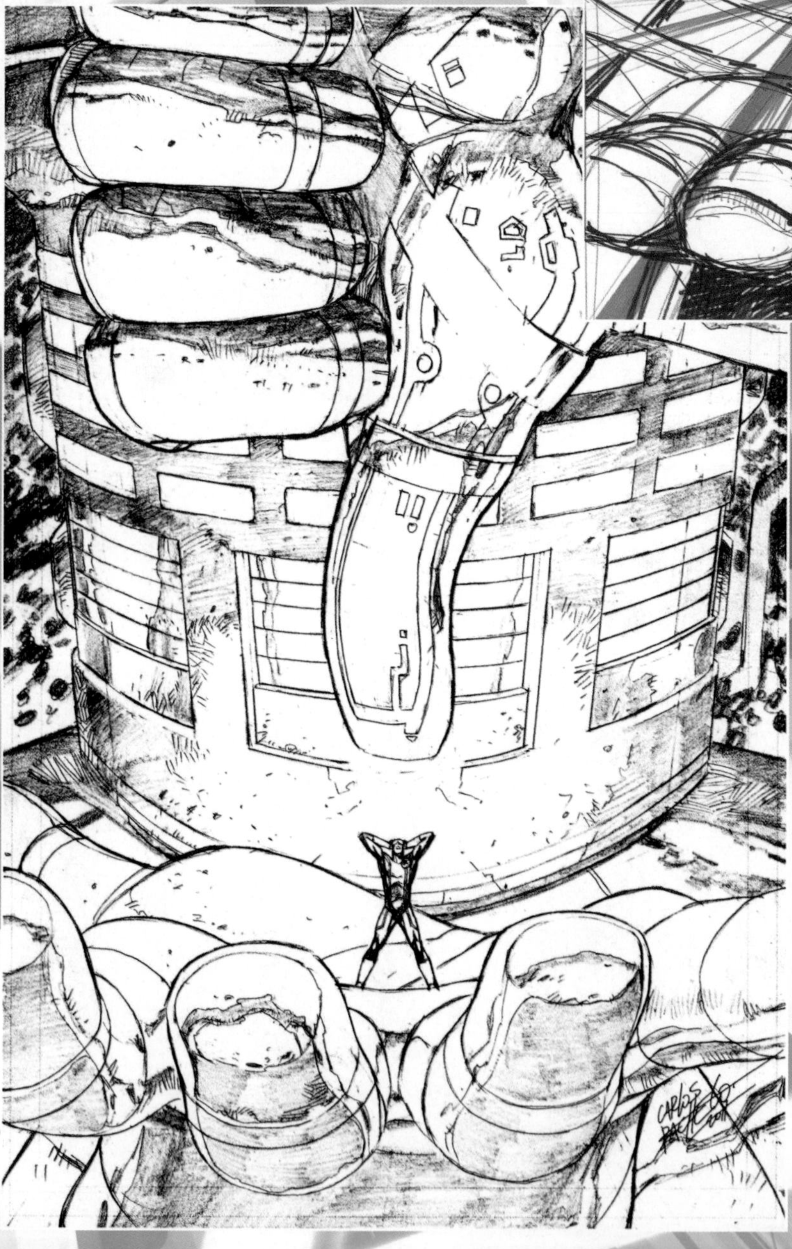

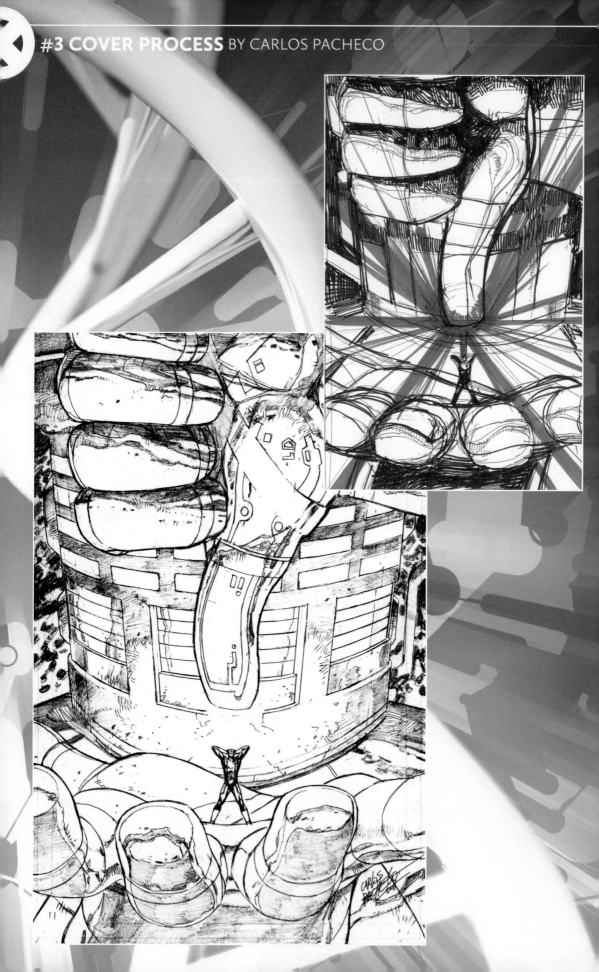

#4 COVER PROCESS BY BRANDON PETERSON

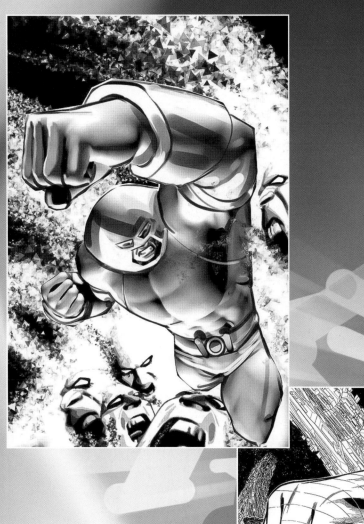

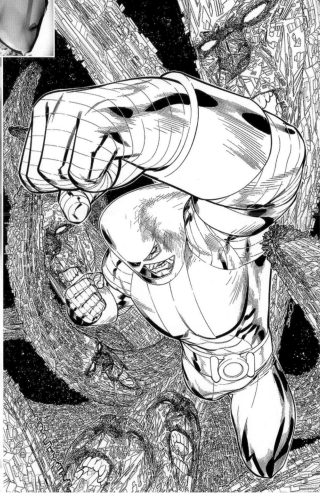

#1, PAGE 7 INKS BY CARLOS PACHECO & CAM SMITH

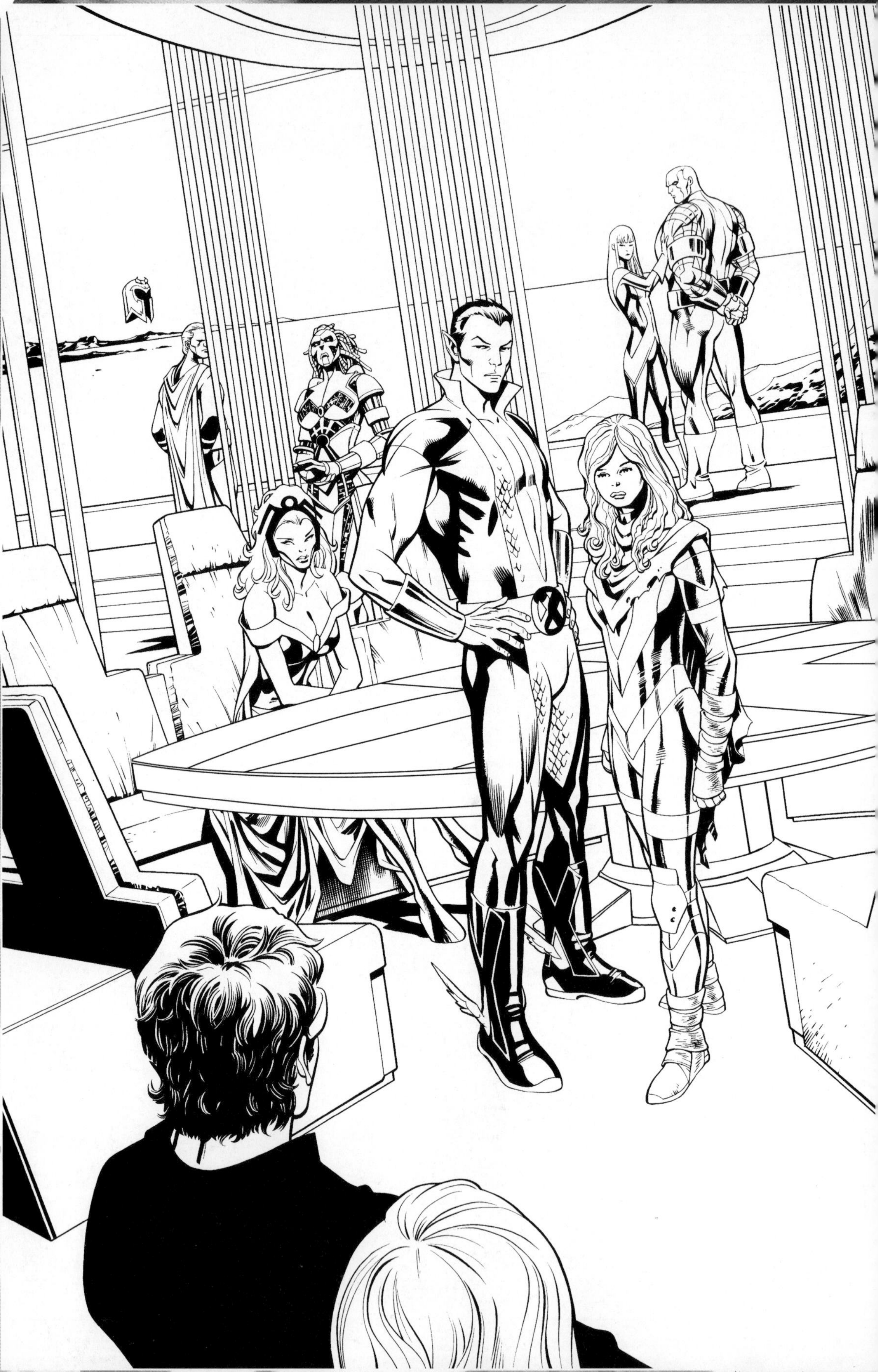

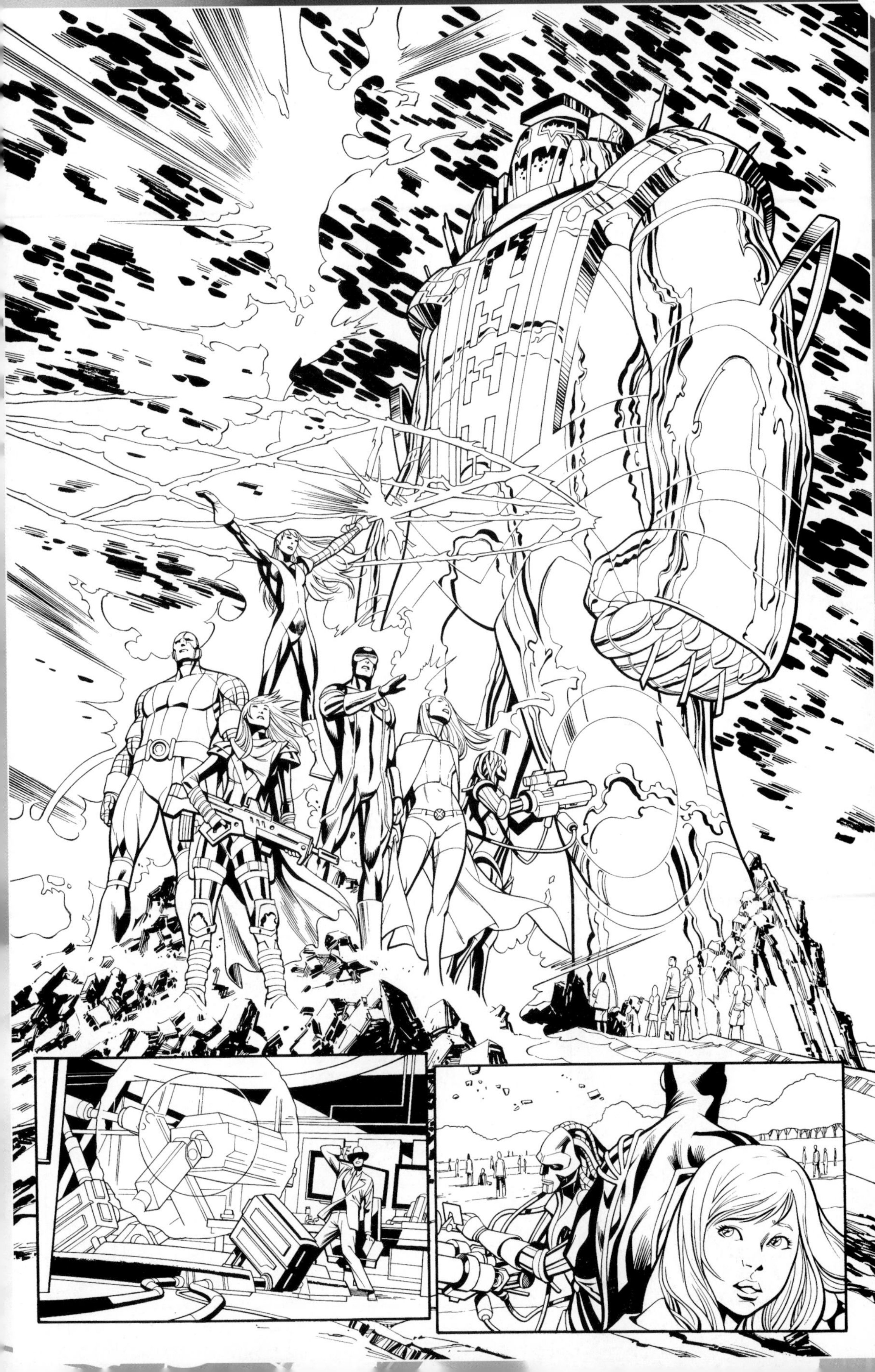

#1, PAGE 20 INKS BY CARLOS PACHECO & CAM SMITH

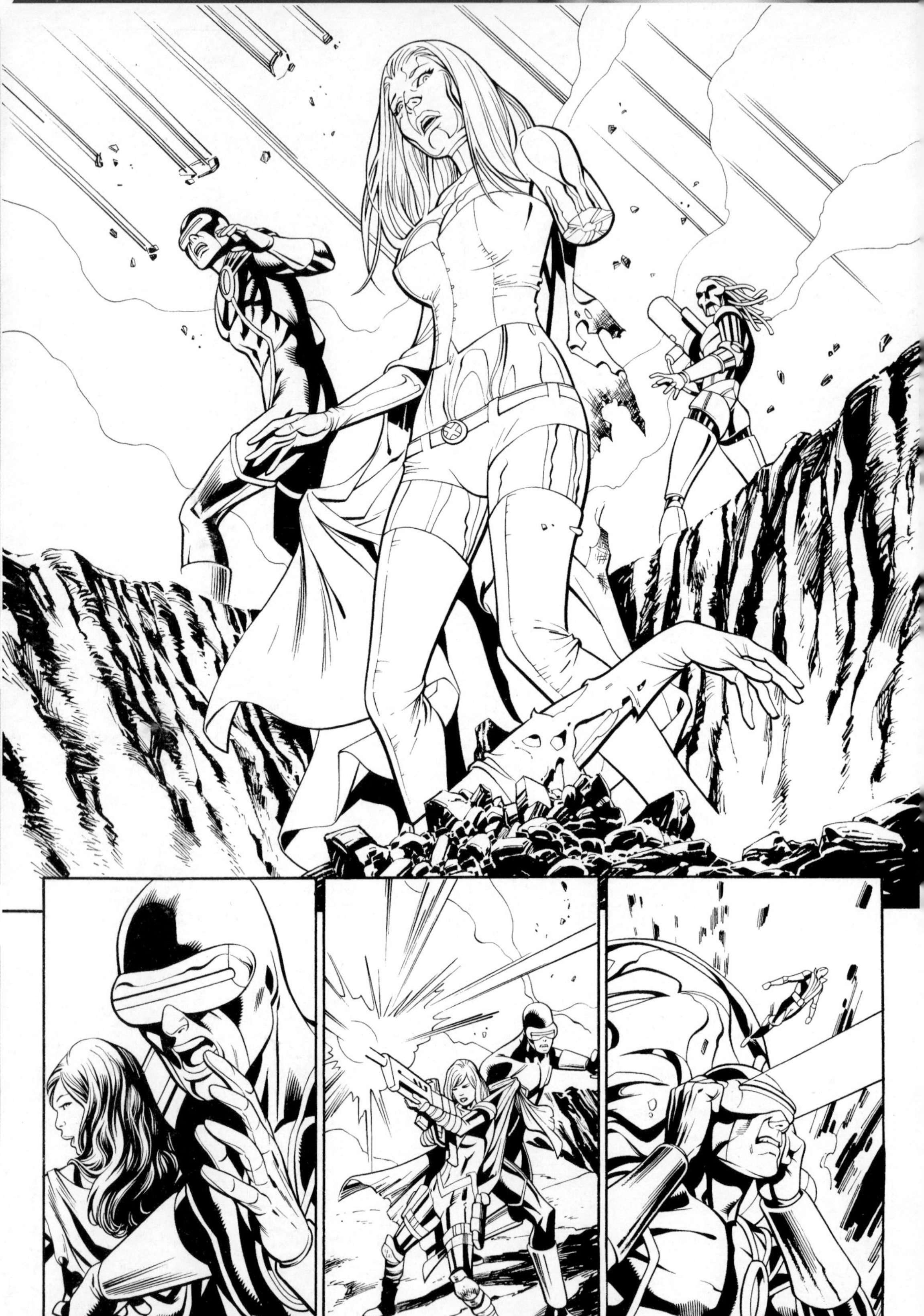